"*A Peculiar Glory* is not just another book defending the reliability of the Scriptures, although it does do that. It is a reminder that without the internal witness of the Spirit, no amount of evidences will ever lead to faith. And that witness works most directly as we read and understand Scripture itself—as it attests itself to us—particularly as we focus on Jesus and the gospel message. Part apologetics, part church history, part almost lyrical poetry, Piper's book should inspire every reader back to the Bible, to its core and to the Jesus whom it reveals, who loves us beyond measure despite all that we are and do—more than enough reason for being his disciples."

Craig L. Blomberg, Distinguished Professor of New Testament, Denver Seminary

"Never has the church been in greater need of recognizing that Scripture is self-attesting. In this important and timely book, Piper shows what it means not only to conform our thinking but also to submit our worship and our lives as a whole to the self-establishing, self-validating truth and authority of the Bible and, in doing that, to the Christ of the Bible."

Richard B. Gaffin Jr., Professor of Biblical and Systematic Theology Emeritus, Westminster Theological Seminary

"*A Peculiar Glory* is a solid theological and exegetical treatment of biblical authority, but much more. Besides the standard arguments, Piper has developed (with the help of Jonathan Edwards) a profoundly original yet biblical approach to the question. It raises the traditional arguments to an exponential level of cogency. Piper says that our most definitive persuasion comes from actually seeing the *glory* of God in his Word. Theologians have traditionally called this the 'internal testimony of the Holy Spirit,' but that theological label does little justice to the experience, the awareness of the glory of God as we meet Jesus in Scripture. That really happens. It is astonishing and powerful. And it explains the difference between an observer's merely theoretical faith and a true disciple's delighted embrace of Christ. This doctrine of Scripture is worthy of the overall emphasis of Piper's writings, the 'desire' for God, 'Christian hedonism,' and the 'dangerous duty of delight.' Perhaps only Piper could have written this book, and I'm delighted that he has done so."

John Frame, J. D. Trimble Chair of Systematic Theology and Philosophy, Reformed Theological Seminary, Orlando

"Piper points us to Scripture—its authority, its historical accuracy, its total truthfulness, and especially its beauty and power. The Scriptures are beautiful and powerful because they disclose to us, as the Spirit opens our hearts, the loveliness and glory of Jesus Christ. Here we find compelling arguments for the truthfulness of the Scriptures and profound meditations on the stunning glory of God. The book captures and expresses the truth of Peter's words in John 6:68, 'Lord, to whom shall we go? You have the words of eternal life.'"

Thomas R. Schreiner, James Buchanan Harrison Professor of New Testament Interpretation, Southern Baptist Theological Seminary

"The classic doctrine of Scripture's self-attestation suffers when it is used as a short-cut method of scoring evidential points or winning an argument without doing any work. But it unfolds its wings and soars to the heavens when handled by somebody who shows that when we read the Bible, we are dealing with God himself in his own holy words. In this book, John Piper throws everything he's got at the message of how God illuminates the mind and gives firm conviction to the heart through the Bible."

> **Fred Sanders,** Professor of Theology, Torrey Honors Institute,
> Biola University

"It's easy to take the Bible for granted. We know that it's the Word of God, but do we really? We know which books belong to it and what distinguishes these texts from ordinary religious literature, right? Of course, we know why we trust Scripture and how to communicate that confidence to others, or do we? Rather than take for granted a high view of Scripture, *A Peculiar Glory* exposes another generation to the source, authority, reliability, and truthfulness of God's written word. Dr. Piper has written another important, accessible, and wise account of the things that matter most."

> **Michael Horton,** J. Gresham Machen Professor of Systematic Theology
> and Apologetics, Westminster Seminary California; author, *Calvin on the
> Christian Life*

"There are few questions more important than 'How do I know the Bible is God's Word?' And there are few people who could address it as well as John Piper. Drawing from the deep theological well of Jonathan Edwards and with a practical eye for the average believer in the pew, Piper helps us recover the foundational importance of a self-authenticating Bible. This book will revolutionize the way you think about God's Word."

> **Michael J. Kruger,** President and Professor of New Testament, Reformed
> Theological Seminary, Charlotte; author, *Canon Revisited*

"In this spirited and tightly argued book, pastor-theologian John Piper seeks to ground our confidence in the Bible's status as the Word of God by directing our attention to the 'peculiar glory' that is manifest through its message and across its pages: the glory of the 'Lion-like majesty' and the 'Lamb-like meekness' that radiates in the face of Jesus Christ. Here is a book on the authority and trustworthiness of Scripture that promises to strengthen our faith in the word of God and to expand our capacity for wonder before the glory of God."

> **Scott R. Swain,** Associate Professor of Systematic Theology and Academic
> Dean, Reformed Theological Seminary, Orlando

"With passion, clarity, a believing respect for Scripture, and a burning desire for God's glory, John Piper has written a robust defense of the complete trustworthiness of Scripture, with debts to Jonathan Edwards and the Westminster Larger Catechism. The language of the book is simple and accessible, but the ideas are deep and its coverage extensive. Scholarship is worn lightly, and the pastoral concern informing the work is pervasively evident. Whether the reader is educationally sophisticated or unsophisticated, the argument is that the peculiar glory of God is on view for all to see, if God gives the grace to do so. I hope this work finds a wide readership."

Graham A. Cole, Dean and Vice President of Education and Professor of Biblical and Systematic Theology, Trinity Evangelical Divinity School

"John Piper has written a robust and pastoral defense of an orthodox doctrine of Scripture. Resisting any who would render well-grounded assurance of Scripture's truthfulness the preserve of experts and academics, his emphasis upon the self-authenticating and life-transforming glory of God they bear is salutary and faith-affirming. We cannot properly regard Scripture without beholding its author. The greatest strength of Piper's treatment lies precisely in the fact that his account of Scripture is so absorbed in the beauty of the one who inspired it."

Alastair Roberts, blogger; participant, Mere Fidelity podcast

"*A Peculiar Glory* should be quickly established as a modern classic on the Bible. Clearly and methodically laying out the case for why we can have absolute confidence in the Bible as God's own word, it gives to faith both muscle and joy. The day John Owen persuaded me that the Christian Scriptures are self-authenticating was a glorious moment of liberation. I hope and expect that John Piper will bring that same liberation to many with this book."

Michael Reeves, President, Union School of Theology; author, *Delighting in the Trinity*; *The Unquenchable Flame*; and *Rejoicing in Christ*

A Peculiar Glory

How the Christian Scriptures
Reveal Their Complete Truthfulness

John Piper

WHEATON, ILLINOIS

Cover design: Josh Dennis

Cover image: Josh Dennis

First printing 2016

Printed in the United States of America

Hardcover ISBN: 978-1-4335-5263-2
ePub ISBN: 978-1-4335-5266-3
PDF ISBN: 978-1-4335-5264-9
Mobipocket ISBN: 978-1-4335-5265-6

Library of Congress Cataloging-in-Publication Data
Names: Piper, John, 1946–
Title: A peculiar glory : how the Christian scriptures reveal their complete truthfulness / John Piper.
Description: Wheaton : Crossway, 2016. | Includes bibliographical references and index. | Description based on print version record and CIP data provided by publisher; resource not viewed.
Identifiers: LCCN 2015039630 (print) | LCCN 2015038465(ebook) | ISBN 9781433552649 (pdf) | ISBN 9781433552656 (mobi) | ISBN 9781433552663 (epub) | ISBN 9781433552632 (hc)
Subjects: LCSH: Bible—Evidences, authority, etc.
Classification: LCC BS480 (print) | LCC BS480 .P635 2016 (ebook) | DDC 220.1—dc23
LC record available at http://lccn.loc.gov/2015039630

Crossway is a publishing ministry of Good News Publishers.

RRD		26	25	24	23	22	21	20	19	18	17	16
15	14	13	12	11	10	9	8	7	6	5	4	3	2	1

To Bethlehem College and Seminary
Sacred Book. Sovereign God. Serious Joy.

In God, whose word I praise,
    in the LORD, whose word I praise,
in God I trust; I shall not be afraid.
    What can man do to me?

PSALM 56:10–11

Contents

PART 1

A Place to Stand

"*. . . the* Lord *revealed himself by the word of the* Lord"

PART 2

What Books and Words Make Up the Christian Scriptures?

"*. . . from the blood of Abel to the blood of Zechariah*"

PART 3

What Do the Christian Scriptures Claim for Themselves?

"*. . . words not taught by human wisdom but taught by the Spirit*"

PART 4

How Can We Know the Christian Scriptures Are True?

". . . by a sight of its glory"

PART 5

How Are the Christian Scriptures Confirmed by the Peculiar Glory of God?

". . . the light of the gospel of the glory of Christ"

Introduction

Is the Bible true? I am not asking if there is truth in it, say, the way there is truth in *Moby Dick*, or Plato's *Republic*, or *The Lord of the Rings*. Aspects of truth can be found virtually everywhere. What I am asking is this: Is the Bible completely true? All of it. Is it so trustworthy in all that it teaches that it can function as the test of all other claims to truth? This book is about how the Bible gives good grounds for the answer yes. The Bible is completely true.

There is a story behind every book. That is certainly true here. This introduction is not that story; my story comes in chapter 1. But I think it will be helpful to signal immediately why glory figures so largely in this book. My seven decades of experience with the Bible have not been mainly a battle to hold on. They have been a blessing of being held on to, namely, by beauty—that is, by glory.

I have stood in front of this window all these years, not to protect it from being broken, or because the owner of the chalet told me to, but because of the glory of the Alps on the other side. I am a captive of the glory of God revealed in Scripture. There are reasons deeper than my experience for focusing on the glory of God. But I cannot deny what I have seen and the power it has had.

Vastly more important than one man's experience is the reality itself. The glory of God is the ground of faith. It is a solid ground. It is objective, outside ourselves. It is the ground of faith in Christ and in the Christian Scriptures. Faith is not a heroic step through the door of the unknown; it is a humble, happy sight of God's self-authenticating glory. Consider the following biblical examples of how the glory of God becomes the ground of knowledge. The fourth example is the focus of this book.

The Heavens

First, how are all human beings supposed to know that God exists and that he is powerful and beneficent and should be glorified and thanked? David, the king of Israel, answered in Psalm 19, "The heavens declare the glory of God, and the sky above proclaims his handiwork" (v. 1).

But there are many people who do not see the glory of God when they look at the heavens. Nevertheless, the apostle Paul says that we should see it and that we are without excuse if we don't, because

> what can be known about God is plain to them, because God has shown it to them. For his invisible attributes, namely, his eternal power and divine nature, have been clearly perceived, ever since the creation of the world, in the things that have been made. So they are without excuse. For although they knew God, they did not honor him as God or give thanks to him. (Rom. 1:19–21)

God has shown everyone the glory of his power and deity and beneficence. If we do not see God's glory, we are still responsible to see it, treasure it as glorious, and give God thanks. If we don't, we are "without excuse."

The Son

Second, how did Jesus's first followers know that he was the Messiah, the Son of the living God? One of those followers answered, "The Word became flesh and dwelt among us, and we have seen his glory, glory as of the only Son from the Father, full of grace and truth" (John 1:14).

But there were others who looked at Jesus, saw his miracles, and heard his words but did not see divine glory. To such people Jesus said, "Have I been with you so long, and you still do not know me?" (John 14:9). He had shown them enough. They were responsible to see the glory—and to know him.

The Gospel

Third, how are people who hear the good news of the Christian gospel supposed to know that it is from God? The apostle Paul answered: by "seeing the light of the gospel of the glory of Christ, who is the image of God," that is, by seeing "the light of the knowledge of the glory of God in the face of Jesus Christ" (2 Cor. 4:4, 6).

But many people hear "the gospel of the glory of Christ" and do not see divine glory. Not seeing the divine glory of Christ in the gospel is blameworthy. It is not an innocent blindness, but a culpable love of darkness. "They are darkened in their understanding . . . due to their hardness of heart" (Eph. 4:18). They are "perishing, because they refused to love the truth and so be saved" (2 Thess. 2:10). The gospel of the glory of Christ is enough. To hear it faithfully and fully presented is to be responsible to see divine glory.

The Scriptures

Fourth, how are we to know that the Christian Scriptures are the word of God? The argument of this book is that the answer to this question is the same as the answer to the three preceding questions. In and through the Scriptures we see the glory of God. What the apostles of Jesus saw face-to-face they impart to us through their words. "That which we have seen and heard we proclaim also to you, so that you too may have fellowship with us; and indeed our fellowship is with the Father and with his Son Jesus Christ" (1 John 1:3).

The glory that they saw in Christ, we can see through their words. The human words of Scripture are seen to be divine the way the human man Jesus was seen to be divine. Not all saw it. But the glory was there. And it is here, in the Scriptures.

Three Sentences behind This Book

This is not a new approach to the question of the truth of Scripture. In fact, one could understand this book as an extended meditation on three sentences.

One of those sentences is from the Westminster Larger Catechism. Question 4 asks, "How doth it appear that the scriptures are the word of God?" One of the answers is: "The scriptures manifest themselves to be the word of God, by . . . *the scope of the whole, which is to give all glory to God.*" This book is an effort to press into that answer as deeply as I can.

A second sentence that gave rise to this book is from Jonathan

Edwards. Edwards cared deeply about the Native Americans of New England in the 1740s. He wrestled with how they could have a well-grounded faith in the truth of Christianity if they were unable to follow complex historical arguments.

> Miserable is the condition of the Houssatunnuck Indians and others, who have lately manifested a desire to be instructed in Christianity, if they can come at no evidence of the truth of Christianity, sufficient to induce them to sell all for Christ, in any other way but this [path of historical reasoning].[1]

His answer was found in 2 Corinthians 4:4–6, which we cited above. He put it like this:

> The mind ascends to the truth of the gospel but by one step, and that is its divine glory. . . . Unless men may come to a reasonable solid persuasion and conviction of the truth of the gospel, by the internal evidences of it, in the way that has been spoken, viz. by a sight of its glory; 'tis impossible that those who are illiterate, and unacquainted with history, should have any thorough and effectual conviction of it at all.[2]

This book is an effort to apply Edwards's concern and his reasoning to the whole of the Scriptures. Can we say, "The mind ascends to the truth of the [Scriptures] but by one step, and that is its divine glory"?

The third sentence at the root of this book is Paul's word from Romans 4: Abraham "grew strong in his faith as he gave glory to God, fully convinced that God was able to do what he had promised" (Rom. 4:20–21). Trusting God's word glorifies God. Why is that true? It is true because trusting a person calls attention to the person's trustworthiness. But that is true *only* if the trust is warranted. Groundless trust does not honor the person trusted. If you trust me with your money when you don't know me or have any good reason, based on my character, to believe I won't steal it, you are not showing me to be trustworthy; you are showing yourself to be a fool. Only warranted trust glorifies the one trusted.

---

[1] Jonathan Edwards, *A Treatise Concerning Religious Affections*, vol. 2, *The Works of Jonathan Edwards*, ed. John Smith (New Haven, CT: Yale University Press, 1957), 304.
[2] Ibid., 299, 303.

Which means that the task I have set myself in this book is to answer the question: What warrant—what good foundation—in the Christian Scriptures provides a well-grounded trust? What basis of belief in the Scriptures as the word of God will, in fact, honor God?

The Glory of the God Who Speaks

Another way to describe what I am aiming at is to distinguish the argument for our confidence in Scripture from the argument that simply says, "We believe the Scriptures because God says they are his word, and God should be believed." My problem with this sentence is not that it is false but that it is ambiguous.

There are false prophets who say, "Thus says the Lord." Yet, "I have not sent them, declares the LORD, but they are prophesying falsely in my name" (Jer. 27:15). What this implies is that when God says, "Thus says the Lord," we are obliged to believe it not *merely* because that's what the word says, but because the glory of the speaker and what he says is manifestly divine. My argument is that the glory of God in and through the Scriptures is a real, objective, self-authenticating reality. Christian faith is not a leap in the dark. It is not a guess or a wager. God is not honored if he is chosen by the flip of a coin. A leap into the unknown is no honor to one who has made himself known.

In the End We Know by Sight, Not Inference

The argument of this book is that the final step of certainty concerning the Scriptures is the step of sight, not inference. The pathway that leads to sight may involve much empirical observation, and historical awareness, and rational thought (see chapter 17). But the end we are seeking is not a probable inference from historical reasoning but a full assurance that we have seen the glory of God. Thus, at the end of all human means, the simplest preliterate person and the most educated scholar come to a saving knowledge of the truth of Scripture in the same way: by a sight of its glory.

Liberating and Devastating

Of course, this is both liberating and devastating. It is liberating because it means the sweetness of well-grounded, God-honoring confidence in

Scripture is not reserved for scholars but is available for all who have eyes to see.

And it is devastating because no human being can see this glory without God's help. This is not because we are helpless victims of blindness but because we are lovers of blindness. "This is the judgment: the light has come into the world, and people loved the darkness rather than the light because their works were evil" (John 3:19). We are not chained in a dark cell, longing to see the sunshine of God's glory. We love the cell, because sin and Satan have deceived us into seeing the drawings on the wall as the true glory and the source of greatest pleasure. Our prison cell of darkness is not the bondage of external constraint but of internal preference. We have exchanged the glory of God for images (Rom. 1:23). We love them. That is our blindness.

What must happen is described by the apostle Paul in 2 Corinthians 4:6. The God who created light in the beginning must shine into our dark cell to reveal himself. "For God, who said, 'Let light shine out of darkness,' has shone in our hearts to give the light of the knowledge of the glory of God in the face of Jesus Christ." The answer to our darkness is the shining of divine glory into our hearts by means of the light of knowledge—the knowledge mediated by God's inspired Scripture. That is what this book is about.

This does not mean that there is nothing we can do in our quest to see the self-authenticating glory of God in Scripture. Jesus gave the apostle Paul an impossible mission. He sent Paul "to open their eyes, so that they may turn from darkness to light and from the power of Satan to God" (Acts 26:18). If it is hopeful for the apostle to move toward the blind, then it is hopeful for the blind to move toward the apostle. Blind or seeing, that is what I hope you will do with me in this book.

The Peculiar Glory

Thus the main burden of this book is parts 4 and 5 (chapters 8–17). In part 4, I probe into what really happens in our experience when we see the glory of God in Scripture; and I try to show how this authenticates the Scripture as God's life-giving, infallible word. In part 5, I argue that the way the Scriptures convince us is by the revelation of a peculiar glory. In other words, the power of Scripture to warrant well-grounded trust is not by generic glory. Not, as it were, by mere dazzling. Not by simply boggling the mind with supernatural otherness. Rather, what we see as inescapably divine is a peculiar glory. And at the center of this peculiar glory is the utterly unique glory of Jesus Christ. This is the heart of the book.

The peculiar glory of God, as he reveals it in the Scriptures, is the way his majesty is expressed through his meekness. I call this a paradoxical juxtaposition of seemingly opposite traits. Jonathan Edwards called it "an admirable conjunction of diverse excellencies." This pattern of God's self-revelation is his lion-like majesty together with his lamb-like meekness. God magnifies his greatness by making himself the supreme treasure of our hearts, even at great cost to himself (Rom. 8:32), and so serving us in the very act of exalting his glory. This peculiar brightness shines through the whole Bible and comes to its most beautiful radiance in the person and work of Jesus Christ, dying and rising for sinners.

I will argue that there is in every human being a "knowledge" of this God—this glory. There is a built-in template that is shaped for this peculiar communication of God's glory. When God opens our eyes (2 Cor. 4:6) and grants us the knowledge of the truth (2 Tim. 2:25), through the Scriptures (1 Sam. 3:21), we know that we have met ultimate reality.

By the instrument of the Scriptures, in the hands of the Holy Spirit, God cuts away the corrosion from the template of his glory. Miraculously we are thus conformed to the peculiar shape of God's glory. Where we saw only foolishness before, now we see the glory of majesty in meekness, and strength in suffering, and the wealth of God's glory in the depth of his giving—that is, in the light of the gospel of the glory of Christ.

Preliminary Questions

Before we direct our full attention to the question of how we know that the Christian Scriptures are the word of God, we must ask: What specific Scriptures are we talking about? Are we talking about the Apocrypha that is contained in the Roman Catholic Bible? Which books actually are parts of the Christian Bible? And what about the handwritten transmission of the Bible during three thousand years until the printing press was invented in 1450? Do we actually have the original words that the authors wrote? Those are the questions we deal with in part 1.

Closer to the heart of the matter, but still preliminary, is the question, What do the Scriptures claim for themselves? This question is preliminary because my argument is not that we believe the Scriptures because they *claim* to be God's word. But it is closer to the heart of the matter, because these claims are, in fact, essential threads in the fabric of the glory-revealing meaning of Scripture. Therefore, they are part of the panorama of glory that gives a well-grounded foundation to our confidence that the Scriptures are the totally true and infallible word of God. This is the focus of part 3.

Not a Masterpiece, but a Window

Part 1 is the story of my life with the Bible, from my childhood to the present. It has at least two purposes. One is to put all my cards on the table so that you know exactly where I stand as I try to deal honestly with the Bible. The other purpose is to draw attention to the way the Bible does its work in a person's life. I point out that I did not simply hold a view of the Bible for seven decades. I was held by a view through the Bible.

As I said at the beginning, the Bible has not been for me like a masterpiece hanging on the wall of an Alpine chalet but rather like a window in the wall of the chalet, with the Alps on the other side. In other words, I have been a Christian all these years not because I had the courage to hold on to an embattled view of Scripture, but because I have been held happily captive by the beauty of God and his ways that I see through the Scriptures.

If your heart says, How can this be? my answer is, Come and see.

PART 1

A Place to Stand

". . . the LORD *revealed himself by*
the word of the LORD*"*

Now to him who is able to keep you from stumbling and to present you blameless before the presence of his glory with great joy, to the only God, our Savior, through Jesus Christ our Lord, be glory, majesty, dominion, and authority, before all time and now and forever. Amen.

JUDE 24–25

1

My Story: Held by the Bible

Everyone stands somewhere, even if we sometimes don't know where we stand. This is true geographically and theologically. You might be blindfolded, and driven around town in a car for an hour, and then let out. You would be standing somewhere but may not know where.

I did this with my wife on her fortieth birthday so she would not know where I was taking her. In her case, she is simply too savvy in the city and could tell by sounds and turns where we were. It didn't work. But for the sake of the illustration, you can see what I mean: you can be standing somewhere and not know where you are standing.

That is true theologically also. Everyone is standing somewhere. I don't mean everyone is dug in somewhere. You might be ready to leave your geographic spot as soon as the blindfold comes off. And the same is true of your theological position. The blindfold I have in mind may be as simple as never having seriously thought about where you're standing. In other words, we may not know where we stand because we've never given it any attention.

But there we are, nonetheless, standing somewhere.

Standing in the Sway of What We Don't Know?

This is true about the Bible. We all stand somewhere in relation to the Bible. A few of us grew up in a Bible-believing home, and we came to believe and love the Bible for ourselves. We stand on it. We believe what it says is true, and we try to bring our lives into harmony with it. But that is not the rule.

My university professors in Germany stood somewhere in relation to the Bible—and it was not where I stood. You may once have stood where I stand and walked away. You may have been badly hurt by people who say they believe the Bible. Or you may have asked too many questions and become disillusioned with the anti-intellectual responses of "Bible-believing" Christians. Or you may be standing just around the corner from where I stand, and all you can see are shadows, but they are very attractive. Or you have just walked through a crisis that made everything feel unstable, and you are grasping for something firm and durable.

Some of you grew up in a home where the Bible was totally absent. You saw it only in the news when people were sworn into office with their hand on it. To this day it may be as absent to your mind as a mathematical equation you have never heard of. But that equation might be true. It might describe the forces of gravity that keep us on the ground. Or it might represent the interaction of oxygen and carbon dioxide that keeps you alive. Or it might signify the thrust needed from a jet engine to keep your plane in the air. In other words, you may be standing in the sway of a life-giving equation and not even know it exists.

It may be that way with the Bible too. It may describe a reality that totally encompasses you without your knowing it. It may describe a power that holds you in being. It may present a path of truth and wholeness and joy, some of which you have intuited and some of which you haven't. Without knowing it, you may enjoy some of that path, and other parts you may hate. But one thing is sure: all of us stand somewhere in relation to the Bible.

The Bible Is More Like a Letter Than an Equation

Likening the Bible to a mathematical equation is not strikingly profound. You can live your whole life with relative happiness, and then die, without regretting that you never knew a single one of those equations. Even though they describe how you walk and breathe and fly, knowing the particular formula doesn't matter.

The Bible isn't like that. And the main reason is that the Bible is more like a letter from the Creator of the universe than it is a record of the laws of nature. The record of natural laws is impersonal. But a letter from the Creator is personal. The main difference between a personal letter and a textbook on physics is that the letter is designed to connect you to the heart and mind of the writer, and the textbook is not. This is the great divide on how we approach the Bible. Does it express the heart and mind of a divine person, or is it merely a record of human religious experience?

This is one of the biggest questions about where we stand: Do we stand consciously in a personal universe or an impersonal one? Do I stand in the awareness that the main thing about the universe is that I am a person created by a Person? Do I live in a universe created by a Person who has purposes and plans for me and for the universe? Or do I stand in an impersonal universe? Does the world have no personal creator or governor? Do I stand as the product only of impersonal material forces?

Cover to cover, the Bible describes the world as personal. A personal God created the world. He created human beings in his own image to manage the world as his stewards.

> God created man in his own image,
>> in the image of God he created him;
>> male and female he created them.

And God blessed them. And God said to them, "Be fruitful and multiply and fill the earth and subdue it, and have dominion." (Gen. 1:27–28)

The least this means is that we are personal the way God is. We are personal in a way that the animals are not. In our personhood, the Bible says, we are meant to image forth the kind of person God is. That is what images are for. Only these images are *living* persons, not statues. Fill the earth with God-imaging persons—according to the Bible, that is human destiny. "Blessed be his glorious name forever; may the whole earth be filled with his glory! Amen and Amen!" (Ps. 72:19).

How Will the Creator Communicate?

This raises the question of whether and how the Creator aims to communicate with the persons he created in his image. Everyone stands somewhere in relation to that question. Not to think about it is a standing place. To say, "No, he doesn't," is a standing place. To say, "He does, through all religions," is a standing place. And to say, "Yes, uniquely and infallibly through the Christian Scriptures, the Bible," that too is a standing place.

And there are reasons why all of us are standing where we are. Some of those reasons are conscious, and some are not. You may have thought about it and concluded: *I just can't know for sure.* Or you may have thought and concluded: *I simply don't approve of the God of the Bible and the way he tells people to live.* Or you may have read it and seen so much moral and spiritual beauty in Jesus that you concluded: *I can't deny what I have seen—this is real.*

I'm in that last category.

So let me clarify where I stand, so we can all be clear from the outset, and you can know what you are dealing with in this book. Then we can raise this question: *Why should we believe this?*

My Standing Place: Home

I grew up in a home where the Bible was assumed to be the infallible word of God. Whether they succeeded or failed, my parents tried to submit to the authority of the Bible. I think they succeeded pretty well. That's probably one reason I never rebelled against them. They tried to form their ideas about God and man and sin and salvation from the Bible. They tried to bring their attitudes and emotions in line with the Bible. And they tried to form their behaviors by the Bible.

That's what you do, if you believe it is a reliable communication from your Creator. In spite of blind spots, and in spite of what the Bible calls "indwelling sin" (Rom. 7:17, 20), I think my parents fundamentally succeeded. The God they worshiped, the Savior they trusted, the joy they experienced, and the love they showed were, I believe, truly the God, the Savior, the joy, and the love of the Bible. It was all real.

There was no claim to perfection, either in knowledge of God or responses to that knowledge. They knew what the Bible itself taught about our knowledge: "Now we see in a mirror dimly, but then face to face. Now I know in part; then I shall know fully, even as I have been fully known" (1 Cor. 13:12). We can know truly, but we cannot know comprehensively or flawlessly while we remain sinners. The day will come when Jesus will return to earth, and the followers of Jesus will be changed. We will sin no more. And even though we will not become omniscient, we will cease to believe wrong things (1 Cor. 13:12).

But for now, we are fallible people, trying to submit as fully as we can to an infallible Book inspired by God. That is what my parents believed and what I grew up believing. As I moved through twenty-two years of formal education, the challenges to this view of the Bible were many and constant. They are many and constant today. And I assume there will be many of them until Jesus comes, because one of the most prominent writers of the Bible predicted it:

> The time is coming when people will not endure sound teaching, but having itching ears they will accumulate for themselves teachers to suit their own passions, and will turn away from listening to the truth and wander off into myths. (2 Tim. 4:3–4)

Those times were already happening when the Bible was written. And there is good reason to believe that as the end of the world approaches (a time of which no one can predict), the Bible will be more embattled than ever.

So, as I moved through college in Illinois, and seminary in California, and graduate school in Germany, I was not surprised that the objections to this view of the Bible intensified at every stage. Can you really continue to hold onto the view of your youth even though you are in graduate school in Germany, where virtually no one shares your view—neither students nor professors?

Not So Much Holding a View as Being Held

It may sound strange, but "holding onto my view" was never the way I experienced it—at least not as I can remember. It felt more like my view of the Bible was holding onto me. Or, as I believe today, God was holding onto me by clarifying and brightening and deepening my view of him in the Bible. I believe that's why the view I received from my parents remained more compelling than any competing view all along the way.

I looked at many competing views of the Bible. I had to. That's what liberal arts education does. It exposes you to great alternative worldviews—as we like to call them. And in seminary, the challenges became more focused on the historicity and formation and preservation of the Bible itself. Then in graduate school, I didn't just read about those views; I had seminars and hallway discussions with the people who held those views and taught them and wrote books about them. In other words, the challenges to my view of the Bible moved from worldview challenges, to historical-critical challenges, to personal challenges.

But simultaneously my view itself was being clarified, brightened, and deepened. It never felt as if the bad guys ganged up to pommel my poor, adolescent, Sunday-school view of the Bible. At every point, it felt like the view grew to be a match for all comers.

The View: Clarified, Brightened, Deepened

Now I need to be careful here, or I am going to create the wrong impression. What I just wrote could sound very intellectual and could give the impression that what was really happening is that I was becoming smarter. I suppose I was learning more and more about presuppositions, and about the logical flaws of certain arguments, and about the misuse of historical data. But that was not decisive. I'm not talking about becoming smarter when I say that my view was being clarified, and brightened, and deepened.

What I mean can be best understood if you take the word *view* not just in an intellectual sense (as in *viewpoint*), but in the aesthetic sense—as in *vista*, or *sight*, or *landscape*. I never recall merely having a view of the Bible, as if it was a book on the table, and I viewed it this way and not that way, nor did I see it as a set of ideas that I could view this way or that way.

Not a Painting on the Wall, but a Window

The Bible was never like a masterpiece hanging in a museum that I viewed this way and that. Rather, it was like a window. Or like binoculars. My view *of* the Bible was always a view *through* the Bible. So when I say that, all along the way, my view was getting clearer and brighter and deeper, I mean the reality seen through it was getting clearer and brighter and deeper. *Clearer* as the edges of things became less fuzzy, and I could see how things fit together rather than just smudging into each other. *Brighter* as the beauty and impact of the whole message was more and more attractive. And *deeper* in the sense of depth perspective—I suppose photographers would say "depth of field." Things stretched off into eternity with breathtaking implications—in both directions past and future. You could sum this up with the phrase *the glory of God*. That's what I was seeing.

That is what was changing to meet the challenges. This was not an intellectual effort. Seeing is not an effort the way thinking is. It happens. You may need to exert yourself to walk up to the edge of the Grand Canyon, but when you get there, seeing is not work. You may need to travel to the Alps or the Himalayas, but when you get there, seeing is not an effort. It is given to you.

I did my walking and my traveling. That's what education is. But I did not make myself see. And that is why I say it is not as though I was holding onto my view of the Bible, but rather that the view was holding onto me. Or God was holding onto me by making the view supremely compelling. If you are standing on the edge of the Grand Canyon, or rafting down the Colorado River *inside* the canyon (as I did in the summer of 2012), it is proper to say you are held by the view, the sight, the vista. That is what the Bible was doing for me. It was holding me; I was not holding it.

When the Clouds Part

Here's an analogy—a living parable—for how it worked.

One of those seven days rafting 190 miles down the Colorado River through the Grand Canyon, it began to rain. That didn't matter much, since we were already wet from the rapids. We were dressed for it. The frustrating part was that it was lunchtime, and there are only so many small beaches where you can tie up and eat.

So we tied up and set up the tables and put up a large umbrella to keep the rain off our peanut butter sandwiches. But the rain was so hard and the wind so strong that the umbrella was useless, and we had to eat soggy sandwiches. We laughed about it, but it was unpleasant and frustrating. For a moment, my "view" was not so clear, and bright, and deep. Maybe being in the Grand Canyon is not so compelling after all. Maybe a dry seat in the hotel back in Las Vegas would be more compelling.

Little did we know what was about to happen. We boarded our two large, blue, motor-driven rafts and set out down river. The rain stopped and the sky started to clear, when suddenly, almost simultaneously, dozens of waterfalls burst out into the river in front of and behind us from the walls of the canyon. Some of these were gigantic, falling a thousand feet. The water coming out of the gorges was red. The guide explained what had happened.

He said that during a hard rain the water in the gorges comes down from the steep sides and builds and builds until it is a rushing river—a rain-made temporary river in a place where it almost never rains—dozens of temporary rivers looking for an outlet. When the water reaches a certain force, it breaks out over the precipice into the canyon as a waterfall. And the red color is owing to the soil it picked up on the way. It was stunning.

Then he said, we might not see the likes of this in the canyon for another hundred years.

That is a parable of how God held onto me by my view of the Bible—that is, my view through the Bible. Just when the view started to seem foggy and rainy and frustrating, and other views of life started to seem more attractive, God would clear the skies and cause even the rain to serve the irresistibly beautiful vista of his glory. He never let any other view of reality outshine the view of the Bible.

So, yes, I still hold the basic view that my parents did and that the Christian church has held through its whole history until the streetlights of the Enlightenment began blinding people to the stars and luring people away from the brightness of God's glory. That is where I still stand—on the edge of the Grand Canyon, and at the foot of the Himalayas, and sometimes rafting right down through the depths of the glory.

More specifically, then, what kind of binoculars is the Bible? What kind of window onto the glory of God is this? Let me move toward a precise description of the kind of book the Bible is by taking you from my days of formal education to where I am today in relation to the church and school and web ministry that I have served.

Teaching College Students as the Vista Expands

When I was twenty-eight, I found my first real job. With my wife and son, I came home from Germany in 1974 and moved straight to St. Paul, Minnesota, where I began to teach biblical studies at Bethel College (now Bethel University). I couldn't believe they were paying me to study and teach the Bible. I would have done it for free, except that I had a wife and a child to support. So the $10,500 annual salary was a needed bonus to the privilege.

I taught New Testament introduction, Greek, and individual New Testament book studies. I loved it. To this day, few things are more gratifying to me than looking at the Bible—and *through* the Bible—long enough to see what is really there and then helping others see it for themselves. I had done it for Sunday school classes all through seminary and graduate school. Now I was doing it for college students. It was deeply satisfying.

Some of my energy was devoted to defining how the view of my parents—my view—related to tough questions such as why there are different accounts of the same event in the four Gospels, especially Matthew, Mark, and Luke (called the Synoptic Gospels). So I wrote a short paper early in my time at Bethel called "How are the Synoptics without Error?"[1] It became a position paper for the Bible faculty for the years I was there.

But, mostly, my energies were devoted to looking through the inerrant window, not at the Bible's "inerrancy" itself. I loved pushing students' noses against the window pane of the first epistle of John, and the first epistle of Peter, and 1 and 2 Thessalonians, and the Gospel of Luke, and doing all I could, with prayer and modeling and asking good questions, to help them see the glory of this Christ-dominated landscape.

The effect of this Bible-saturated life was that a vision of God's greatness and glory and centrality was becoming more clear and bright and deep. I found that one aspect of this glory, namely, God's sovereignty over all things, was relentlessly controversial in all my classes. No matter the text or the subject of the class, that issue would come

---

[1] Available at http://www.desiringgod.org/articles/how-are-the-synoptics-without-error.

up. Students would see it shining in the distance (some might have said lurking or prowling). And not a few of them did not like what they saw.

This did not surprise me, but it did trouble me. I had been in their shoes all through my own college days. And I had gone to seminary as a person who was happy to put limits on God's sovereignty by my *self*-determining will (which I liked to call "free will"). This is the air we breathe in America, and it is the default assumption of the human heart. By nature and culture, we resonate with William Earnest Henley's "Invictus":

> It matters not how strait the gate,
> > How charged with punishments the scroll,
> I am the master of my fate,
> > I am the captain of my soul.

One of the reasons this feels so obvious is that moral accountability seems impossible without ultimate human self-determination. And if anything is clear in the Bible, it is that human beings are morally accountable to God. I had never really considered whether this assumption—that moral responsibility requires human autonomy—was in the Bible. I just assumed it was. But I did have to admit that defending my own volitional supremacy did not produce a robust experience of worship.

Only in seminary was I able to see that one of the highest, reddest, most magnificent of all the waterfalls in the canyon of God's glory was the absolute sovereignty of God. I wrote on my final exam in a course on systematic theology, "Romans 9 is like a tiger going around devouring free-willers like me." The battle had been painful, and there were tears along the way. But now the fight was over. What had seemed like an assault on my freedom became the ground of my hope.[2]

Romans 9 and the Call to the Pastorate

So I knew what these students were feeling. What was troubling is that when I tried to show them what I had found in Romans 9, for example,

---

[2] If any reader would like to see how I worked all this out, one place to look would be John Piper, *The Pleasures of God: Meditations on God's Delight in Being God* (Colorado Springs, CO: Multnomah, 2012), chaps. 2, 4, 5.

many of them were not persuaded. They argued that it simply does not mean what Piper says it means. And they had books and teachers to back them up.

Eventually, when my time for a sabbatical came, I took it from the spring of 1979 till January 1980 to write the most thorough treatment of Romans 9:1–23 that I was capable of. I put my eye to those twenty-three verses and looked as hard as I could, day and night, for those months. The book was published as *The Justification of God* in 1983.[3] I was writing it first for my own conscience's sake and then for my students. Was I really seeing what is there? I inherited from my parents not only a high view of the Bible but also a sober view of my sinfulness and fallibility. I was not without error. The Bible was. So I was writing the book to test what I saw in Romans 9.

But something utterly unexpected happened. As I worked on Romans 9 day after day for months, the vision of God's magisterial sovereignty not only became more and more clear, but it took hold of me in a way I had never planned.

When I was a child and a teenager, folks would ask me, "Are you going to be a preacher like your dad?" My father was a traveling evangelist—a great preacher in my estimation, and I respected and loved him deeply. I still do. But I would always answer no. The simple reason was that I couldn't speak in front of a group without freezing up. It was a horrible condition for an adolescent. And to this day, I do not make light of it. God lifted that burden in part when I was in college and seminary. I was able to teach. But teaching seemed very different from preaching.

But during that sabbatical, the God of Romans 9 seemed to be saying through the window of his word: "I will be proclaimed, not just analyzed. I will be heralded, not just studied and explained." And little by little there grew in me a desire—totally unexpected—to leave academia and preach this great and glorious God of Romans 9.

I wanted to see what would happen. I wanted to put to the test whether preaching the whole counsel of God—with a vision of God that many students found offensive—could grow and sustain and nurture and delight and guide and empower a church with people from all age

---

[3] John Piper, *The Justification of God: An Exegetical and Theological Study of Romans 9:1–23* (Grand Rapids, MI: Baker, 1983).

ranges and different educational and ethnic backgrounds. On the one hand, this felt like a challenge to exalt the greatness of God, but on the other hand, it felt like a challenge to the authority and truthfulness of the Bible.

Could I preach the God of the Bible as he really was in the text? Could all the things the Bible says about God and about man and salvation and holiness and suffering really be heralded with unvarnished clarity so that a people would be built up, and souls would be saved, and missions would be advanced, and justice would roll down like rivers, and joy would abound even in sorrow?

Looking through the Book from behind the Pulpit

I could not resist this call. It became overwhelming on the night of October 14, 1979. That next morning my wife said she had seen it coming and would happily support the move. I resigned my teaching post and accepted the call to be the preaching pastor at Bethlehem Baptist Church in Minneapolis, Minnesota, where I served for thirty-three years until the spring of 2013.

My answer to the question *Can the God of Romans 9, with his absolute sovereignty over all things, including salvation and suffering, be preached without compromise for the growth and strength and mission of the church?* is yes. For thirty-three years, week in and week out, I gazed at the words of Scripture until I saw through them to the Reality and then preached what I saw. I do not recall a single weekend when I was not excited to preach what God had shown me. Sometimes this was controversial. But I tried to be so faithful to the text of the Bible, and so transparent about how I saw what I saw, that the people would trust me. I did not want them to depend on my authority but on God's authority in the Bible. I resonated with the apostle Paul when he said,

> My speech and my message were not in plausible words of wisdom, but in demonstration of the Spirit and of power, so that your faith might not rest in the wisdom of men but in the power of God. (1 Cor. 2:4–5)

In one sense, I viewed my whole ministry as a demonstration of the truth and authority of God's word, preached with as much clarity and brightness and depth as I was able, with God's help. Would my "view" of the Bible that I inherited from my parents prove as compelling to others as it was to me? The question was not mainly, *Would they come to "hold" my view?* The question was, *Would the view of God's glory in the Scriptures hold them as it has held me?* That was the test. History, and finally eternity, will answer.

An Eldership of One Mind on the Whole Counsel of God

When I came to Bethlehem Baptist Church in 1980, there was a very broad affirmation of faith, doctrinally speaking. I am very much in favor of a broad affirmation of faith as a qualification for *membership* in the local church. I think that's right. The door into the local body of believers, it seems to me, should be roughly the same size as the door into the universal body of believers.

But the door into the eldership—that is, the door into the council that will give an account to God for the souls of the flock as teachers and leaders (Heb. 13:17; 1 Tim. 3:2; 5:17)—should be much narrower. When Paul addresses the elders of the church, his stress is that they not shrink back from teaching anything in God's counsel, but give the flock the "whole counsel of God" (Acts 20:20, 27–28). That implies that elders must make an effort to find and clarify and preserve this whole counsel of God.

Little by little through the years at Bethlehem, I was preaching and teaching and leading in such a way that I hoped would lead the elders to have one mind about what this whole counsel looked like. After about fifteen years, I thought we were ready to work toward putting our unified grasp of God's word into a document we could all agree on. This affirmation of faith then would become the criteria, under Scripture, of what the elders would be expected to believe and teach.

The aim, of course, was that the people would joyfully see this as truth from the Bible and gladly embrace it. But since people were joining the church all the time at different levels of biblical understanding, and since people did not always agree with everything in the document, we did not make this affirmation of faith a criterion for membership. It represented where the elders would try to lead the people, not where people had to be in order to join the church.

In other words, the aim was that the elders would define a place to stand—including a place to stand regarding the nature of the Bible. That is section 1 in the document. This process of refining what has become the Bethlehem Baptist Church Elder Affirmation of Faith (now embraced also by Bethlehem College and Seminary, and the Treasuring Christ Together network of churches, and the ministry of desiringGod. org) took several years.

I did the first draft and then sent the document to a dozen respected leaders outside Bethlehem for feedback, to be sure it avoided eccentricities. I wanted it to be a fresh statement of biblical truth, exalting the glory of God, and interwoven with the truth that God is most glorified in us when we are satisfied in him. But I did not want it to be idiosyncratic or quirky or novel. We do not think God has shown us truth that no one else has seen. We believe it is wise and humble to aim at reclaiming the glory of long-held biblical truth rather than claiming new discoveries.

The elders worked on it for a long time, and we were in no rush. We were working for the generations to come, not just for ourselves. We hoped to put in place an affirmation of faith that God might be pleased to use for decades to protect and ignite the truth in the institutions and personal lives that had grown up at the church. So twenty years after my arrival, the elders unanimously settled on the wording of the affirmation, and the church voted that from that time on all the elders would embrace this truth as the core of what we would preach and teach.

Section 1 concerns the Scriptures—the subject matter of this book. This is where we stand. This is the standing place that defines this book. This is the view we "hold." But more importantly, it is the nature of the window onto the vista of God's glory that has *held* us—held me for over sixty years.

1. Scripture, the Word of God Written

1.1 We believe that the Bible, consisting of the sixty-six books of the Old and New Testaments, is the infallible Word of God, verbally inspired by God, and without error in the original manuscripts.

1.2 We believe that God's intentions, revealed in the Bible, are the supreme and final authority in testing all claims about what is true and what is right. In matters not addressed by the Bible, what is true and right is assessed by criteria consistent with the teachings of Scripture.

1.3 We believe God's intentions are revealed through the intentions of inspired human authors, even when the authors' intention was to express divine meaning of which they were not fully aware, as, for example, in the case of some Old Testament prophecies. Thus the meaning of Biblical texts is a fixed historical reality, rooted in the historical, unchangeable intentions of its divine and human authors. However, while meaning does not change, the application of that meaning may change in various situations. Nevertheless it is not legitimate to infer a meaning from a Biblical text that is not demonstrably carried by the words which God inspired.

1.4 Therefore, the process of discovering the intention of God in the Bible (which is its fullest meaning) is a humble and careful effort to find in the language of Scripture what the human authors intended to communicate. Limited abilities, traditional biases, personal sin, and cultural assumptions often obscure Biblical texts. Therefore the work of the Holy Spirit is essential for right understanding of the Bible, and prayer for His assistance belongs to a proper effort to understand and apply God's word.

Here I Stand

This is where I stand with hope and joy and love. This is the window of the Word through which the vision of God has exerted its compelling power. I do not merely hold a view of Scripture. I am held. The glory of God shining through his Word has been an irresistible treasure. Nothing in this world comes close to the beauty and the value of God and his ways and his grace.

After almost seven decades of seeing and savoring the glory of God in Scripture, the doxology of Jude 24–25 is very personal:

> Now to him who is able to keep you from stumbling and to present you blameless before the presence of his *glory* with great joy, to the only God, our Savior, through Jesus Christ our Lord, be *glory*, majesty, dominion, and authority, before all time and now and forever. Amen.

In my case—and I think it is what Jude intends—the "glory, majesty, dominion, and authority" of God are ascribed to him here because this is what, in fact, did the keeping. He has kept me—held me—by his glory by revealing his glory to my heart year after year so that other glories would not lure me away. This he has done through his word. For me, the glory of God and the word of God are inseparable. I have no sure sight of God's glory except through his word. The word mediates the glory, and the glory confirms the word.

We turn now to a more important story than my own—the story of how the Bible came to be and how it has confirmed its truth and authority for two thousand years. How do we know what the Bible is—which books are in it? How do we know it's true? How has the Bible provided a well-grounded faith that the Bible itself is the word of God?

This wonderful story of God's work in the world—to create his written word and to build his church by his word—is woven together with my story. It is also woven together with yours. Everyone will be drawn into this story one way or the other. It could not be otherwise, since we are not dealing with a tribal deity and a provincial book. We are dealing with the Creator of the universe and a book that he inspired as a gift for all the peoples of the world. I invite you to come with me. I know of no greater quest than this: Is the Bible God's word? Are the Christian Scriptures true? How do we know?

PART 2

What Books and Words Make Up the Christian Scriptures?

". . . from the blood of Abel to the blood of Zechariah"

Truly, I say to you, until heaven and earth pass away, not an iota, not a dot, will pass from the Law until all is accomplished.

MATTHEW 5:18

2

Which Books Make Up
the Old Testament?

We believe that the Bible, consisting of the sixty-six books of the Old and New Testaments, is the infallible Word of God, verbally inspired by God, and without error in the original manuscripts.

It is a stupendous claim that any book written by human hands is the infallible word of God. If the claim is true, and if the book claims to teach the only path to eternal life, then that book is more important than any other book. It has more to offer us than any other book. And what it offers is of infinite importance.

What the Christian Scriptures Offer

One of Jesus's followers said to him, "Lord, to whom shall we go? You have the words of eternal life" (John 6:68). In other words, any attempt to find eternal life apart from the words of Jesus will fail. This is what the emissaries of Jesus taught when he had been raised from the dead: "There is salvation in no one else, for there is no other name under heaven given among men by which we must be saved" (Acts 4:12).

That conviction was rooted in what Jesus himself had taught: "Truly, truly, I say to you, whoever hears my word and believes him who sent me has eternal life" (John 5:24). And this was an exclusive claim: "I am the way, and the truth, and the life. No one comes to the Father except through me" (John 14:6). So his followers taught, "Whoever has the Son has life; whoever does not have the Son of God does not have life" (1 John 5:12).

To reject the words of Jesus's apostles when they preached in his name, and wrote the New Testament, was to spurn eternal life. "Paul and Barnabas spoke out boldly, saying, 'It was necessary that the word of God be spoken first to you. Since you thrust it aside and judge yourselves unworthy of eternal life, behold, we are turning to the Gentiles'" (Acts 13:46). To thrust this word of God away is to thrust away life.

So, I say it again: if the claim of such a book is true, then that book is more important than any other book. It has more to offer us than any other book. And what it offers is of infinite importance.

What Book Are We Talking About?

This means that even before we show how this book reveals its truth, we need to clarify what book we are talking about. If we are going to gaze through the window of this book in the hope of finding everlasting life and inexpressible joy, then we need to know which book we are talking about. And that life and joy are precisely what we hope to find. The fullest life possible. And inexpressible joy.

If that is not what we find at the end of our quest, then we are wasting our time. And, be assured, that is precisely what the book claims to offer: "I came that they may have life and have it abundantly" (John 10:10). "Though you do not now see [Jesus], you believe in him and rejoice with joy that is inexpressible and filled with glory, obtaining the outcome of your faith, the salvation of your souls" (1 Pet. 1:8–9). Fullness of everlasting life and inexpressible joy in the greatest person in the universe, Jesus, the Son of God.

Which Books Are in the Book?

So the specific question is: What Bible are you talking about? The answer in our Affirmation of Faith is "the Bible, consisting of the sixty-six books of the Old and New Testaments." If you are new to the Bible, those terms may be new to you. You will discover when you look at the table of contents in the Bible that there are two parts. The first is called the Old Testament; the second is the New Testament. The word *testament* is an old word for *covenant,* which is a biblical word for God's commitment to keep certain promises to his people on certain terms. The Old Testament contains the books that deal with God's interaction with the world and with Israel before the coming of Jesus. The New Testament contains books that deal with God's breaking into history in Jesus Christ and the founding of the Christian church and Christian mission. There are thirty-nine books in our[1] modern-language Old Testament and twenty-seven books in our modern-language New Testament.

Old Testament		
Genesis	2 Chronicles	Daniel
Exodus	Ezra	Hosea
Leviticus	Nehemiah	Joel
Numbers	Esther	Amos
Deuteronomy	Job	Obadiah
Joshua	Psalms	Jonah
Judges	Proverbs	Micah
Ruth	Ecclesiastes	Nahum
1 Samuel	Song of Solomon	Habakkuk
2 Samuel	Isaiah	Zephaniah
1 Kings	Jeremiah	Haggai
2 Kings	Lamentations	Zechariah
1 Chronicles	Ezekiel	Malachi

---

[1] When I refer to "our," I mean "Protestant," because the Roman Catholic Old Testament includes books from the Apocrypha. See below.

New Testament		
Matthew	Ephesians	Hebrews
Mark	Philippians	James
Luke	Colossians	1 Peter
John	1 Thessalonians	2 Peter
Acts	2 Thessalonians	1 John
Romans	1 Timothy	2 John
1 Corinthians	2 Timothy	3 John
2 Corinthians	Titus	Jude
Galatians	Philemon	Revelation

You can see that the Bible is a book of "books"—history, prophecy, poetry, proverbs, letters, and more—from various human authors across fifteen hundred years. It is astonishing that sixty-six such varied "books" would be gathered into one Bible (from the Greek *biblion*, which means "book") with a coherent historical development from creation in the past to the coming kingdom of God on earth in the future.

These books are sometimes called the "canon" of Scripture. It might be important for you to know this, because whole books and many articles have been written discussing what books actually belong in the "canon" and the process that eventually determined what books would be in the "canon" (the process of canonization). The word *canon* originally meant (in its Greek root, *kanōn*) "straight staff," or "measuring rod," and then a guide or a model or a test of truth or beauty.

We can see it used this way in the New Testament: "And as for all who walk by this rule [*kanoni*], peace and mercy be upon them, and upon the Israel of God" (Gal. 6:16). The earliest use of the word *canon* in reference to the books of the Bible seems to be at the Council of Laodicea in AD 363: "No psalms of private authorship can be read in the churches, nor *uncanonical* books, but only the *canonical* books of the Old and New Testaments."[2]

---

[2] Samuel Macauley Jackson, *The New Schaff-Herzog Encyclopedia of Religious Knowledge*, vol. 1 (New York: Funk and Wagnalls, 1908), 385.

The Canon of the Old Testament

There are several important things to know about the formation of the Old Testament canon. The first is that the list of thirty-nine books in our Old Testament are the same books that make up the Jewish Bible, which they call the Tanach (a word built on the first letters of three groupings of the sixty-six books, *Torah, Nebiim, Chetuvim*, which are the Hebrew words for Law, Prophets, Writings).

The Jewish Bible organizes differently the thirty-nine books that are in our Old Testament (which of course the Jewish people would never call an "Old Testament" since for mainstream Judaism, Jesus is not yet recognized as the Messiah, and so the New Testament is not part of their Bible). In their Tanach are twenty-four books, which include all of our thirty-nine and no more. The reason the number is twenty-four instead of thirty-nine is that the Jewish Bible treats as one book several that the Christian Bible counts as two or more. Here is the way they organize the books and the order in which they occur:

- *Torah* (Law): Genesis, Exodus, Leviticus, Numbers, Deuteronomy

- *Nebiim* (Prophets): Joshua, Judges, Samuel (1 and 2), Kings (1 and 2), Isaiah, Jeremiah, Ezekiel, the Minor Prophets (treated as one book, which in the Christian Bible are twelve: Hosea, Joel, Amos, Obadiah, Jonah, Micah, Nahum, Habakkuk, Zephaniah, Haggai, Zechariah, Malachi)

- *Chetuvim* (Writings): Psalms, Job, Proverbs, Ruth, Song of Solomon, Ecclesiastes, Lamentations, Esther, Daniel, Ezra-Nehemiah (treated as one book), Chronicles (1 and 2)

Thus the canon of the Jewish Bible (the Tanach) begins with Genesis and ends with 2 Chronicles. The Christian Bible begins with Genesis and ends with the prophet Malachi. The books are ordered differently. This will be an important fact when we come to ask what Bible Jesus used.

Why Is the Christian Old Testament Ordered Differently?

Interestingly, the reason our organization of the Old Testament books is different from the Jewish Hebrew Bible is that the Christian organization was based on the widely used Greek translation of the Hebrew

Bible. This translation is called the Septuagint and is often abbreviated LXX (the Roman numeral for seventy) because the tradition is that it was translated into Greek by seventy scholars.

The reason this is interesting is that even though the organization of the Christian Bible is based on the organization of the Septuagint, our Bible does *not* contain all the Old Testament books contained in the Septuagint. In other words, the early Christians were willing to use the Septuagint as a helpful translation, but they did not agree with the Septuagint as to which books should be in the authoritative canon of the Word of God. The Christian church believed that the Hebrew Bible contained the only authoritative books.

Besides the thirty-nine books that are in the Old Testament we have today (and in the Hebrew Bible), other Jewish books were written in the period between the Old and New Testaments. These include:

1 Esdras	Epistle of Jeremiah
2 Esdras	Prayer of Azariah
Tobit	Susanna
Judith	Bel and the Dragon
Additions to Esther	Prayer of Manasseh
Wisdom of Solomon	1 Maccabees
Ecclesiasticus (or Sirach)	2 Maccabees
Baruch	

These books came to be called, as a group, the "Apocrypha," which comes from the Greek *apokryphos*, which means "hidden" or "secret" or "obscure." Neither in Jesus's day nor in ours did the Jewish people consider the Apocrypha to have the authority of the canonical books. For example, one of the most authoritative voices in the Jewish community, the Babylonian Talmud (Yomah 9b), says, "After the latter prophets Haggai, Zechariah, and Malachi had died, the Holy Spirit departed from Israel." The point was not that the Spirit was inactive in the world but that his unique work of inspiring authors of Scripture had ceased.

Similarly the Jewish book of 1 Maccabees 4:45–46 (written about 100 BC) spoke of the cessation of prophecy: "So they tore down the altar and stored the stone in a convenient place on the temple hill *until there should come a prophet* to tell what to do with them" (emphasis added). And again the author refers to great distress "such as had not been *since the time that prophets ceased to appear among them*" (1 Macc. 9:27, emphasis added).

Josephus, the Jewish historian who was born about AD 37, wrote, "From Artaxerxes [at the end of Old Testament era] to our own times a complete history has been written, but has not been deemed worthy of equal credit with the earlier records, because of *the failure of the exact succession of the prophets*" (*Ag. Ap.* 1:41, emphasis added). In other words, he knew the writings of the Apocrypha and did not regard them as canonical. Similarly, the Jewish mystic Philo, who died about AD 50, knew the Aprocrypha and did not consider these writings authoritative on par with the Hebrew canon.[3]

What this means is that while the early Christian church adapted its ordering of the Old Testament books to the order in the Septuagint, the church did not follow the Septuagint by including the apocryphal books in the Christian Old Testament.

The New Testament Witness to the Old Testament Canon

When we turn to the New Testament witness about the Old Testament canon, it is striking that, according to Roger Nicole, the New Testament quotes various parts of the Old Testament as divinely authoritative more than 295 times, but not once does it cite any statement from the books of the Apocrypha, or any other writings, as having divine authority.[4] One of the New Testament books, Jude (in 14–15), does quote the pseudepigraphal book 1 Enoch 60:8 and 1:9, and Paul quotes pagan authors in Acts 17:28 and Titus 1:12, but none of these citations is quoted as Scripture or as having divine authority.

When the apostle Paul referred to the "Scripture" as inspired by God in 2 Timothy 3:16 ("All Scripture is breathed out by God"), he was referring to the "sacred writings" that Timothy had been taught by his Jewish mother and grandmother:

---

[3] Roger Beckwith, *The Old Testament Canon of the New Testament Church* (Grand Rapids, MI: Eerdmans, 1985), 117; F. F. Bruce, *The Canon of Scripture* (Downers Grove, IL: InterVarsity, 1988), 29–30.

[4] Roger Nicole, "New Testament Use of the Old Testament," in *Revelation and the Bible*, ed. Carl Henry (London: Tyndale Press, 1959), 137–41. We will have more to say about the New Testament's witness to the Old Testament in chap. 6.

> As for you, continue in what you have learned and have firmly believed, knowing from whom you learned it and how from childhood you have been acquainted with the sacred writings, which are able to make you wise for salvation through faith in Christ Jesus. (2 Tim. 3:14–15)

Those who had taught Timothy from his youth were his mother and grandmother: "I am reminded of your sincere faith, a faith that dwelt first in your grandmother Lois and your mother Eunice and now, I am sure, dwells in you as well" (2 Tim. 1:5). We know from Acts 16:1 that Timothy's mother was Jewish. Therefore, there is good reason to believe that he had been raised as a good Jew with the understanding that the Hebrew canon, not the Apocrypha, was the inspired, authoritative word of God. And as Paul affirms its inspiration in 2 Timothy 3:16, he makes no attempt to include any other books than those that would be assumed as part of the "sacred writings" of his and Timothy's Jewish upbringing.

What Was Jesus's Bible?

There is no record of any dispute between Jesus and the Jewish leaders of his day over what the extent of the Scriptures was. He seemed to assume that their Bible was his Bible, and he made remarkable claims about its authority, like, "The Scripture cannot be broken" (John 10:35). Given the hostilities between the greatest Jewish authorities and Jesus, and given Jesus's pervasive dependence on the Hebrew Scriptures, it is almost certain that Jesus would have been criticized by his adversaries if he took the position that the Jewish Scriptures should be supplemented by other books such as the Apocrypha. There is no evidence that Jesus did so. And there is no evidence that he was ever criticized for his understanding of the extent of the Hebrew canon. Jesus and his adversaries disagreed over the meaning of the Hebrew Scriptures, not their scope.

So when Jesus referred to the whole Hebrew Bible, we are not surprised that he would use terms that reflect the standard Jewish division into Law, Prophets, and Writings. For example, in Luke 24:44 he said,

> These are my words that I spoke to you while I was still with you, that everything written about me in the *Law of Moses* and the *Prophets* and the *Psalms* must be fulfilled.

I think Robert Stein is right when he says that the use of the word "Psalms," instead of "Writings," is owing to the fact that Psalms was the first and the largest book in the Writings and probably came to stand for the whole.[5] Having mentioned the three parts of the Hebrew Scriptures, Luke says in the next verse, "Then he opened their minds to understand the *Scriptures*" (Luke 24:45). In other words, what Jesus had just designated "Law of Moses, Prophets, and Psalms," Luke now calls "the Scriptures." This is a strong indication that Jesus's Bible was not the Septuagint, with its added books and its different arrangement, but the Hebrew Bible, the structure of which he took for granted.

The most significant demonstration that Jesus's Bible contained only the books of the Hebrew Bible, not including the apocryphal books of the Septuagint, is the assumption he shared with his people that the Bible began with Genesis and closed with 2 Chronicles (unlike the Septuagint). We can see this in Luke 11:49–51:

> The Wisdom of God said, "I will send them prophets and apostles, some of whom they will kill and persecute," so that the blood of all the prophets, shed from the foundation of the world, may be charged against this generation, from the blood of Abel to the blood of Zechariah, who perished between the altar and the sanctuary. Yes, I tell you, it will be required of this generation.

At first, we may be puzzled why Jesus spoke of the blood of the prophets extending "from the blood of Abel to the blood of Zechariah." Calling Abel a prophet is probably explained in that his blood cried out prophetically against his murderer: "The LORD said, 'What have you [Cain] done? The voice of your brother's blood is crying to me from the ground'" (Gen. 4:10).

But what about Zechariah? His stoning is recorded in the Old Testament book of 2 Chronicles 24:20–21:

> Then the Spirit of God clothed Zechariah the son of Jehoiada the priest, and he stood above the people, and said to them, "Thus says God, 'Why do you break the commandments of the LORD, so that

---

[5] R. H. Stein, *Luke* (Nashville: B&H, 1992), 620. Psalms "probably refers to the third major section of the Old Testament, called the 'Writings,' which contains the rest of the books in the Old Testament [after the Law and the Prophets]. The first (in the Hebrew arrangement) and largest book in this section is the Psalms."

you cannot prosper? Because you have forsaken the LORD, he has forsaken you.'" But they conspired against him, and by command of the king they stoned him with stones in the court of the house of the LORD.

Why is this Zechariah (who is *not* the prophet who wrote the Old Testament book of Zechariah) treated as the final prophet in the line of martyred prophets? Chronologically, the last martyr in the Old Testament was Uriah the Son of Shemaiah, whose death is described in Jeremiah 26:20–23. He died during the reign of Jehoiakim, who reigned from 609 to 598 BC. That was about two hundred years *after* the Zechariah that Jesus refers to.

The reason is that 2 Chronicles, where Zechariah's murder is described, was the last book of the Hebrew canon. So when Jesus said, "from the blood of Abel to the blood of Zechariah," he meant all the prophets from the beginning to the end of the Bible—the Hebrew Scriptures. This means that Jesus was using the Hebrew Bible, which, unlike the Septuagint, ended with Chronicles.

One of Our Earliest Witnesses to the Old Testament Canon

The point I am trying to make is that the Bible that Jesus considered to be his Bible did not include the books of the Apocrypha but only the books that are in our Old Testament today.[6] This limitation on the books that have supreme authority is confirmed by the way the New Testament authors cite the books of the Hebrew Bible as Scripture but do not cite the apocryphal books that way. To be sure, the New Testament authors quoted from the Septuagint because they were all writing in Greek, and this was the widely used Greek translation of the Hebrew Bible. But even though the Septuagint contains the Apocrypha, the New Testament writers did not cite those books as Scripture.

One of the earliest witnesses to the Old Testament canon that we have in our Bible today is Melito, Bishop of Sardis, around AD 170:

> When I came to the east and reached the place where these things were preached and done, and learnt accurately the books of the

---

[6] The Roman Catholic Church and some other Christian traditions include the Apocrypha in the books they consider authoritative.

Old Testament, I set down the facts and sent them to you. These are their names: five books of Moses, Genesis, Exodus, Numbers, Leviticus, Deuteronomy, Joshua the son of Nun, Judges, Ruth, four books of Kingdoms, two books of Chronicles, the Psalms of David, the Proverbs of Solomon and his Wisdom, Ecclesiastes, the Song of Songs, Job, the prophets Isaiah, Jeremiah, the Twelve in a single book, Daniel, Ezekiel, Ezra.[7]

No apocryphal books are mentioned by Melito, and the only missing book from our Old Testament canon is Esther, which was controverted for some time and may have been suppressed for political reasons at the time, because it spoke of a Jewish uprising.

Embracing Jesus's Bible

Our purpose so far has not been to answer the question of why Jesus believed the Old Testament was the word of God or why we should. Our purpose has simply been to identify what Jesus's Bible was. What books were included in it? And is this the same as the Old Testament that we have in our modern-language Bibles today?

Our conclusion is that when we say, "We believe that the Bible consists of the sixty-six books of the Old and New Testaments," we mean that thirty-nine of those sixty-six are the books of the Old Testament that Jesus and the apostles counted as authoritative, and these thirty-nine are the same as the twenty-four books of the Hebrew Bible that Jesus knew as authoritative Scripture. Now we turn with a similar question to the second part of our Bible. Which books make up the canon of the New Testament?

---

[7] Melito's list is found in Eusebius, *Ecclesiastical History*, 4.26.13–14.

When the Spirit of truth comes, he will guide you into all the truth, for he will not speak on his own authority, but whatever he hears he will speak, and he will declare to you the things that are to come. He will glorify me, for he will take what is mine and declare it to you.

JOHN 16:13–14

3

Which Books Make Up
the New Testament?

We believe that the Bible, consisting of the sixty-six books of the Old and New Testaments, is the infallible Word of God, verbally inspired by God, and without error in the original manuscripts.

When Jesus Christ came into the world, there was no New Testament. He and all his apostles were Jews. They all believed in the Hebrew Bible as God's word. Our Old Testament, in Hebrew, was their Bible. There were no other inspired writings in the minds of Jesus and his earliest followers.

This is important as we consider how the New Testament came into being and came to have an authority equal to that of the Old Testament. Jesus and the early Christians were Bible people. That is, they lived and breathed the air of biblical authority. They assumed the existence of a canon of books—a Hebrew Bible—that had absolute authority over their lives. The concept of a canon—a written, God-given, authoritative rule—was not foreign to them. It was assumed as part of their Jewish culture.

From our relatively secular atmosphere, it is difficult to imagine how prominent and unquestioned these Scriptures were for first-century Jews. Consider how Jesus and the early Christians spoke of them:

> Beginning with Moses and all the Prophets, [Jesus] interpreted to them in all the *Scriptures* the things concerning himself. (Luke 24:27)

> You search the *Scriptures* because you think that in them you have eternal life; and it is they that bear witness about me. (John 5:39)

> Paul went in, as was his custom, and on three Sabbath days he reasoned with them from the *Scriptures*. (Acts 17:2)

> Whatever was written in former days was written for our instruction, that through endurance and through the encouragement of the *Scriptures* we might have hope. (Rom. 15:4)

What this means for the emergence of the New Testament canon of Scripture is both positive and negative. Positively, the concept of a people ruled by a canon of authoritative writings was already prominent. Therefore, it did not prove strange for the early church, growing organically in the soil of first-century Judaism, to be a people ruled by an authoritative written canon. Indeed, it would have been strange if they were not governed by such a book.

But, negatively, the Hebrew Bible was considered a closed canon, as we have seen. No books would ever be added to the Old Testament— not to this day. The prophets had ceased to speak with divine inspiration. This would mean that any claim to have books of equal authority with the Old Testament canon would be astonishing and controversial.

New Authority Comes into the World, the Living Word

But what changed everything was the uniqueness of Jesus Christ himself. God did not send a new book into the world first. He sent his Son into the world. As one New Testament book puts it, "Long ago, at many times and in many ways, God spoke to our fathers by the prophets, but in these last days he has spoken to us by his Son" (Heb. 1:1–2). What opened the way to a new canon of authoritative writings was not the arrival of new spokesmen for God, who would be called apostles, but rather the arrival of God himself.

"In the beginning was the Word, and the Word was with God, and the Word was God. . . . And the Word became flesh and dwelt among us, and we have seen his glory, glory as of the only Son from the Father, full of grace and truth" (John 1:1, 14). Not surprisingly Jesus, the Son of God, was recognized by his followers as having an authority equal to and beyond the Old Testament Scriptures. This is what he claimed for himself. The glory of God incarnate would create—and confirm in the hearts of his people—the existence of a new canon of Scripture.

The shocking claims of Jesus about himself created a new authority in the world—an authority equal to, and beyond, that of the Hebrew Bible. This has always been the stumbling block for those who do not recognize the staggering nature of what happened in the coming of Jesus—that God himself had entered the world as the God-man.

All the efforts to turn Jesus into a nondivine, remarkable, even revolutionary Jewish teacher shatter again and again on the outrageous claims he made about himself, even in the places where you would least expect them. For example, the Sermon on the Mount. There was an old liberalism a hundred years ago (which has its representatives today) that loved the Sermon on the Mount as the most radical collection of Jesus's ethical teachings. Here the old liberals hoped to be rid of the mythological claims about a supernatural person and instead find a simple religion of the fatherhood of God, the brotherhood of man, and the ethic of love. They loved the following words from this famous sermon:

Blessed are the peacemakers. (Matt. 5:9)

Whatever you wish that others would do to you, do also to them. (Matt. 7:12)

Judge not, that you be not judged. (Matt. 7:1)

Love your enemies. (Matt. 5:44)

But just when they thought Jesus was a good Moses-like, Confucius-like, Mahatma-like, Mao-like teacher, suddenly, right there in the Sermon on the Mount, the imperial, supernatural "I" or "me" or "my" smacked them in the face:

> Not everyone who says to me, "Lord, Lord," will enter the kingdom of heaven, but the one who does the will of my Father who is in heaven. On that day many will say to me, "Lord, Lord, did we not prophesy in your name, and cast out demons in your name, and do many mighty works in your name?" And then will I declare to them, "I never knew you; depart from me, you workers of lawlessness." (Matt. 7:21–23)

This is staggering. Imagine hearing an ordinary Jewish teacher talk like this. He is saying: "At the last judgment, I will be the one you will give an account to. I will be there as the Judge, and I will decide who enters heaven and who goes to hell." In other words, this teacher of the Sermon on the Mount says he is the judge of the universe. This is simply breathtaking. Such talk would eventually get Jesus killed. But the radiance of God's glory in such authority would also give rise to a New Testament canon.

Or again in the first chapter of the Sermon on the Mount (Matt. 5:17), Jesus shocks us with his claims. We think he is going to say, "Do not think that I have come to abolish the Law or the Prophets; I have not come to abolish them but to *confirm* them." That's not what he says. He says, "I have not come to abolish them but to *fulfill* them."

The glory of God that proved God's reality to the Old Testament prophets was fulfilled in Jesus. He was the light of God's glory in the world. "Jesus said to them, 'The light is among you for a little while longer. Walk while you have the light'" (John 12:35). But many did not see his brightness as the light of God's glory: "Though he had done so many signs before them, they still did not believe in him" (John 12:37).

The apostle John explained this blindness by quoting the prophet Isaiah: "He has blinded their eyes and hardened their heart" (John 12:40; Isa. 6:10). Then John gives this astonishing explanation: "Isaiah said these things because he saw [Jesus's] glory and spoke of him" (John 12:41). In other words, the light of the world, who was walking among them in the person of Jesus, is the light of the glory of God revealed in

Isaiah 6. This is the heart of what it means for Jesus to say, "I came to fulfill." And this is the basis for how the disciples—and how we—come to know that his words are true.

Jesus was not just another member in the long line of wise men and prophets. He was the end of the line. In his own person and work, the Law and the Prophets were fulfilled. Which is why, six times in Matthew 5, Jesus stunningly confronted Scripture and tradition with his supremely authoritative words, "But I say to you" (Matt. 5:22, 28, 32, 34, 39, 44).

And just when the Beatitudes are sounding like the words of a lowly, wise spiritual guide, Jesus tells us that we are blessed for being reviled on *his* account. Not *God's*, but *his*! "Blessed are you when others revile you and persecute you and utter all kinds of evil against you falsely on *my* account." And what's more, he says we can rejoice in that day, because we are in the same category with the prophets who were persecuted on *God's* account. To be a follower of Jesus is to be rewarded with the prophets of God.

The point is that the divine majesty of the person of Jesus is woven inseparably into every layer of the teachings of Jesus. There is no portrait of Jesus in the New Testament as a merely human teacher of ethics. There is only the Lord of glory. The fulfiller of history. The judge of the universe.

An Authority above the Scriptures

Accordingly, Jesus was recognized by the early church as having authority equal to and beyond the Old Testament Scriptures.

> He was teaching them as one who had *authority*, and not as their scribes. (Matt. 7:29)

> You have heard that it was said, "An eye for an eye and a tooth for a tooth." *But I say to you*, Do not resist the one who is evil. But if anyone slaps you on the right cheek, turn to him the other also. (Matt. 5:38–39)

> Heaven and earth will pass away, but *my words will not pass away*. (Mark 13:31)

The men of Nineveh will rise up at the judgment with this generation and condemn it, for they repented at the preaching of Jonah,
and behold, *something greater than Jonah is here.* The queen of the
South will rise up at the judgment with this generation and condemn it, for she came from the ends of the earth to hear the wisdom
of Solomon, and behold, *something greater than Solomon is here.*
(Matt. 12:41–42)

Jesus said to him, "I am the way, and *the truth*, and the life. No one
comes to the Father except through me." (John 14:6)

Jesus came and said to them, "All *authority* in heaven and on earth
has been given to me." (Matt. 28:18)

The point here is that the person and the teaching of Jesus must inevi-
tably lead to an expansion of the canon of the early church. A people
who for centuries have been accustomed to be governed by a written
revelation of God, the Hebrew Bible, are now confronted with the divine
author of that very book (cf. 1 Pet. 1:11), present in human form, teaching with absolute authority. The glory of God that stood forth in God's
word in the Old Testament had come into the world. "We have seen his
glory, glory as of the only Son from the Father, full of grace and truth"
(John 1:14). This glory created and confirmed a new canon. The Old
Testament did not cease to be God's word ("Do not think that I have
come to abolish the Law or the Prophets," Matt. 5:17). Rather, the new
revelations coming through Christ would be preserved as the govern-
ment of the people of God. A New Testament canon came into being.

Jesus's Preparation for the New Testament Canon

Jesus himself pointed in this direction. By his words, he prepared the
early church to expect that he was planning an authoritative canon of
teaching concerning himself and his word to govern his church when
he was gone. As John Frame says, "Crass as it may sound to modern
religious speculators, it is evident from biblical history that God intends
to rule his church through a book."[1] But not only was Jesus planning
this book; he himself would provide for it through the appointment

---

[1] John Frame, *Apologetics to the Glory of Christ: An Introduction* (Phillipsburg, NJ: P&R, 1994), 122.

of authoritative spokesmen called "apostles." And he promised that he would send the Holy Spirit to guide them. These spokesmen would write the books, by the guidance of the Spirit, which would become the New Testament canon that would govern the thinking and acting of the church until Jesus comes a second time to reign bodily on the earth.

> When day came, he called his disciples and chose from them *twelve*, whom he named *apostles*: Simon, whom he named Peter, and Andrew his brother, and James and John, and Philip, and Bartholomew, and Matthew, and Thomas, and James the son of Alphaeus, and Simon who was called the Zealot, and Judas the son of James, and Judas Iscariot, who became a traitor. (Luke 6:13–16)

Why twelve? Probably because they were symbolically like the twelve tribes of Israel. Only they would be the foundation of a new Israel—all those who would believe in the Messiah of Israel, Jesus Christ. In the last book of the New Testament, the book of Revelation, the church is portrayed first as a bride and then as a city coming down to earth. The wall of the city had twelve gates and twelve foundations. The gates represent the new Israel: "On the gates the names of the twelve tribes of the sons of Israel were inscribed" (Rev. 21:12).

And the foundations represent the apostles: "The wall of the city had *twelve foundations*, and on them were the *twelve names of the twelve apostles* of the Lamb" (Rev. 21:14). This is how the early church understood what Jesus was doing when he chose twelve apostles: the apostles would teach the church, and their teaching would become the foundation of the church in perpetuity. The apostle Paul put it like this: "You [Gentiles] are no longer strangers and aliens, but you are fellow citizens with the saints and members of the household of God, built on *the foundation of the apostles and prophets*, Christ Jesus himself being the cornerstone" (Eph. 2:19–20).

When Judas, one of the Twelve, proved to be a betrayer (which Jesus knew from the beginning would happen, John 6:64), the other apostles knew what they must do. He must be replaced. And the criteria must be the same that Jesus used. In fact, in the end, the risen and ascended Lord Jesus himself made the choice. The leader of the eleven stood up and said,

"So one of the men who have accompanied us during all the time that the Lord Jesus went in and out among us, beginning from the baptism of John until the day when he was taken up from us—one of these men must become with us a witness to his resurrection." And they put forward two, Joseph called Barsabbas, who was also called Justus, and Matthias. And they prayed and said, "You, Lord, who know the hearts of all, show which one of these two you have chosen to take the place in this ministry and apostleship from which Judas turned aside to go to his own place." And they cast lots for them, and the lot fell on Matthias, and he was numbered with the eleven apostles. (Acts 1:21–26)

Jesus Promises the Spirit of Truth

Not only had Jesus planned that there would be authorized spokesmen to provide foundational teaching for the church, but he also promised to send the Holy Spirit to guide them in what they teach. The night before he was crucified, Jesus said to the Twelve,

> These things I have spoken to you while I am still with you. But the Helper, the Holy Spirit, whom the Father will send in my name, he will teach you all things and bring to your remembrance all that I have said to you. (John 14:25–26)

And:

> I still have many things to say to you, but you cannot bear them now. When the Spirit of truth comes, he will guide you into all the truth, for he will not speak on his own authority, but whatever he hears he will speak, and he will declare to you the things that are to come. He will glorify me, for he will take what is mine and declare it to you. (John 16:12–14)

The earthly teaching of Jesus was not all he had to say to his church: "I still have many things to say to you." His plan was to complete his foundational teaching for the church (Eph. 2:20) through the Holy Spirit. "When the Spirit of truth comes, he will guide you into all truth." What the church would need to know about the glory of Christ, which is not fully revealed in his earthly ministry, will be completed by the ministry of the Spirit. "He will glorify me." The promise that the Holy Spirit would reveal the glory of Christ alerts us to the way Scriptures would be confirmed in the life of the early church. The light of that glory would shine through the inspired word into the hearts of God's people and verify the divine origin and character of the Scriptures (2 Cor. 4:4–6).

Paul and the Twelve

The apostle Paul was not one of the original twelve apostles. But he wrote thirteen of the twenty-seven books that are now our New Testament. The place of his foundational authority in the early church, along with the Twelve, was fully established during his lifetime. But it was not unchallenged. How did he come to have this apostolic authority?

Paul was called by the risen Christ to be an apostle to the Gentiles (non-Jews). Paul began one of his earliest letters this way: "Paul, an apostle—not from men nor through man, but through Jesus Christ and God the Father, who raised him from the dead" (Gal. 1:1). At first, this was a suspicious surprise to the Twelve. But after a meeting together Paul reports,

> When they [Peter, James, and John] saw that I had been entrusted with the gospel to the uncircumcised, just as Peter had been entrusted with the gospel to the circumcised (for he who worked through Peter for his apostolic ministry to the circumcised worked also through me for mine to the Gentiles), and when James and Cephas and John, who seemed to be pillars, perceived the grace that was given to me, they gave the right hand of fellowship to Barnabas and me, that we should go to the Gentiles and they to the circumcised. (Gal. 2:7–9)

So Paul was accepted and affirmed by the Twelve as a genuine apostle of the risen Lord Jesus. Paul himself was utterly stunned by the risen Jesus breaking into his life on the Damascus Road as he was persecuting Christians (Acts 9:1–9). He acknowledged that the risen Christ had appeared "to Cephas [another name for Peter], then to the twelve. Then he appeared to more than five hundred brothers at one time, most of whom are still alive, though some have fallen asleep. Then he appeared to James, then to all the apostles" (1 Cor. 15:5–7). And then, in a sense of overwhelming unworthiness, he says,

> Last of all, as to one untimely born, he appeared also to me. For I am the least of the apostles, unworthy to be called an apostle, because I persecuted the church of God. But by the grace of God I am what I am, and his grace toward me was not in vain. On the contrary, I worked harder than any of them, though it was not I, but the grace of God that is with me. (1 Cor. 15:8–10)

As an apostle, having equal authority with the Twelve, Paul experienced the fulfillment of Jesus's promise of the Holy Spirit to guide his teaching. He spoke repeatedly of the authority that the Lord had given him for the sake of the churches (2 Cor. 10:8; 13:10), and he claimed that his words were more authoritative than those who claimed to speak with gifts of prophecy, but were not apostles: "If anyone thinks that he is a prophet, or spiritual, he should acknowledge that the things I am writing to you are a command of the Lord. If anyone does not recognize this, he is not recognized" (1 Cor. 14:37–38).

Paul as a Writer of Scripture

That is a spectacular claim of authority. What was it rooted in? It was rooted in the fact that Paul had seen the actual historical, risen Jesus Christ and knew that this Jesus, as the Lord of the universe, had commissioned him as an apostle and had sent the Holy Spirit in a special way to fulfill what he had promised when he was on the earth: "The Holy Spirit, whom the Father will send in my name, he will teach you all things and bring to your remembrance all that I have said to you" (John 14:26). This is what he said about his own teaching:

> Now we have received not the spirit of the world, but the Spirit who is from God, that we might understand the things freely given us by God. And we impart this in words not taught by human wisdom but taught by the Spirit, interpreting spiritual truths to those who are spiritual. (1 Cor. 2:12–13)

That is Paul's claim to be inspired by the Spirit in fulfillment of the promise of Jesus.

And the claim was recognized by the other apostles. Peter said in his second letter, "Our beloved brother Paul also wrote to you *according to the wisdom given him*" (2 Pet. 3:15). Paul said that his wisdom in teaching the church was "taught by the Spirit." Peter said it was "given him." Richard Bauckham comments, "The appeal to Paul's teaching in his letters is reinforced by reference to the fact that the apostle wrote under divine inspiration."[2]

A Foundational Authority for All of History

In other words, as Jesus promised, the Holy Spirit had come and was guiding Jesus's apostles into truth. Jesus did not leave his people without a real, present, objective expression of his own authority. And he was establishing that authority by the inspiration of the Holy Spirit. The risen Christ was continuing to shepherd his flock through the mouth of the apostles. He would provide a foundation for the church through their writings so that a canon of writings would emerge that would have the authority of the Lord Jesus till he comes again.

The early church—and all succeeding generations—would be able to recognize that authority because Jesus promised that the Holy Spirit, in these writings, would "glorify me" (John 16:14). The same divine glory that convinced his first disciples that he was the truth (John 1:14) will shine through his new Scriptures and convince the church that these are the very words of God.

Jesus did not intend, through the history of the church, to keep sending more and more spokesmen with this kind of authority. That is why the apostolic teaching is called the "foundation" of the church, not the ongoing structure (Eph. 2:20). It is also why one of the later books of the New Testament refers to "the faith that was *once for all delivered to the saints*":

> Beloved, although I was very eager to write to you about our common salvation, I found it necessary to write appealing to you to contend for the faith that was once for all delivered to the saints. (Jude 3)

---

[2] Richard J. Bauckham, *2 Peter, Jude*, vol. 50, Word Biblical Commentary, ed. David A. Hubbard, Glenn W. Barker, Ralph P. Martin (Dallas: Word, 1998), 329.

The apostolic witness to Christ in that first generation was meant by Jesus to be foundational for all of history. With the authority of Jesus Christ himself, the writings of this band of apostolic spokesmen would stand alongside the Hebrew Bible as the true and authoritative instruction of God for his people throughout the history of the world.

And as Jesus said, this new canon of books—this New Testament— would not be a contradiction or a correction of the Old Testament, but a fulfillment: "Do not think that I have come to abolish the Law or the Prophets; I have not come to abolish them but to fulfill them" (Matt. 5:17). To be sure, many instructions and rules and religious practices and rituals from the Old Testament are no longer to be practiced. But this is not because these practices and rules were wrong, but because they were temporary and were pointing forward to the day when Jesus Christ would fulfill them and thus end them. The coming of Christ did not abolish them, but it did make them obsolete (Heb. 8:13).

The new people of God—the followers of the Messiah, the true Israel—is not an ethnically, politically, geographically defined people any longer. Christianity has no geographic center. It has no single ethnic identity. It is not a political nation-state. It has no system of sacrificing animals, no tabernacle, no succession of priests, no divinely authorized feast days, no requirements of circumcision or dietary particulars. All of these Old Testament patterns were temporary. Jesus has fulfilled them and ended them.

The New Scriptures

That is what the apostles were authorized by Jesus to make plain: Who is this Jesus Christ? What did he accomplish in his life, death, resurrection, and ascension? What is he doing now in his universal reign as Lord? What will he do when he comes again? And what is the mission of his church, the way of salvation for the world, and the way his people should live until he comes? This is what the New Testament teaches. Thus the New Testament completes the Old Testament without nullifying its authority or contradicting its truth. It is the word of the risen Christ, through the Holy Spirit, guiding his people in their understanding of how the work of God in the world—recorded and celebrated in the Old Testament—is to be completed in the remainder of history.

Thus already in the New Testament, the writings of the apostles were treated on par with the God-inspired writings of the Old Testament Scriptures. For example, the apostle Peter saw Paul's writings as part of an enlarging canon of Scripture alongside the Old Testament. We have already seen that Peter regarded Paul's writings as inspired by the Holy Spirit. Now we observe that he also saw them, accordingly, as Scripture—on par with the Old Testament canon. Peter wrote,

> [Paul wrote to you] as he does in all his letters when he speaks in them of these matters. There are some things in them that are hard to understand, which the ignorant and unstable twist to their own destruction, as they do *the other Scriptures.* (2 Pet. 3:16)

If I say, "Abraham Lincoln and the *other presidents* are worthy of serious study," it is clear that I am regarding Lincoln as one of the presidents. Similarly here, when Peter refers to Paul's writings "and the *other Scriptures,*" he regards Paul's writings as Scripture. Richard Bauckham again comments, "The inclusion of Paul's letters in this category certainly means they are regarded as inspired, authoritative writings (as v. 15 in fact says), ranked alongside the Old Testament and probably various other books, including other apostolic writings."[3]

Therefore, in the coming of Jesus Christ, and his appointment of apostles, and his promise of the Holy Spirit to guide them into truth, and the consciousness of his apostles that this was in fact happening, there is a built-in trajectory toward a New Testament canon. That canon would provide the true and authoritative record of the life and teaching of Jesus and the foundational teachings of his authoritative spokesmen. What remained for the early church to do was to discern which writings were the fulfillment of Jesus's promise to the apostles.

Discerning Which Books Were Apostolic

The rise of heretical teachings and the emergence of spurious books that claimed apostolic origin spurred the process of canonization. How did that happen? From what we have seen so far, it is not surprising that the dominant characteristic of a writing in establishing its authority

---

[3] Ibid., 333.

in the early church was its link with the authority of Jesus through its apostolicity. What does *apostolicity* mean?

Everyone agrees that it does not mean simply "written by an apostle," because the term is applied to books such as the Gospels of Mark and Luke, which were not written by apostles but by people in close association with an apostle (Luke with Paul, and Mark with Peter). But apostolicity, as a force that compelled the affirmation of the early church, probably means more than "written in close association with an apostle." What the apostles possessed from the risen Christ through the Holy Spirit was a supernatural spiritual wisdom both to understand things incomprehensible to the "natural man" and to teach them in words "taught by the Spirit." Paul writes,

> No one comprehends the thoughts of God except the Spirit of God. Now we have received not the spirit of the world, but the Spirit who is from God, that we might understand the things freely given us by God. And we impart this in words not taught by human wisdom but taught by the Spirit, interpreting spiritual truths to those who are spiritual. (1 Cor. 2:11–13)

So there is a double supernatural work involved here. There is a *comprehending* of the thoughts of God because they had received God's Spirit, and there is a *teaching* "in words not taught by human wisdom but taught by the Spirit." Jesus had promised this divine help by the Spirit (John 14:25–26; 16:12–14). It was an extension of his unique capacities to know and speak for God. It was an extension of the radiance of the self-authenticating glory of Christ that was present in his incarnate person (John 1:14) and promised through his Spirit (John 16:14).

Apostolicity as Supernatural Communication

Therefore, apostolicity is not merely a historical connection with Jesus or his emissaries. Apostolicity is the supernatural transmission of naturally incomprehensible reality to spiritually discerning people ("those who are spiritual," 1 Cor. 2:13), through writing that is "taught by the Spirit." This means that the recognition by the church of the apostolicity of the twenty-seven books of the New Testament was neither a mere historical judgment about who wrote the books nor a mere preference for some over others. Rather, the historical judgments and the corporate preferences were the outworkings of the supernatural encounter between the unique work of God in the writings ("words not taught by human wisdom") and providentially discerning Christians endowed with the Holy Spirit ("interpreting spiritual truths to those who are spiritual").

What this means is that the question about how the books of the Christian canon got there is another form of the question *How do we know this is the word of God?* It is not as though there was a purely historical process, or merely ecclesiastical-selective process of canonization, and then later a spiritual question about whether these books are the word of God. Rather, the very process of canonization was governed by the spiritual and supernatural reality of the books and by the spiritual discernment of the church. The glory of God manifest in the books was not powerless in this process. It did its work historically in canon formation, as it does its work personally in heart illumination.

Michael Kruger's recent book *Canon Revisited: Establishing the Origins and Authority of the New Testament Books* moves in this direction. He says,

> The apostles were mouthpieces of Christ and were given the task of delivering and preserving this redemptive message—which was originally delivered orally but eventually was embodied in a more permanent, written form. The New Testament books were considered authoritative not because the church declared them to be so, or even because they were written directly by an apostle, but because they were understood to bear the essential apostolic deposit. For this reason, Ridderbos is able to assert, "In its redemptive-historical sense, the canon is not the product of the church, rather the church is to be the product of the canon."[4]

Or, as the New Testament scholar F. F. Bruce said a generation earlier,

> The New Testament canon was not demarcated by the arbitrary decree of any Church Council. When at last a Church Council—the Synod of Hippo in A.D. 393—listed the 27 books of the New

---

[4] Michael J. Kruger, *Canon Revisited* (Wheaton, IL: Crossway, 2012), 193–94, citing Herman N. Ridderbos, *Redemptive History and the New Testament Scripture* (Phillipsburg, NJ: P&R, 1988), 25.

Testament, it did not confer upon them any authority which they did not already possess, but simply recorded their previously established canonicity.[5]

That list of books, with the traditional apostolic connections, consists of:

- Matthew: apostle
- Mark: Peter's interpreter and assistant (as Papias, Bishop of Hierapolis, AD 60–140, wrote: "Mark became Peter's interpreter and wrote accurately all that he remembered"[6])
- Luke: close associate and partner of Paul (known from the book of Acts)
- John: apostle
- Thirteen epistles of Paul: apostle
- Hebrews: from the Pauline circle (as we see in Heb. 13:22, where the author refers to "our brother Timothy")
- James: Jesus's brother who was closely associated with the original twelve apostles (Gal. 1:19)
- 1 and 2 Peter: apostle
- 1, 2, and 3 John: apostle
- Jude: brother of Jesus and James (Jude 1; Matt. 13:55)
- Revelation: John the apostle

Compelling Allegiance

When F. F. Bruce refers to "their previously established canonicity," the question remains how that authority compelled the allegiance of the early Christians. What we have argued is that this question and our question about the divine origin and truth and authority of the Bible are essentially the same question. What this means for our approach in this book is that we should draw our chapters on the canon to a close and move to the more fundamental question of how any of us can know that these books are the word of God. Our question is the same question the church faced as the canon was emerging.

What we have seen is that the twenty-seven books that make up

---

[5] F. F. Bruce, *The Books and the Parchments* (Old Tappan, NJ: Revell, 1963), 112–13. Other partial lists of the emerging canon are known from much earlier than this first complete list in AD 393.
[6] Eusebius, *Ecclesiastical History*, 3.39.15.

our New Testament grew organically out of the appearance of a new authority in the world.[7] Jesus Christ was not merely a final or a great prophet. He was the presence of God in the flesh. Therefore, he confirmed and fulfilled and stood above the authority of the Old Testament. Accordingly his own authority would extend over the new people of God that he was calling into being.

He planned for this and sent his Spirit to make sure that the apostles would be led into all truth. They would speak with his authority by the Spirit, and they would glorify him. The manifestation of this glory through the inspired, apostolic writings would confirm to the early church—as it continues to do for God's people today—that these writings are the word of God.

It was inevitable that in addressing the question *Which books make up the New Testament?* we would pass over into the question *How do we know these books are the word of God?* So, in a sense, we have gotten ahead of ourselves. That question will be answered more fully in chapters 8–17. So if the pointers feel tantalizing now, let that be encouraging rather than frustrating. The fuller explanation is coming. For now, it was necessary to point out that the spiritual forces at work in confirming the New Testament canon to the church were the same spiritual forces that are at work in confirming the Scriptures to Christians today.

There are two more steps to take before we can focus fully on how we know these books are God's word. First, in the next chapter, we need to ask the question *Do we have the very words that the New Testament writers wrote—have they been preserved faithfully for us?* Second, we will need to ask, in chapters 5–7, what, in fact, the Scriptures claim for themselves.

---

[7] Of course, the very idea of a limited canon of twenty-seven books implies that there were contenders for inclusion that did not make the cut. These are of many kinds. A quick overview can be found at http://en .wikipedia.org/wiki/New_Testament_apocrypha. One way to think about the major contenders is to use the categories provided by Eusebius, a church historian who died about AD 340 (*Ecclesiastical History*, 3.25.1–7). When he gave his list of books that the church took seriously, they fell into four categories: (1) recognized books, (2) disputed books, (3) rejected books (e.g., *Apocalypse of Peter*, *Epistle of Barnabas*, *Didache*, *Gospel of Hebrews*), and (4) heretical books (e.g., *Gospel of Peter*, *Gospel of Thomas*, *Gospel of Matthias*, *Acts of Andrew*, *Acts of John*). One helpful discussion of these is found in Kruger, *Canon Revisited*, 266–87.

Then the LORD said to me, "You have seen well, for I am watching over my word to perform it."

JEREMIAH 1:12

4

Do We Have the Very Words of the Biblical Authors?

. . . verbally inspired by God, and without error in the original manuscripts.

When we confess our belief that "the infallible Word of God [is] *verbally inspired by God*," the word "verbally" means that we believe God guided the biblical authors in their selection of the very *words* that they wrote to communicate his divine meaning. This is not identical with dictation, since the biblical authors are themselves selecting the words, under God's guidance. Though there are rare times when God dictates the very words a prophet is to speak, typically the biblical authors write with their own styles and personalities, which are guided by God. "Men spoke from God as they were carried along by the Holy Spirit" (2 Pet. 1:21).

This has implications for the theme of this chapter: Do we have the very words that the biblical authors wrote? If God cared about the very words of the text as he guided the authors to write it, then it is a crucial question whether we have access to these words or not.

Of course, the Bible was written originally in Hebrew and Greek. So if we are reading English, or some other language, we are not reading the text in the language in which it was first written. We will come back to the issue of accurate translation later on. But for now, the question remains: Do we have access to the very Greek and Hebrew words that the biblical authors wrote? The fact that we believe in "verbal inspiration" makes that question of utmost importance.

Jesus Thought That Words Matter

Words matter. Jesus, according to the Gospel of John, makes this clear. For example, after the resurrection of Jesus, he was with the apostles, and John tells us of this exchange between Jesus and Peter:

> When Peter saw [John], he said to Jesus, "Lord, what about this man?" Jesus said to him, "If it is my will that he remain until I come, what is that to you? You follow me!" So the saying spread abroad among the brothers that this disciple was not to die; yet Jesus did not say to him that he was not to die, but, "If it is my will that he remain until I come, what is that to you?" (John 21:21–23)

I can easily imagine some people today saying that Jesus is being too picky about his words here. Peter asked him about John. Jesus answers, "If it is my will that he remain until I come, what is that to you?" He meant, "If I want him to remain alive until my second coming from heaven, don't bother about that; be a faithful disciple yourself, whether you live or die."

Evidently, when these words were reported, someone was careless with Jesus's meaning. They took him to mean: "John is going to live till Jesus's second coming!" To correct this rumor, John gives the exact words that Jesus used. He says in effect, "Listen carefully to the very words. Jesus did not *say* what you thought he did. He did not use words that carry that meaning. What he said was, 'If it is my will that he remain until I come, what is that to you?'"

The point is that Jesus and John stood by words. They spoke as though words mattered, not just impressions. Not just inferences. They would agree that if someone has misunderstood what you said, the way toward a resolution is to return to the very words of what you said. We all feel this way when our meaning is distorted. We protest, "I didn't *say* that!" And if they say (as they probably did in this case with Jesus), "Well, you gave the impression that . . . ," you will say, "But what I *said* was . . ." This is how important words are.

One of the strongest statements of Jesus's concern for preserving his own words, as well as the very words of the Old Testament, is Matthew 5:17–18:

> Do not think that I have come to abolish the Law or the Prophets; I have not come to abolish them but to fulfill them. For truly, I say to you, until heaven and earth pass away, not an iota, not a dot, will pass from the Law until all is accomplished.

The words "iota" and "dot" probably refer to the smallest Hebrew letter (*yod*) and to the tiny hook that distinguishes some Hebrew letters from others. This is Jesus's way of emphasizing the importance of the details of Scripture, including the very words. D. A. Carson comments, "In any event Jesus here upholds the authority of the Old Testament Scriptures right down to the 'least stroke of a pen.' His is the highest possible view of the Old Testament."[1]

Peter Cared about Words

Peter seems to have learned from Jesus the importance of getting an author's words right, and thus the danger of twisting words, because in his second letter (in a passage we've already seen), he warns against those who take the words of Paul and distort them to suit their own error:

> There are some things in [Paul's letters] that are hard to understand, which the ignorant and unstable *twist* to their own destruction, as they do the other Scriptures. You therefore, beloved, knowing this beforehand, take care that you are not carried away with the *error* of lawless people and lose your own stability. (2 Pet. 3:16–17)

If lawless people twist Paul's written epistles into meanings that lead to destruction, what is the remedy? Part of the remedy is preserving and presenting the very words Paul wrote. How else will other people be persuaded that Paul did not teach what the word-twisters say he taught? The

---

[1] D. A. Carson, "Matthew," in *Matthew, Mark, Luke*, vol. 8, Expositor's Bible Commentary, ed. Frank E. Gaebelein (Grand Rapids, MI: Zondervan, 1984), 145.

way they will be persuaded is by showing them the words Paul actually wrote so that they can see the meaning for themselves. Therefore, Peter is telling us how important it is to have the very words of the biblical writers.

Paul's Vigilance over His Words

Paul wrote at least one of his letters, if not many or all, by using a kind of secretary (called an "amanuensis") to take his dictation. In Romans 1:1 Paul begins the way he begins most of his letters, by identifying himself: "Paul, a servant of Christ Jesus, called to be an apostle, set apart for the gospel of God." And in the letter he refers to himself as "I" about a hundred times. No one doubts that the apostle Paul wrote this letter. But how did he write it? In Romans 16:22 we read, "I Tertius, who wrote this letter, greet you in the Lord." This is Paul's assistant who had, evidently, been taking dictation.

But there is good evidence that Paul was jealous for his readers to know that though he may sometimes use an aide to do the actual transcription, the words are his. One of the ways we feel Paul's concern is how many times he takes up the pen himself and actually tells us that is what he is doing, so as to vouch for the letter. For example:

> I, Paul, write this greeting with my own hand. This is the sign of genuineness in every letter of mine; it is the way I write. (2 Thess. 3:17)

> I, Paul, write this greeting with my own hand. (1 Cor. 16:21)

> I, Paul, write this greeting with my own hand. (Col. 4:18)

> See with what large letters I am writing to you with my own hand. (Gal. 6:11)

> I, Paul, write this with my own hand. (Philem. 19)

Most scholars think that when Paul says, "I write this greeting with my own hand," he means he did not write the whole letter with his own hand but through a secretary. Supporting that idea is the fact that when it comes to his letter to Philemon, Paul does not limit his claim to the greeting, but says, "I, Paul, write this with my own hand." Philemon is only twenty-five verses long, and it may well be that Paul wrote all of it himself, since he did not mention writing the greeting. The words from Galatians 6:11 do not refer to a greeting either ("See with what large letters I am writing to you"). So we can't be sure whether he penned all of it himself.

Why did Paul bother to take up the pen and draw attention to his own handwriting (2 Thess. 3:17) and greeting? We know that he was aware of forgeries—people trying to spread their own views by claiming Paul's authority through letters that he did not write. For example, he wrote to the Thessalonians:

> Now concerning the coming of our Lord Jesus Christ and our being gathered together to him, we ask you, brothers, not to be quickly shaken in mind or alarmed, either by a spirit or a spoken word, or *a letter seeming to be from us*, to the effect that the day of the Lord has come. (2 Thess. 2:1–2)

So one reason Paul may have put his name and distinctive handwriting at the end of some of his letters was to make sure his letters were not seen as forgeries. In any case, he was manifestly eager for his readers to have his own words, not those of another. He was eager not only that his readers have his very words but that they *know* that they have them. This is our concern as well. Do we have the original words of Scripture, and do we know that we do?

The connection between this concern and our belief in *verbal* inspiration is made by Paul himself at least twice, once in regard to the Old Testament and once in regard to the New Testament, that is, in regard to his own letters.

Divine Inspiration of the Very Words of the Old Testament

With regard to the Old Testament, Paul links divine inspiration with words, not just prophets. God's inspiration—his "breathing out" the Scriptures—affects not only the human instrument but also the human product. Writings are inspired, not just people. Here is what Paul says to his younger protégé Timothy in this regard:

> Continue in what you have learned and have firmly believed, knowing from whom you learned it and how from childhood you have

been acquainted with the sacred *writings* [*grammata*], which are able to make you wise for salvation through faith in Christ Jesus. All Scripture [*graphē*] is breathed out by God and profitable for teaching, for reproof, for correction, and for training in righteousness, that the man of God may be complete, equipped for every good work. (2 Tim. 3:14–17)

First, Paul refers to the holy *writings*, which in Timothy's upbringing, as we have seen, would have been the Hebrew Bible (Acts 16:1; 2 Tim. 1:5; 3:14). Then he calls those writings "Scripture," which is another name for "writing." Then he says that these writings were "breathed out by God" (*theopneustos*). The writings themselves are inspired. This does not mean that the writers were not inspired. We know that is not true, from what Peter said in 2 Peter 1:20–21:

[Know] this first of all, that no prophecy of *Scripture* [*graphēs*] comes from one's own interpretation. For no prophecy was ever produced by the will of man, but *men spoke from God as they were carried along by the Holy Spirit.*

I take verse 20 to mean that no prophecy was ever put in Scripture *merely* according to what a human author thought it meant. Rather, Peter is clarifying that when a prophecy "comes" (literally, "happens" or "is," *ginetai*), and thus becomes part of Scripture, this does not happen by a *merely* human agency of the prophet's effort to understand what God is revealing.[2] Rather, as verse 21 makes clear, God's revelations to the prophets who wrote Scripture were guarded from human distortion because the prophets were "carried along by the Spirit" (not their own unaided efforts to understand), so that what was spoken, and then written, was no mere human interpretation of the mind of God.

Paul would not disagree with this—that the inspiration of *Scripture* happened through "*men* as they were carried along by the Holy Spirit." Paul would be enthusiastic to affirm this, and then he would simply add—which is what he does in 2 Timothy 3:16—that the implication of this process is that the *writings themselves* are thus God-breathed,

---

[2] Richard J. Bauckham gives an extensive defense of this interpretation, *2 Peter, Jude*, vol. 50, Word Biblical Commentary, ed. David A. Hubbard, Glenn W. Barker, Ralph P. Martin (Dallas: Word, 1998), 228–33.

not just the prophets who wrote. That was the point of the protective work of the Holy Spirit, to secure a "prophetic word (*prophētikon logon*) more fully confirmed" (2 Pet. 1:19). The aim of the process of inspiration was a sure "*word*" (2 Pet. 1:19), a "*Scripture*" (2 Pet. 1:20), a holy *writing* (2 Tim. 3:15).

Divine Inspiration of the Very Words of the New Testament

The same vigilance over the very words of God shows up in Paul's claim for his own inspiration by the Holy Spirit.

> Now we have received not the spirit of the world, but the Spirit who is from God, that we might understand the things freely given us by God. And we impart this in words [*logois*] not taught by human wisdom but taught by the Spirit, interpreting spiritual truths to those who are spiritual. (1 Cor. 2:12–13)

Paul does not claim to be inspired the way a poet today might say, "I was inspired to write a poem last night." The poet means that he was moved with an emotional creativity and energy that resulted in his poetic effort. But Paul means that his very words were governed by the Spirit of God—"*words* not taught by human wisdom but taught by the Spirit" (1 Cor. 2:13). God aims to communicate with us through words. He cares, therefore, that the words not be ill-chosen to accomplish his purpose. So the Holy Spirit worked in and through the human authors so that the words were really their own way of writing, but expressed God's meaning with the words he willed for them to use.

The Divine Will in the Human Will

This understanding of the divine will and the human will at work together is not restricted to the writing of Scripture. It pervades all human life. For example, consider Joseph, one of Jacob's twelve sons, who was sold by his brothers into slavery in Egypt. When he was promoted to ruler in Egypt, he said to his brothers, "As for you, you meant evil against me, but God meant it for good" (Gen. 50:20). It does not say, "You meant it for evil, but God *used* it for good," as though God's intention and action came in *after* they sold Joseph. No. It says that they had a meaning *in* their action, and God had a meaning *in* their action. The two intentions were both real and simultaneous.

Jonathan Edwards has a dramatic way of describing the interplay of the simultaneous divine action and the human action. For example, in relation to our sanctification he says,

> We are not merely passive in it, nor yet does God do some and we do the rest, but God does all and we do all. God produces all and we act all. For that is what he produces, our own acts. God is the only proper author and fountain; we only are the proper actors. We are in different respects wholly passive and wholly active.[3]

And in this concurrence of the divine and human activity, our activity is really ours, bearing all the marks of our own personality. Sinclair Ferguson points out how this is true in the creation of inspired Scripture as well:

> Undoubtedly the human writers of Scripture were conscious that they were expressing their own thoughts as they wrote. But at the same time they were under the sovereign direction of the Spirit. Theologians call this two-dimensional reality "concurrence."[4]

In this way, we can understand that the words of Scripture are both divinely determined and yet truly of human origin. They are really God's words and man's.

Does It Make Sense to Affirm the Inerrancy of Manuscripts We Don't Have?

Since the words of Scripture are so important to Jesus and his apostles, we must ask, therefore, whether we have access to the words that the inspired authors wrote. This question leads us into the field called "textual criticism," which refers to the branch of biblical scholarship that specializes in studying the ancient manuscripts of the Bible to discern how similar to the original manuscripts are the Greek and Hebrew texts we use today.

---

[3] Jonathan Edwards, *Writings on the Trinity, Grace, and Faith*, vol. 21, *The Works of Jonathan Edwards*, ed. Sang Hyun Lee (New Haven, CT: Yale University Press, 2003), 251.
[4] Sinclair Ferguson: *From the Mouth of God: Trusting, Reading, and Applying the Bible* (Edinburgh: Banner of Truth, 1982), 11.

We regard this matter as so important that it finds expression in our Affirmation of Faith.[5] "We believe that the Bible is . . . verbally inspired by God, and without error *in the original manuscripts.*"

It is true that we do not presently possess any of the actual manuscripts that the biblical authors produced (the very parchments they wrote on). What does that imply for our thinking about the inerrancy of Scripture? For several decades, I have heard people object to this phrase in our Affirmation, "in the original manuscripts." They often say, "We don't have the originals, so what good does it do to assert anything about them; we should make assertions about what we have, not what we don't have." In other words, it doesn't matter what you say about the inspiration and inerrancy of manuscripts you don't have. Is that true? I don't think so. Consider the analogy that follows.

An Illustration of the Importance of Nonextant Original Documents

Suppose I wrote you a letter (the old-fashioned way, on real paper) with careful instructions about how to get to my house for an important meeting. And suppose I asked you to share this information with others who need to come to the meeting. So (imagine yourself living in the 90s!) you scan the letter into a computer twice on two different days. Then you send out the scanned letter in two batches of emails to those who should come.

But, unfortunately, in one version of the scanned letter, the scanner had misread the original letter and had converted my address on "Fanny Street" to "Parry Street." In the other version of the scanned letter, the address was correct. "Fanny Street" came through accurately. Then suppose that the original letter was lost.

The people receiving the emails discover that their instructions for how to get to my house do not agree; so they come to you and ask which is correct. But you say that you have lost the original. Does anyone say: "Oh, well, it doesn't matter whether the original was correct or not; we'll just guess"?

No, some research is done—the text criticism mentioned above. For

---

[5] I am referring again to the Bethlehem Baptist Church Elder Affirmation of Faith, which not only the church but also Bethlehem College and Seminary and desiringGod.org are governed by.

example, a computer genius in the group suggests that you do some tests with the scanner. Remarkably, you discover that in dozens of tries the scanner never converts a P to an F but often converts an F to a P. And it never converts "rr" to "nn" but often converts "nn" to "rr." So you conclude that the original letter almost certainly read, "Fanny Street," which got converted to "Parry Street," not the other way around. And so you all get to the important meeting.

Now everyone getting to the meeting depended on the firm belief that the original letter was accurate and that every effort to get back to that wording was crucial—*even though the original letter no longer existed*. Similarly, if the wording of Scripture *in the original manuscripts* is not affirmed as inerrant, there would be little incentive to try to get back as close as possible in our text-critical studies, which form the basis of all our translations.

Original Manuscripts Have Objective Historical Reality

There is a strange cynicism that often accompanies the assertion that affirming the inerrancy of the original manuscripts doesn't really matter. It is sometimes expressed with rhetorical questions such as: "Don't you think the Bible in your hand today is inerrant?" And thus this question postures as a higher view of inerrancy.

The answer to the question is: *Our Greek and Hebrew versions and our translations are inerrant to the degree that they faithfully render the divine meaning carried by the inspired human words of the original manuscripts.*

This view represents a higher (that is, more accurate) view of inerrancy than the one represented by saying that every translation is inerrant and that the inerrancy of the original manuscripts doesn't matter. Occasionally, translations differ from each other in matters that make a difference in important matters of faith. So to say that they are all inerrant (in spite of such differences) is to weaken the meaning of inerrancy to the point where it loses objective reality.

On the other hand, to say that the inerrancy of the original manuscripts matters elevates the objective reality of inerrancy. It is a historical reality. God really did inspire the writings of the Bible so that his ideas were inerrantly carried in the words of the original manuscripts.

This historical reality is an objective standard that we can approach through textual criticism. Without this conviction, the contemporary versions and translations are set adrift in a sea of subjectivism with no objective standard to measure their faithfulness. Thus, affirming the inerrancy of the original manuscripts is a higher, more faithful, view of inerrancy. This is why our Affirmation of Faith says, "We believe that the Bible is . . . verbally inspired by God, and without error *in the original manuscripts.*"

Controversy and Consensus

In the past decade, one of the most intentional attacks on Christian belief has come in this field of textual criticism. Some scholars have argued that the Bible, as we have it, does not give a sure foundation for historic Christian belief.[6] Serious and responsible books[7] have been written to answer these arguments, and the debate goes on. I don't see this present book as the place for the kind of detailed historical argument that would be required if we were to respond to the arguments against the reliability of the text we have.

Moreover, I am convinced that in the end none of us settles the issue of biblical authority *decisively* on the basis of historical arguments. If that were the way God intended us to arrive at certainty of truth, the vast majority of people in the world would be excluded from the knowledge they need for living and dying as Christians. I will argue in the coming chapters how ordinary people, with little chance of following complex and obscure textual and historical arguments, may

---

[6] Most notably, biblical scholar Bart Ehrman has written and spoken about his own departure from Christian orthodoxy and has argued that the Bible, as we have it, does not give a sure foundation for historic Christian belief. Bart D. Ehrman, *The Orthodox Corruption of Scripture: The Effect of Early Christological Controversies on the Text of the New Testament* (1993; repr. Oxford, UK: Oxford University Press, 2011); Bart D. Ehrman, *Misquoting Jesus: The Story Behind Who Changed the Bible and Why* (New York: HarperOne, 2007).

[7] Timothy Paul Jones, *Misquoting Truth: A Guide to the Fallacies of Bart Ehrman's "Misquoting Jesus"* (Downers Grove, IL: InterVarsity, 2007); J. Ed Komoszewski, M. James Sawyer, and Daniel B. Wallace, *Reinventing Jesus: What the Da Vinci Code and Other Novel Speculations Don't Tell You* (Grand Rapids, MI: Kregel, 2006); Daniel B. Wallace, *Revisiting the Corruption of the New Testament: Manuscript, Patristic, and Apocryphal Evidence* (Grand Rapids, MI: Kregel, 2011); Daniel B. Wallace, "The Reliability of the New Testament Manuscripts," in *Understanding Scripture: An Overview of the Bible's Origin, Reliability, and Meaning,* ed. Wayne Grudem, C. John Collins, Thomas R. Schreiner (Wheaton, IL: Crossway, 2012); Robert B. Stewart, ed., *The Reliability of the New Testament: Bart Ehrman and Daniel Wallace in Dialogue* (Minneapolis, MN: Fortress, 2011); Craig Evans, *Fabricating Jesus: How Modern Scholars Distort the Gospels* (Downers Grove, IL: InterVarsity, 2008); Craig Blomberg, *Can We Still Believe the Bible?: An Evangelical Engagement with Contemporary Issues* (Grand Rapids, MI: Brazos, 2014); Michael Bird, ed., *How God Became Jesus: The Real Origins of Belief in Jesus' Divine Nature: A Response to Bart D. Ehrman* (Grand Rapids, MI: Zondervan, 2014).

discern whether the Christian Scriptures are the word of God. We may rejoice that God always raises up scholarly Christians to interact with scholarly opponents of Christian faith. But it is wrong to think that all believers need to follow those debates in order to have a justified faith in Scripture.

A Personal Story from Graduate School

My aim here is to describe the historic consensus of biblical scholars concerning the access we have to the original writings of the Bible. A personal anecdote captures the convictions of many mainline biblical scholars about the reliability of the Greek and Hebrew texts we use today. When I was doing my doctoral studies in Germany, my topic was Jesus's command to love our enemies. I was a brand-new doctoral student at the University of Munich. About nine months into my studies, my turn came to present a paper to my *Doktorvater*, Leonhard Goppelt, and the half dozen doctoral students who gathered at his house every month or so.

I decided to present my first paper on the text-critical issues in Matthew 5:43–48, which is one of the most important paragraphs dealing with Jesus's command of enemy-love. I attempted to assume nothing and to demonstrate as rigorously and as closely as I could that we have access to the wording that Matthew originally penned in Greek in that paragraph.

When I was finished presenting my very detailed (and, no doubt, boring) paper, which I assumed would be an early chapter in my dissertation, Dr. Goppelt thanked me for the work I had done and then said as gently as he could, "Mr. Piper," which he pronounced Peeper, "this will not be necessary for the rest of the texts you deal with. You may simply take your starting point from the established critical edition of the Greek text. We are assured that the text-critics have provided us with a reliable text." That was, and is, the general view of mainline biblical scholarship. It is not a uniquely conservative or evangelical view.

So let me sketch here why that kind of confidence is typical among historical scholars, even among those who are not conservative, or even Christian.

The State of the Union in Textual Criticism

The first printed Greek New Testament was published in 1516 by Erasmus. Before that, all copying was by hand. We owe our Bible to the meticulous love and care given by countless monks and scholars of the first fifteen hundred years of the Christian era. The challenge of getting back to the original manuscripts that the biblical authors wrote is the challenge of working with those hand-copied documents. That is why they are called *manu*scripts. Before 1516 they were all *hand*written. I will focus on the New Testament for illustrative purposes.

How many Greek manuscripts of the New Testament writings do we possess today? About 5,800. The following statistics are taken from the Institut für Neutestamentliche Textforschung, Münster, Germany, as of 2011. To my knowledge, no discoveries of any manuscripts have happened since then.

322	Uncial texts (all capital letters)
2,907	minuscule texts (all small letters)
2,445	lectionary portions (text portions contained in church readings)
127	papyri (manuscripts written on papyrus)
5,801	Total

It is a wonder of our day that many of these manuscripts are visible online at the Center for the Study of New Testament Manuscripts.[8]

To get a perspective on the astonishing number of manuscript fragments we have, it helps to compare the quantity of our fragments with other surviving historical documents. Daniel Wallace, who is regarded as "evangelical Christianity's premier active textual critic today,"[9] described the situation in 2012 like this:

> New Testament scholars face an embarrassment of riches compared to the data the classical Greek and Latin scholars have to contend with. The average classical author's literary remains number no more than twenty copies. We have more than 1,000 times the manuscript data for the New Testament than we do for the average Greco-Roman author. Not only this, but the extant manuscripts of

---

[8] http://www.csntm.org/manuscript; accessed 3-27-2015.
[9] http://www.thegospelcoalition.org/blogs/justintaylor/2012/03/21/an-interview-with-daniel-b-wallace-on-the-new-testament-manuscripts/; accessed 2-19-15.

the average classical author are no earlier than 500 years after the time he wrote. For the New Testament, we are waiting mere decades for surviving copies.[10]

For example:

Caesar's *Gallic Wars* (composed between 58 and 50 BC): There are about ten manuscripts available and the oldest is nine hundred years after the event.

Parts of the *Roman History* of Livy (composed between 59 BC and AD 17): These are preserved in about twenty manuscripts only one of which, containing only fragments, is as old as the fourth century.

The *Histories* and the *Annals* of the Roman historian Tacitus (composed around AD 100): These are preserved (partially) only in two manuscripts, one from the ninth century and one from the eleventh.

The *History* of Thucydides (who lived 460–400 BC): This is known to us from only eight manuscripts, the earliest belonging to AD 900, and a few papyrus scraps from the beginning of the Christian era.

Significantly, historians have never despaired of having reliable knowledge of these important writers. F. F. Bruce says,

No Classical scholar would listen to an argument that the authenticity of Herodotus or Thucydides is in doubt because the earliest manuscripts of their works which are of any use to us are over 1,300 years later than the originals.[11]

No other ancient book comes close to the kind of wealth of diverse preservation that we have for the New Testament. Not only is the number of manuscripts remarkable, but also the antiquity. The oldest fragment we have, for example, is a papyrus that comes from about AD 130 and contains John 18:31–33, 37ff. One of the oldest manuscripts of the entire New Testament comes from about AD 350. It is called *Codex Sinaiticus* because it was discovered in a monastery on Mount Sinai.

---

[10] Ibid.

[11] F. F. Bruce, *The New Testament Documents: Are They Reliable?*, 6th ed. (Grand Rapids, MI: Eerdmans, 1981), 11.

The huge number of manuscripts of the New Testament has two complementary results. First, there are *many variations* in wording among them because they were all copied by hand and subject to human error. Second, *variations tend to be self-correcting* because of the enormous number of manuscripts we have to compare. Again, F. F. Bruce comments,

> Fortunately, if the great number of MSS [manuscripts] increases the number of scribal errors, it increases proportionately the means of correcting such errors, so that the margin of doubt left in the process of recovering the exact original wording is not so large as might be feared; it is in truth remarkably small.[12]

Do We Have Access to What Was Originally Written?

What does this mean for our question *Do we have access today to the words that the biblical writers wrote?* Remembering that they wrote in Greek and Hebrew, not English, the answer is yes, we do, in every way that makes a difference in the truthfulness and authority of the Bible. Following are several summary statements from scholars to this effect.

Paul Wegner, in his *Student's Guide to Textual Criticism of the Bible*, writes,

> It is important to keep in perspective the fact that only a very small part of the text is in question—approximately 10 percent of the Old Testament and 7 percent of the New Testament. Of these, most variants make little difference to the meaning of any passage, as Douglas Stuart explains: "It is fair to say that the verses, chapters, and books of the Bible would read largely the same, and would leave the same impressions with the reader, even if one adopted virtually every possible alternative reading to those now serving as the basis for current English translations."[13]

Daniel Wallace has debated Bart Ehrman and reports his reaffirmed persuasion:

---

[12] Ibid., 14.
[13] Paul Wegner, *A Student's Guide to Textual Criticism of the Bible* (Downers Grove, IL: IVP Academic, 2006), 298, citing Douglas Stuart, "Inerrancy and Textual Criticism," in *Inerrancy and Common Sense*, ed. Roger R. Nicole and J. Ramsey Michaels (Grand Rapids, MI: Baker, 1980), 98.

Ever since the 1700s, with Johann Albrecht Bengel who studied the meaningful and viable textual variants, scholars have embraced what is called "the orthodoxy of the variants." For more than two centuries, most biblical scholars have declared that no essential affirmation [of Christian doctrine] has been affected by the variants. Even Ehrman has conceded this point in the three debates I have had with him.[14]

Similarly D. A. Carson sums up the situation this way: "What is at stake is a purity of text of such a substantial nature that nothing we believe to be doctrinally true, and nothing we are commanded to do, is in any way jeopardized by the variants."[15]

The Muslim Counterclaim

What this implies, among many other things, is that there is no historical evidence at all for a different Jesus, or a different Christianity, than the one we have in the New Testament we all use. You can disbelieve it and say that it was all somehow fabricated, but you can't bring forward any evidences of a different Jesus or a different faith from the one found in the New Testament. They don't exist.

This is relevant in responding to Islam. One of the popular claims of Islam is that even though Allah gave a book to Jesus, that book is lost, and all the other (Christian) records of who Jesus was and what he did are corruptions of original sources. As one Muslim website puts it, "The original teachings are simply lost from this earth. Only the Glorious Quran is the original Word of Allah Almighty. Nothing else stands. All of the other books contain corruptions and lies in them."[16]

This claim is essential for Islam because the Islamic view of Jesus is radically different from the view in the New Testament:

Islam affirms that Jesus was born of a virgin, that he lived a sinless life, that he performed mighty miracles, and that he will come again at the end of history. It even calls him a word from God. However,

---

[14] "An Interview with Daniel B. Wallace on the New Testament Manuscripts," http://www.thegospel coalition.org/blogs/justintaylor/2012/03/21/an-interview-with-daniel-b-wallace-on-the-new-testament -manuscripts/; accessed February 19, 2015.
[15] D. A. Carson, *The King James Version Debate* (Grand Rapids, MI: Baker, 1979), 56.
[16] http://www.answering-christianity.com/injil_and_gospels_according_to_islam.htm; accessed February 20, 2015.

it explicitly denies the deity of Christ and repudiates the title "Son of God" as blasphemous. It also (according to the majority view) denies he died on the cross, claiming that Jesus' visage was imposed on someone else, who was then crucified, and that Jesus was taken up into heaven without tasting death. Islam explicitly denies the possibility of substitutionary atonement.[17]

Thus the Quran, Sura 4:156–57, says,

> For their [the Jews'] saying: "We slew the Messiah, Jesus son of Mary, the Messenger of God"—yet they did not slay him, neither crucified him, only a likeness of that was shown to them. Those regarding him: they have no knowledge of him, except the following of surmise; and they slew him not of a certainty—no indeed; God raised him up to Him; God is All-mighty, All-wise.[18]

Muslims claim that the reason the New Testament depicts a supernatural Jesus who was the Son of God and was crucified and raised from the dead is that Christians changed and distorted original writings. But there is no evidence that such writings existed, which means that the Muslim claim is an *inference* based on Mohammed's view of Jesus. This is crucial to see. The claim that Jesus did not die, and that Christianity is wrong, therefore, at its core, is a faith claim based on a seventh-century teacher, Mohammed. There are no ancient manuscripts of the New Testament that support a Muslim view that Christians corrupted the earliest testimonies. All the manuscripts that touch on the end of Jesus's life portray Jesus as crucified, dead, buried, and raised. There is no historical evidence at all for an uncrucified Jesus Christ.

We Have the Word of God

The point of this chapter has not been to prove the truth of Christian Scripture but rather to show that the Greek and Hebrew Scriptures we have today are essentially the same as the ones written by the original authors. In chapters 8–17 we will address the question of how we know they are true.

---

[17] Zane Pratt, "Ten Things Every Christian Should Know about Islam," accessed February 20, 2015, http://www.thegospelcoalition.org/article/10-things-every-christian-should-know-about-islam/print/.
[18] Quoted in Evertt W. Huffard, "Culturally Relevant Themes about Christ," in *Muslims and Christians on the Emmaus Road*, ed. J. Dudley Woodberry (Monrovia, CA: MARC, 1989), 165.

For now, it is worth hearing the conclusion of one of the great textual critics, Sir Frederic G. Kenyon:

> It is reassuring at the end to find that the general result of all these discoveries and all this study is to strengthen the proof of the authenticity of the Scriptures, and our conviction that we have in our hands, in substantial integrity, the veritable Word of God.[19]

Since the Greek and Hebrew texts on which our modern language translations are based today are essentially the same as what the inspired authors wrote, we may turn now to our final two tasks. First, what do these Scriptures claim for themselves? Do they actually claim to be the infallible word of God (chapters 5–7)? And second, how can we know if such a claim is true (chapters 8–17)?

---

[19] Frederic G. Kenyon, *The Story of the Bible*, 2nd ed. (Grand Rapids, MI: Eerdmans, 1967), 113.

PART 3

What Do the Christian
Scriptures Claim for Themselves?

*"... words not taught by human
wisdom but taught by the Spirit"*

The words of the LORD are pure words,
like silver refined in a furnace on the ground,
purified seven times.

PSALM 12:6

5

The Old Testament

Is the Bible the reliable word of God—is it inspired by God, and true, and free from error? If we are going to pursue an answer to that question, then it would be wise to consult with the Bible first, to see what it claims for itself. In fact, we are not the ones who initiated this interaction with the Bible. The Bible was there first. The Bible itself was making claims for itself—and making claims on us—before we ever decided to engage with the Bible.

God's word does not wait for us to give it permission to be God's word. If it is God's word, it is God's word—with or without us. If we fail to recognize that God is speaking, that is no excuse. We are accountable from the start. So it is fitting, in more ways than one, that we listen to the Bible concerning the Bible before we even frame the final question about truth.

The Threads and the Tapestry

To be clear, my approach to the truth of Scripture is not that we are convinced that Scripture is true simply because it claims to be. In saying this, I am not denying that if God says his word is true, that is a good reason to believe it. No one is better positioned to know God's word is true than God himself. Rather, what I will argue in chapters 8–17 is that the Scriptures give well-grounded warrant to our confidence in their truth by more than their claims to be true.

I will argue that those truth claims are threads in a tapestry whose divine glory is self-authenticating. Or, to change the image, the truth claims of Scripture are facets in the diamond of Scripture's luminous meaning, which reveals its divine glory in a way similar to the way the human Jesus reveals his divine glory. That's how I will argue in chapters 8–17. But the truth claims of Scripture are indeed beautiful and important threads of the tapestry of its meaning. Therefore, chapters 5–7 are devoted to seeing these threads as clearly as we can. It may be—indeed, it is my prayer—that in reading the Bible's unique and glorious witness to its own grandeur, you will see not just a divine claim but a divine reality.

We have had glimpses already of Jesus's view of the Old Testament (Matt. 5:17–18) and his plan for the New Testament (John 14:24–26; 16:12–14). We have seen Paul's view of the Old Testament (2 Tim. 3:15–17) and his own apostolic inspiration (1 Cor. 2:13). And we have seen Peter's view of Paul's writings (2 Pet. 3:16). But those were only glimpses. There is, to change the metaphor one more time, a vast panorama of the Bible's own presentation of its divine truthfulness and authority. We will not be able to fit the extent of that panorama within the lens of this chapter or this book. It is too vast.[1] So in chapters 5–7, I will simply open the lens a little more widely so that we have a better sense of the extent of the claims and the force and nature of what we are called to believe—and what is being displayed for us to see.

The Old Testament Writers Are in the Drama, Not Outside It

The Old Testament never comments on the Old Testament as a collection of writings. The writers were conscious of God's speaking to them and through them (as we will see), but they never stood outside the Old Testament and commented on it as a whole. But Jesus does do this. So does the apostle Paul. And all the New Testament writers treat the Old Testament as the authoritative deposit of God's word. But the Old Testament writers themselves were actors on the stage of the Old Testament drama that God was composting and directing. They never

---

[1] One of the most impressive renderings of the beauty and vastness of the Bible's own view of itself is Wayne Grudem, "Scripture's Self-Attestation and the Problem of Formulating a Doctrine of Scripture," in *Scripture and Truth*, ed. D. A. Carson and John D. Woodbridge (Grand Rapids, MI: Zondervan, 1983), 19–59.

stood outside the drama and commented on its authority as a completed canon of Scripture.

So when we ask how the Old Testament writers testified to its truth and authority, the answer is not that they affirmed the truthfulness of the Old Testament the way Jesus does (Matt. 5:17–18; John 10:35). Jesus knew it as a complete collection of books that were already functioning for the Jewish people as a unified expression of God's word. But the writers of the Old Testament were still in the middle of the process of bringing the Old Testament into being.

Therefore, what we hear from them are expressions not about the Old Testament as a whole but rather about the way God was revealing himself to them and to others through them. The impact these expressions had was to make Israel aware that the Creator of the universe was speaking to them through the words of men. We take this so much for granted in the Christian church that we may fail to be amazed at how staggering this really is.

God is so great that he holds the galaxies in existence and calls the trillions of stars by name (Isa. 48:26)—think of it: by name, trillions of names—and he is not the least stressed or wearied by this (Isa. 40:28). This God condescends (infinitely!) to speak to human beings. What we want to see, as we read, is how he did this. Then we can stand back and ask how all that gave rise to the Old Testament.

So consider with me some of the ways that the Old Testament bears witness to God's astonishing willingness to speak in human language.

God Speaks in Human Language

The first and most basic thing to observe is that throughout the Old Testament from Adam and Eve (Gen. 2:16) to Malachi (who, in four short chapters, uses the phrase "says the LORD of hosts" twenty times), God speaks in human language directly to human beings. "Now the LORD said to Abram, 'Go from your country and your kindred and your father's house to the land that I will show you'" (Gen. 12:1). "God spoke all these words, saying, 'I am the LORD your God, who brought you out of the land of Egypt, out of the house of slavery'" (Ex. 20:1–2). "I heard the voice of the Lord, saying, 'Whom shall I send, and who will go for us?'" (Isa. 6:8).

How God actually speaks to men is never explained. It is doubtful that there is an "explanation" that a human could make sense of. One of the partners in this communication, namely, God, is of such a supernatural nature that he exceeds our ability to fully comprehend him or his ways (Isa. 55:8; Rom. 11:33–34). This mystery has caused many people to be skeptical that what the Old Testament describes really is possible. Skeptical scholars who want to hold onto some kind of biblical authority have minimized this kind of verbal transaction between God and man and put all the emphasis on God's communication through events rather than divine words. This resistance to the plain and pervasive claims of the Old Testament caused James Barr, who was no evangelical, to protest,

> Direct verbal communication between God and particular men on particular occasions . . . is, I believe, an inescapable fact of the Bible and of the Old Testament in particular. God can speak specific verbal messages, which he wills, to the man of his choice. . . . If we persist in saying that the direct, specific communication must be subsumed under revelation through events in history and taken as subsidiary interpretation of the latter, I shall say that we are abandoning the Bible's own representation of the matter for another which is apologetically more comfortable.[2]

God Speaks to People through People

Not only does God speak directly to human beings throughout the Bible; he also commissions some of those people to speak to others what he has said. In fact, this is clearly God's more normal way of making his word known in the world. The Old Testament is not a record of God treating each individual as a receiver of direct, divine communication without other persons being involved. The typical way for God to communicate to most people is through other people—his chosen spokesmen.

Thus, for example, God said to Nathan the prophet, "Go and tell my servant David, 'Thus says the Lord: Would you build me a house to dwell in?'" (2 Sam. 7:5). And God came to Isaiah and said, "Go and

---

[2] James Barr, "The Interpretation of Scripture II: Revelation through History in the Old Testament and in Modern Theology," *Interpretation* 187 (1963): 201–2.

say to Hezekiah, 'Thus says the Lord, the God of your father David, I have heard your prayer, I have seen your tears; behold, I will add fifteen years to your life'" (Isa. 38:5 NASB). And he says to Jeremiah, "Go and say to the men of Judah and the inhabitants of Jerusalem, 'Will you not receive instruction by listening to My words?'" (Jer. 35:13 NASB). In all these cases—and they are typical—God does not intend to communicate directly to David and Hezekiah and the men of Judah without a prophet. He means to speak to them *through* a prophet.

Therefore, we find the statement that God spoke "through" his prophet: "Thus Zimri destroyed all the household of Baasha, according to the word of the Lord, which He spoke against Baasha *through Jehu the prophet*" (1 Kings 16:12 NASB). But this explicit statement that God's words are passing "through" the prophet does not lessen the expectancy that they are the very words of God. When God's words come *through* the prophet, they are still God's words: "You shall speak *my words* to them, whether they hear or refuse to hear, for they are a rebellious house" (Ezek. 2:7). They are God's words because God superintends the prophet's speaking so that his mouth is like God's mouth: "Now therefore go, and I will be with your mouth and teach you what you shall speak" (Ex. 4:12).

The great prophecy of the ideal prophet who would eventually come in the person of Jesus Christ expresses this most forcefully:

> I will raise up for them a prophet like you from among their brothers. And I will *put my words in his mouth*, and he shall speak to them all that I command him. And whoever will not listen to my words that he shall speak in my name, I myself will require it of him. But the prophet who presumes to speak a word in my name that I have not commanded him to speak, or who speaks in the name of other gods, that same prophet shall die. (Deut. 18:18–20; cf. Acts 3:22–23)

Often in the prophetic books, this close identification between God's words and the prophet's words means that the prophet speaks in the first-person singular ("I") as if God himself were standing there speaking: "I am the Lord, and there is no other, besides me there is no God" (Isa. 45:5).

Not surprisingly, therefore, trusting the words of prophets when they are speaking for God is treated as trusting God himself. "When [the Levites] went out, Jehoshaphat stood and said, 'Hear me, Judah and inhabitants of Jerusalem! Believe in the LORD your God, and you will be established; *believe his prophets, and you will succeed*" (2 Chron. 20:20). One implication of this is that God was at work to secure the accuracy of his prophets' speech so that what the people understood from them would have the same truthfulness as if God were speaking directly.

Stepping back to look at the whole Old Testament, this amazing reality of divine speech through authorized human beings is seen for the pervasive reality that it is. In the English Standard Version, the phrase "thus says the Lord" occurs 417 times. And the phrase "declares the Lord" occurs 358 times. These frequencies really should take our breath away. This book—the Old Testament—is saturated with the explicit claim that our Creator and Sustainer and Redeemer is actually speaking intelligibly to the world he has made.

In one sense, God's intelligible communication to us through other human beings seems obvious, and in another sense, it seems incredible. It seems obvious because he is God and can do whatever he pleases. If he wants to communicate by human words, he will. But on the other hand, there is, after all, an infinite qualitative difference between God and the creature of God. If there ever was a vast "cultural" difference between a translator and a receptor people, this is it—an infinite difference. How can the eternal, and infinite Creator make himself intelligible to minds and hearts that are of an infinitely different order? This is as mysterious as the coming of God into the world himself in Jesus Christ. Both are unfathomable. And both are real. And when we take the divine-human Bible in our hands, we should feel a similar wonder to what we may feel when we touch the skin of the risen God-man, Jesus Christ.

God Intends for His Revelation to Be Written

Then we notice that God intends for there to be a written form of this divine revelation. He says to Moses, "Write this as a memorial in a book and recite it in the ears of Joshua" (Ex. 17:14). And again, "Write these words, for in accordance with these words I have made a covenant with you and with Israel" (Ex. 34:27). "And Moses wrote down all the words of the LORD" (Ex. 24:4; cf. Deut. 27:3). In the rest of the Old Testament, there are dozens of references to the written Law of Moses (1 Kings 2:3; 1 Chron. 16:40; Ezra 3:2; Neh. 8:14; Dan. 9:13).

And not only did God instruct Moses to write down the revelation he had received, but he instructed the prophets to do the same. To Jeremiah God says, "The word that came to Jeremiah from the LORD: 'Thus says the LORD, the God of Israel: Write in a book all the words that I have spoken to you'" (Jer. 30:1–2). "This word came to Jeremiah from the LORD: 'Take a scroll and write on it all the words that I have spoken to you against Israel and Judah and all the nations, from the day I spoke to you, from the days of Josiah until today" (Jer. 36:1–2, 28). And similarly God said to Habakkuk, "Write the vision; make it plain on tablets, so he may run who reads it" (Hab. 2:2; cf. Ezek. 43:11).

Accordingly, therefore, the written prophetic books regularly begin with the indication that the written book is a composition of the prophet's revelations from God.

> The words of Jeremiah, the son of Hilkiah, one of the priests who were in Anathoth in the land of Benjamin, to whom *the word of the LORD came* in the days of Josiah the son of Amon, king of Judah, in the thirteenth year of his reign. (Jer. 1:1–2)

> In the thirtieth year, in the fourth month, on the fifth day of the month, as I was among the exiles by the Chebar canal, the heavens were opened, and I saw visions of God. On the fifth day of the month . . . *the word of the LORD came to Ezekiel* the priest. (Ezek. 1:1–3)

> *The word of the LORD that came to Hosea*, the son of Beeri, in the days of Uzziah, Jotham, Ahaz, and Hezekiah, kings of Judah, and in the days of Jeroboam the son of Joash, king of Israel. (Hos. 1:1)

> *The word of the LORD that came to Micah* of Moresheth in the days of Jotham, Ahaz, and Hezekiah, kings of Judah, which he saw concerning Samaria and Jerusalem. (Mic. 1:1)

The word of the LORD *that came to Zephaniah* the son of Cushi, son of Gedaliah, son of Amariah, son of Hezekiah, in the days of Josiah the son of Amon, king of Judah. (Zeph. 1:1)

The Sum of Your Word Is Truth

What emerges from this survey of the Old Testament's self-attestation is a culture in Israel that knows itself confronted by God through his all-authoritative word, which comes not directly to every individual, but through persons chosen by God and enabled to speak his word reliably, including its written form. The emergence of a collection of such writings—the canon of the Hebrew Bible—is therefore exactly what we would expect.

And as this collection of writings emerges, it would be handled with extraordinary care, because not only did the writings claim to be the word of God, but they also made explicit one of the clear implications of that fact, namely, their complete truthfulness.

> God is not man, that he should lie,
>> or a son of man, that he should change his mind.
> Has he said, and will he not do it?
>> Or has he spoken, and will he not fulfill it? (Num. 23:19)

The Glory of Israel will not lie or have regret, for he is not a man, that he should have regret. (1 Sam. 15:29)

> The words of the LORD are pure words,
>> like silver refined in a furnace on the ground,
>> purified seven times. (Ps. 12:6)

> The sum of your word is truth,
>> and every one of your righteous rules endures forever.
>>> (Ps. 119:160)

> Forever, O LORD, your word
>> is firmly fixed in the heavens.
> Your faithfulness endures to all generations. (Ps. 119:89–90)

> Every word of God proves true;
>> he is a shield to those who take refuge in him.

Do not add to his words,
> lest he rebuke you and you be found a liar. (Prov. 30:5–6)

Our Expectations Are High

The writers of the Old Testament do not make comments about the canon of the Old Testament as a whole. They are *in* the drama, not watching it from outside. But they make astonishing claims about God's speaking directly to men and through men. There is a claim that God intends for his revelation to be written down. And there are claims of God's unqualified truthfulness. All of this means that our expectations are high as we turn to Jesus—who claimed to be the very fulfillment of the Old Testament—and as we ask, *What was his estimate of these writings?*

Do not think that I have come to abolish the Law or the Prophets; I have not come to abolish them but to fulfill them. For truly, I say to you, until heaven and earth pass away, not an iota, not a dot, will pass from the Law until all is accomplished.

MATTHEW 5:17–18

6

Jesus's Estimate of the

Old Testament

In one sense, Jesus was in the drama, and in one sense, he could view it from outside. How so? The drama of God's interaction with the world goes on after the Old Testament. It continues today. God is at work in the world sustaining, governing, saving, and guiding it toward the day when Jesus will come again and establish his kingdom of worship and righteousness and peace. But within this drama of God's activity in the world, Jesus was sent to speak God's unbreakable word to his people in person, and then, by his Spirit, through writings—the New Testament Scriptures.

To be sure, God dwells in all Christians by his Spirit (Rom. 8:9), and he has a personal relationship with each of them. They speak to him as to a loving Father. And he makes himself known to them personally, by his word. It is a living, personal, precious fellowship (John 14:18–23; Gal. 2:20; 1 Pet. 2:3). But neither in the Old Testament times nor in the New Testament times, nor today, did God—or does God—deliver his infallible word directly to all his children. That kind of infallible communication he has reserved for the book—the Scriptures, the inspired writings.

We do not receive the kind of revelation directly and personally that God has given through his apostles and prophets in the Bible. When the apostle Paul confronted those in the church at Corinth who claimed to receive revelations from God, he did not deny it, but he subordinated it to his own apostolic word: "If anyone thinks that he is a prophet, or spiritual, he should acknowledge that the things I am writing to you are a command of the Lord. If anyone does not recognize this, he is not recognized" (1 Cor. 14:37–38).

God may lead us to see things and know things, but all our revelatory experiences with God are subordinate to Scripture. Therefore, we are not infallible. God is. And the word he inspired is. We may experience the powerful, personal dimension of God's word as the Holy Spirit makes it real and personal to us (Rom. 5:5). But God has bound his infallible word to the writings—the Scriptures.

Thus, there is a sense that Jesus and we are *inside* the drama of redemptive history and a sense in which we can view it as whole through God's inspired word. We are in the story. And we can read the story. The written record of God's dealings with creation is our only authoritative guide for understanding the story we are in. Only God sees things whole and sees them perfectly. He has inspired a book that gives the only infallible record of God's nature and will and plan.

Therefore, when Jesus comes into the world, he is coming as part of the ongoing history of redemption. Indeed, he comes as the capstone of the history of redemption (Matt. 5:17), the fulfillment of what the Old Testament was pointing toward (Rom. 10:4; cf. Luke 24:27). But here is the crucial thing concerning the Old Testament. When Jesus comes, he finds the Old Testament is complete and closed. He does not write the last chapter of the Old Testament canon. The canon is closed. The drama goes on. But Act 1 of biblical history is complete, and fixed, and written. Though Jesus was active in the Old Testament (cf. John 12:41), he now meets the Old Testament from the outside. It is a book. And he is reading it, though he once was acting to bring the book into being. As the apostle Peter said,

> Concerning this salvation, the prophets who prophesied about the grace that was to be yours searched and inquired carefully, inquiring what person or time the *Spirit of Christ in them was indicating when he predicted the sufferings of Christ* and the subsequent glories. (1 Pet. 1:10–11)

He was writing the story. Now he is reading it. The question before us now is: *What was his estimate of this book, the Hebrew Scriptures—what we call the Old Testament?*

Jesus and the Psalms

In a word, Jesus's esteem for and confidence in the Old Testament was perfect. It was a book that in the fullness of its scope must be fulfilled and in the minutiae of its detail could not be broken. This is what he taught.

With regard to inspiration, Jesus spoke of the Psalms as the voice of men who were guided by the Holy Spirit:

> As Jesus taught in the temple, he said, "How can the scribes say that the Christ is the son of David? *David himself, in the Holy Spirit, declared,*
>
>> 'The Lord said to my Lord,
>> "Sit at my right hand,
>>   until I put your enemies under your feet."'
>
> David himself calls him Lord. So how is he his son?" (Mark 12:35–37)

The word "in" ("David himself, *in* the Holy Spirit, declared") can mean a position (in) or instrumentality (by). You can serve "in" a nursing home, and you can serve "in" the strength that God supplies. This second use is what Jesus means: David spoke "in" the guidance and control of the Holy Spirit. This is what David had said about his own songs: "The Spirit of the LORD speaks by me; his word is on my tongue" (2 Sam. 23:2).

This was the apostles' understanding of David's inspiration as well. Peter said on the day of Pentecost, fifty days after the resurrection of Jesus, "Brothers, the Scripture had to be fulfilled, which *the Holy Spirit spoke beforehand by the mouth of David* concerning Judas" (Acts 1:16; Ps. 69:25; cf. Acts 4:25; Heb. 3:7; 10:15). In fact, this is precisely the way Peter described the inspiration of *all* prophecy, namely, "men spoke from God as they were carried along by the Holy Spirit" (2 Pet. 1:21).

God Said What Moses Said

There is good reason to believe that Jesus thought of the entire Old Testament as having this kind of connection between the human authors and the guiding work of God's Spirit. When Jesus was dealing with the issue of divorce, he based his view on the words of Moses in the creation story of Genesis 2. The words Jesus uses are clear evidence that he saw the words of Moses as the words of God:

> Pharisees came up to him and tested him by asking, "Is it lawful to divorce one's wife for any cause?" He answered, "Have you not read that *he who created them from the beginning made them male and female, and said,* 'Therefore a man shall leave his father and his mother and hold fast to his wife, and the two shall become one flesh'? So they are no longer two but one flesh. What therefore God has joined together, let not man separate." (Matt. 19:3–6)

My point here is a bit detailed, but look carefully. Who said, "Therefore a man shall leave his father and mother"? Answer: "He who created them . . . said . . ." That is, God said. But in Genesis 2:24, God is not being quoted. The verse that Jesus quotes (Gen. 2:24) is simply part of the narrative that Moses wrote ("Therefore a man shall leave his father and his mother and hold fast to his wife, and they shall become one flesh").

What this means is that Jesus saw the narratives of Moses as what God himself said. He did not think that we have God's word only in those places where Moses quotes the voice of God. All the Scripture that Moses wrote was the voice of God. This confirms what we saw earlier—that God intended the *voice* of his prophets to be put in *writing* with the same authority that they had in the moment of prophetic preaching. Jesus confirms for us that writing is what the Old Testament is.

The Scriptures Cannot Be Broken

The inference Jesus drew from this kind of inspiration of the Scriptures was that none of them can be broken. It is a sweeping claim. Jesus had just said to the Jews, "I and the Father are one." They picked up stones to kill him (John 10:30–31). Here is their accusation and the way Jesus defended himself (since his hour had not yet come):

The Jews answered him, "It is not for a good work that we are going to stone you but for blasphemy, because you, being a man, make yourself God." Jesus answered them, "Is it not written in your Law, 'I said, you are gods'? If he called them gods to whom the word of God came—*and Scripture cannot be broken*—do you say of him whom the Father consecrated and sent into the world, 'You are blaspheming,' because I said, 'I am the Son of God'?" (John 10:33–36)

Our concern here is not with the strangeness of the reference to "gods."[1] Our concern is the seeming incidental insertion of the words "and the Scripture cannot be broken." It is Jesus's way of saying, "Yes, this is a small, seemingly incidental, perhaps even obscure, reference from Psalm 82:6 (I said, 'You are gods, sons of the Most High, all of you'), but my view—which I assume you all share—is that not even the small parts of the Scripture can be wrong." Remember, this was also the implication of Jesus's words, "Not an iota, not a dot, will pass from the Law until all is accomplished" (Matt. 5:18).

So what we have seen so far is that Jesus believed the Holy Spirit was at work guiding the writers of Scripture and that this included not just the parts where God is quoted directly but the other narrative and poetic parts as well, and that this implies that in the mind of Jesus, these Scriptures, therefore, cannot be broken—they cannot be wrong.

Will They Lead You to Err?

This impeccability of the Old Testament Scriptures is why knowing them keeps us from error—that is, knowing them rightly will keep us from erring in the matter they are addressing. Jesus makes this point in Mark 12, where the Sadducees try to make the doctrine of the resurrection look ludicrous. They set Jesus up like this:

Teacher, Moses wrote for us that if a man's brother dies and leaves a wife, but leaves no child, the man must take the widow and raise up offspring for his brother. There were seven brothers; the first took a wife, and when he died left no offspring. And the second took her, and died, leaving no offspring. And the third likewise. And the seven

---

[1] If you're interested in the reference to "gods," I addressed this in a sermon in 2011. The written manuscript, along with audio and video, are available at http://www.desiringgod.org/sermons/i-and-the -father-are-one.

left no offspring. Last of all the woman also died. In the resurrection, when they rise again, whose wife will she be? For the seven had her as wife. (Mark 12:19–23)

Jesus responds to them, "Is this not the reason you are wrong, because you know neither the Scriptures nor the power of God?" (Mark 12:24). That is, you err because you don't know the Scriptures. If you knew them, and the power of God they teach, and the implications they carry for the resurrection of the body, you would have been protected from error in this matter.

Jesus helps us see here why the doctrine of the inerrancy of Scripture matters. It's not merely because we want to assert that documents don't err but, more importantly, so that *we* don't err. In preserving the *Bible* from error, God is loving *us*. The Scriptures are meant to protect people. Truth leads to freedom (John 8:32), and error leads to bondage (2 Tim. 2:25–26). Truth saves (2 Thess. 2:10); error destroys (2 Thess. 2:11). Truth enlightens (Ps. 43:3; Eph. 5:9); error deceives (Prov. 12:17; 2 Cor. 11:13). Truth gives life (1 John 5:20); error brings death (2 Sam. 6:7). Therefore, God is concerned not only for his own glory in being a God of truth (Rom. 3:7); he is concerned also for *us* when he guards his word from error.

Jesus Defeats the Devil with the Word

As the perfect God-*man*, battling the temptations of Satan in the wilderness, Jesus uses the written word of God the way we should. He sets us an example. He overcomes his adversaries by the truth and power of God's word. This is amazing because Jesus is God, and could have—as he often did—dispatched Satan with one word of *his own*. But in this case, Jesus is modeling his human reliance on the Father's word.

When Satan tempts him in the wilderness, he overcomes him in every case by quoting Scripture. He does this though he is the Son of God—that is the very point of the temptation ("If you are the Son of God . . ."). As the Son of God, he has the power in himself to tell Satan to depart the same way he told two thousand demons to depart in Mark 5:12–13. But instead of using that power, he gives us an example. Watch for the word "written":

The tempter came and said to him, "If you are the Son of God, command these stones to become loaves of bread." But he answered, "It is *written*,

> 'Man shall not live by bread alone,
> but by every word that comes from the mouth of God.'"

Then the devil took him to the holy city and set him on the pinnacle of the temple and said to him, "If you are the Son of God, throw yourself down, for it is written,

> 'He will command his angels concerning you,'

and

> 'On their hands they will bear you up,
> lest you strike your foot against a stone.'" (Matt. 4:3–6)

And Jesus countered the Devil's misuse of Scripture with a true use:

Again it is *written*, "You shall not put the Lord your God to the test." (Matt. 4:7)

Again, the devil took him to a very high mountain and showed him all the kingdoms of the world and their glory. And he said to him, "All these I will give you, if you will fall down and worship me." Then Jesus said to him, "Be gone, Satan! For it is *written*, 'You shall worship the Lord your God and him only shall you serve.'" (Matt. 4:8–10)

In every case Jesus overcame his adversary—a very powerful supernatural adversary—by quoting what is *written*—the Old Testament Scriptures. The result? "Then the devil left him, and behold, angels came and were ministering to him" (Matt. 4:11).

He did the same thing with his human adversaries. When he saw the way the behavior of the scribes and Pharisees did not fit their teaching of the Mosaic law, his way of responding was to criticize not the law of Moses but the inconsistency of the teachers. He explicitly affirmed that the problem was not the law: "The scribes and the Pharisees sit on *Moses'* seat, so do and observe whatever they tell you, but not the works they do. For they preach, but do not practice" (Matt. 23:2–3). In other words, even if the word of God comes through hypocritical channels (such as Pharisees), it is still the word of God. It gets its authority not from the humans who teach it but from God, who inspired it.

Jesus's Estimate of the Old Testament as a Litmus Test of Spiritual Sight

There are at least two occasions when Jesus called attention to the peculiar nature of the Old Testament as a kind of litmus test for a person's openness to other truth. In other words, he showed that if you don't believe God's word in the Old Testament, there is a kind of blindness that will probably keep you from seeing truth about hell and about Jesus. The implication of these two passages seems to be that the Old Testament is not an ordinary book but has a kind of inspiration and authority that makes it different in the effect it has on how you view other truth.

The Rich Man and Lazarus

The first occasion is the story of the rich man and Lazarus, the poor man at his gate. Both men die and go to different places:

> The poor man died and was carried by the angels to Abraham's side. The rich man also died and was buried, and in Hades, being in torment, he lifted up his eyes and saw Abraham far off and Lazarus at his side. And he called out, "Father Abraham, have mercy on me, and send Lazarus to dip the end of his finger in water and cool my tongue, for I am in anguish in this flame." But Abraham said, "Child, remember that you in your lifetime received your good things, and Lazarus in like manner bad things; but now he is comforted here, and you are in anguish. And besides all this, between us and you a great chasm has been fixed, in order that those who would pass from here to you may not be able, and none may cross from there to us." And he said, "Then I beg you, father, to send him to my father's house—for I have five brothers—so that he may warn them, lest they also come into this place of torment." (Luke 16:22–28)

To this request Abraham says, "They have Moses and the Prophets; let them hear them" (v. 29). In other words, God has given a revelation to your brothers, and it is sufficient. But the point here is that it is *more* than sufficient.

The rich man protests that the Scriptures are not sufficient: "No, father Abraham, but if someone goes to them from the dead, they will repent" (v. 30). In other words, what they need is an outward miracle to wake them up. The voice of God is not enough; there must be something more sensational.

Then Abraham says something truly amazing: "If they do not hear Moses and the Prophets, neither will they be convinced if someone should rise from the dead" (v. 31). This is remarkable for two reasons. One is that we instinctively feel that seeing someone rise from the dead would be more compelling than reading Scripture. So why would Abraham say what he does?

Why Would Resurrection Not Convince?

The other reason Abraham's words are remarkable is that miraculous signs and wonders (such as resurrections and healings and exorcisms) were viewed positively by the apostles as witnesses to the truth of their message—and God used them to testify to the truth of his word. For example, Barnabas and Paul in Iconium were "speaking boldly for the Lord, *who bore witness to the word of his grace, granting signs and wonders* to be done by their hands" (Acts 14:3). And Hebrews 2:3–4 reminds us that salvation "was declared at first by the Lord, and it was attested to us by those who heard, *while God also bore witness by signs and wonders and various miracles* and by gifts of the Holy Spirit distributed according to his will." So miracles have value in the process of convincing people of the truth of God's word.

The effect of a resurrection at the hands of the apostles can be seen in Acts 9:36–42. A disciple named Tabitha had died. Her friends asked Peter to come and pray over her. He does, and God raises her from the dead. What was the effect? "Calling the saints and widows, he presented her alive. And it became known throughout all Joppa, and many believed in the Lord" (Acts 9:41–42).

What then did Abraham mean when he said to the rich man in the flames, "If they do not hear Moses and the Prophets, neither will they be convinced if someone should rise from the dead" (Luke 16:31)?

The first thing we can say is this: miracles by themselves do not convince sinners of the true spiritual beauty of Jesus Christ. Miracles may convince sinners that Jesus can do miracles and that he would, therefore, make a very useful king (John 6:15, 26). Miracles even convinced his own brothers that he was a miracle worker. They urged him to go to Jerusalem to show off his power, "for no one works in secret if he seeks to be known openly. If you do these things, show yourself to the world" (John 7:4). But on this, John commented, "For not even his brothers believed in him" (John 7:4–5; see 2:22–25). They were persuaded by the miracles, *and* they were not yet truly believers.[2]

So when Abraham said, "If they do not hear Moses and the Prophets, neither will they be convinced if someone should rise from the dead," he probably meant this: *wherever there is a spiritual deafness to the voice of God in the Old Testament, mere external miracles will not cure that spiritual deafness.* Something more is required when reading the Scripture. And something more is required when looking at a miracle. The same deadness that blinds to the one blinds to the other. And either—the Scripture or a miracle—may be the occasion for that deadness being removed. But as long as it is there, no resurrection will be persuasive.

God may grant ears to hear and eyes to see when a resurrection happens (or not, John 11:45–53), just like he may grant ears to hear and eyes to see when the Scriptures are heard (or not, Luke 4:16–30). But the decisive cause in both cases is the illuminating work of God, not the external word or work. One may read the Scripture and see a miracle and *not* see the glory of God. Seeing the glory of God in the word of God or in the work of God is a gift of God (2 Cor. 4:6; 2 Tim. 2:25–26).

If that gift is given in the faith-filled reading of the Old Testament (as in the case of Anna and Simeon, Luke 2:25–38), then the illumined heart will be able to recognize the arrival of the Messiah. In other words, the presence of a miracle does not create the seeing heart but confirms it. But if the reading of the word of God meets only with spiritual

---

[2] We will deal more with this issue of how the glory of God is seen in the miracles of Jesus in chap. 15.

blindness, then no mere external miracle, observed by the physical eyes, will remove the blindness (John 5:38; 10:25).

"If You Believed Moses"

The second occasion where Jesus called attention to the peculiar nature of the Old Testament as a kind of litmus test for a person's openness to other truth is John 5:39–47. Jesus said to the Jewish leaders,

> You search the Scriptures because you think that in them you have eternal life; and it is they that bear witness about me, yet you refuse to come to me that you may have life. I do not receive glory from people. But I know that you do not have the love of God within you. I have come in my Father's name, and you do not receive me. . . . If you believed Moses, you would believe me; for he wrote of me. But if you do not believe his writings, how will you believe my words?

This again shows that blindness to the Old Testament witness to Jesus is the same blindness that keeps a person from recognizing Jesus when he comes. This means that Jesus believed there was a kind of self-authenticating beauty and truth in the Old Testament that proved to be the litmus test of whether you were spiritually prepared to see the glory of Christ when he reveals himself in history and in the gospel. This is one of the highest estimates that can be given to the Old Testament—the estimate of Jesus.

Jesus Saw His Life, Death, and Resurrection as a Fulfillment of Scripture

We have already seen that Jesus fully expected everything written in the Old Testament, including its smallest affirmations, to be fulfilled:

> Do not think that I have come to abolish the Law or the Prophets; I have not come to abolish them but to fulfill them. For truly, I say to you, until heaven and earth pass away, not an iota, not a dot, will pass from the Law until all is accomplished. (Matt. 5:17–18)

What we have not seen yet is the pervasive way Jesus not only predicts such fulfillment of Scripture but also points out repeatedly during his life when and how it was happening. Here are a few examples.

- What happens to Jesus in his final days is the fulfillment of Scripture:

  And taking the twelve, he said to them, "See, we are going up to Jerusalem, and *everything that is written about the Son of Man by the prophets will be accomplished.* For he will be delivered over to the Gentiles and will be mocked and shamefully treated and spit upon. And after flogging him, they will kill him, and on the third day he will rise." (Luke 18:31–33)

- Jesus's cleansing of the temple was a fulfillment of Isaiah 56:7:

  He entered the temple and began to drive out those who sold and those who bought in the temple, and he overturned the tables of the money-changers and the seats of those who sold pigeons. And he would not allow anyone to carry anything through the temple. And he was teaching them and saying to them, "*Is it not written*, 'My house shall be called a house of prayer for all the nations'? But you have made it a den of robbers." (Mark 11:15–17)

- The people's blindness in response to the parables fulfills the prophecy of Isaiah 6:9–10:

  This is why I speak to them in parables, because seeing they do not see, and hearing they do not hear, nor do they understand. Indeed, *in their case the prophecy of Isaiah is fulfilled* that says:

  > "You will indeed hear but never understand,
  > and you will indeed see but never perceive."
  >   (Matt. 13:13–14)

- He describes his entire ministry as the fulfillment of Isaiah 61:1–2:

  He came to Nazareth, where he had been brought up. And as was his custom, he went to the synagogue on the Sabbath day, and he stood up to read. And the scroll of the prophet Isaiah was given to him. He unrolled the scroll and found the place where it was written,

"The Spirit of the Lord is upon me,
    because he has anointed me
    to proclaim good news to the poor.
He has sent me to proclaim liberty to the captives
    and recovering of sight to the blind,
    to set at liberty those who are oppressed,
to proclaim the year of the Lord's favor."

And he rolled up the scroll and gave it back to the attendant and sat down. And the eyes of all in the synagogue were fixed on him. And he began to say to them, "*Today this Scripture has been fulfilled in your hearing.*" (Luke 4:16–21)

- The ministries of both Jesus and John the Baptist are being played out according to Scripture (Isa. 52:13–53:12; 1 Kings 19:1–2):

  They asked him, "Why do the scribes say that first Elijah must come?" And he said to them, "Elijah does come first to restore all things. And how *is it written of the Son of Man that he should suffer many things and be treated with contempt?* But I tell you that Elijah has come, and they did to him whatever they pleased, *as it is written of him.*" (Mark 9:11–13)

- Jesus saw his betrayal by Judas as a fulfillment of Psalm 41:9:

  The Son of Man goes *as it is written of him*, but woe to that man by whom the Son of Man is betrayed! It would have been better for that man if he had not been born. (Mark 14:21)

  I am not speaking of all of you; I know whom I have chosen. But *the Scripture will be fulfilled*, "He who ate my bread has lifted his heel against me." (John 13:18)

- Jesus saw the disciples' abandonment as fulfillment of Zechariah 13:7:

Jesus said to them, "You will all fall away, *for it is written,* 'I will strike the shepherd, and the sheep will be scattered.'" (Mark 14:27)

- Jesus saw his arrest as a criminal as fulfillment of Isaiah 53:12:

I tell you that *this Scripture must be fulfilled in me*: "And he was numbered with the transgressors." For what is written about me has its fulfillment. (Luke 22:37)

Do you think that I cannot appeal to my Father, and he will at once send me more than twelve legions of angels? *But how then should the Scriptures be fulfilled, that it must be so?* (Matt. 26:53–54)

- Jesus taught that we should be quick to believe all that the Old Testament prophets have spoken and that all the Scriptures pointed to him:

He said to them, "O foolish ones, and slow of heart to believe *all that the prophets have spoken*! Was it not necessary that the Christ should suffer these things and enter into his glory?" And beginning with Moses and all the Prophets, he interpreted to them *in all the Scriptures* the things concerning himself. (Luke 24:25–27)

His Estimate Is Supreme

In chapter 2 we saw that the Bible Jesus knew and loved was the same Hebrew Bible that stands behind our Old Testament. So his estimate of his Bible is essentially his estimate of our Old Testament.

In this chapter we have seen that his estimate of this Old Testament is supreme. Jesus had an unparalleled position in history for making such an estimate. His relationship with the Old Testament was unique. He was there at its composition, guiding the prophets (1 Pet. 1:11), and then he came into history and looked at the very book he guided into being. No one else took stock of the Old Testament in this way. He alone, in all of history, was active as an author, a theme, a fulfillment, and an assessor of the Old Testament. Therefore, his assessment carries extraordinary force.

He taught that everything in it must be fulfilled; that the Psalm writers spoke by the Holy Spirit; that Moses's words in Scripture were the very words of God; that not one part of the Scriptures can be broken; that faithfulness to the Scriptures will keep us from error; that it can defeat the most powerful adversaries; that it is a litmus test to show if the eyes of our hearts are open to know Jesus; and that it is a virtual script being acted out in the triumph of Jesus through his sufferings, death, and resurrection.

And if the skeptic should object, *How can we know that all these reports about what Jesus taught about the Old Testament are historical?* there are two kinds of answers. One is from the nature of the history, and the other is from the work of the Spirit.

From the standpoint of history, the most skeptical scholars who think that much of the New Testament did not really happen nonetheless concede that the Jesus of history was an ardent believer in the Old Testament. They may think he was wrong. But the denial that he embraced the divine authority of the Old Testament is not seriously defended. There is simply no historical layer of evidence to support it, they say.

From the standpoint of the Holy Spirit, there are good reasons to believe that the Jesus we meet in the New Testament Gospels is the real divine-human Jesus of history, and that his estimate of the Old Testament and his plan for the New Testament are trustworthy. This is what we will turn to later in chapters 8–17. But before we do, there is one more group of witnesses we should hear concerning what the Bible claims for itself—namely, the apostles.

If anyone thinks that he is a prophet, or spiritual, he should acknowledge that the things I am writing to you are a command of the Lord. If anyone does not recognize this, he is not recognized.

1 CORINTHIANS 14:37–38

7

The Authority of the Apostles

Since the formation of the New Testament canon was largely a recognition of the reality of what the New Testament claimed for itself—and what it proved to *be* by God's inspiration—we have already dealt significantly with this theme, in chapter 3 on the canon of the New Testament. But there is more to see. What I try to answer in this chapter is, *What claims did the apostolic writings make for themselves?*

The Authority of the Apostles Comes from Jesus

The first and most important thing to say is that apart from the supreme authority of Jesus Christ, the apostolic writings claim nothing for themselves. All their authority is self-consciously derivative. Jesus Christ is the one who has "all authority in heaven and on earth" (Matt. 28:18). He is the one

> to whom alone the Father has given "authority over all flesh" (John 17:2);

> who alone claimed, "All things have been handed over to me by my Father, and no one knows the Son except the Father, and no one knows the Father except the Son and anyone to whom the Son chooses to reveal him" (Matt. 11:27);

> who alone could say, "I am the way, and the truth, and the life" (John 14:6);

who alone could say, "I will build my church, and the gates of hell shall not prevail against it" (Matt. 16:18);

who alone taught in such an unparalleled way that "the crowds were astonished at his teaching, for he was teaching them as one who had authority, and not as their scribes (Matt. 7:28–29);

who alone, when he "comes in his glory, and all the angels with him . . . will sit on his glorious throne. . . . Before him will be gathered all the nations, and he will separate people one from another as a shepherd separates the sheep from the goats" (Matt. 25:31–32);

who alone could say, "Heaven and earth will pass away, but my words will not pass away" (Matt. 24:35);

who alone "rebuked the wind and the raging waves, and they ceased, and there was a calm" (Luke 8:24);

who alone commanded demons with complete authority, "'Be silent and come out of him!' And when the demon had thrown him down . . . he came out of him, having done him no harm. . . . And they were all amazed and said to one another, 'What is this word? For with authority and power he commands the unclean spirits, and they come out!'" (Luke 4:35–36);

who alone, claiming to forgive sins, which only God can do, said, "'That you may know that the Son of Man has authority on earth to forgive sins'—he said to the paralytic—'I say to you, rise, pick up your bed, and go home'" (Mark 2:10–11);

who alone would dare say, "Whatever the Father does, that the Son does likewise" (John 5:19).

These are the things that the apostles saw and heard and remembered and recorded. "He is Lord of all" (Acts 10:36). He is God (John 1:1; 20:28; Rom. 9:5; Col. 2:9; Heb. 1:8–9). The words of the Old Testament that were applied to Yahweh, the apostles applied to the risen Jesus (Rom. 10:11; 1 Cor. 1:31; 2 Cor. 10:17; Eph. 4:8; Phil. 2:10). He is, therefore, "our only Lord and Master" (Jude 4).

Jesus, a New and Unique Authority in the World

Herman Bavinck, the Dutch Reformed theologian of the Free University of Amsterdam, summed up the place Jesus held in the minds of his New Testament witnesses as follows:

> Throughout the New Testament Jesus's witness is considered divine, true, infallible. He is the Logos who makes known the Father (John 1:18; 17:6), the faithful and true witness (Rev. 1:5; 3:14; cf. Isa. 55:4), the Amen in whom all the promises of God are "yes" and "amen" (Rev. 3:14; 2 Cor. 1:20). There was no guile (*dolos*) on his lips (1 Peter 2:22). He is the apostle and high priest of our confession (Heb. 3:12; 1 Tim. 6:13). He does not speak *ek tōn idiōn* [from himself], like Satan who is a liar (John 8:44), but God speaks through him (Heb. 1:2). Jesus was sent by God (John 8:42) and bears witness only to what he has seen and heard (John 3:32). He speaks the words of God (John 3:34; 17:8) and only bears witness to the truth (5:33; 18:37). For that reason his witness is true (John 8:14; 14:6), confirmed by the witness of God himself (5:32, 37; 8:18).[1]

In other words, as we saw in chapter 3, Jesus Christ was a new and absolutely unique and supreme authority in the world. He was the arrival of God in history. His authority was, therefore, absolute. It was supreme over the Old Testament, which he regarded as unbreakable (John 10:35), and it was now supreme over the church, which he said he would build with such irresistible power that the gates of hell could not hold out against its advance (Matt. 16:18).

Jesus's Aim to Govern His People through Scripture

Another Dutch scholar, Norval Geldenhuys, contemplated the absolute authority of Jesus and his purposes for the world and drew out the implication for the role Scripture would have. Jesus's purpose was to spread a movement, in his name and for his glory, to all the peoples of the world (Matt. 28:18–20). He aimed to gather a redeemed people into churches (Matt. 18:17). And he aimed that they would live under the authority of his teaching till the end of the age (Matt. 7:24–27).

---

[1] Herman Bavinck, *Reformed Dogmatics: Prolegomena* (Grand Rapids, MI: Baker Academic, 2003), 397–98.

Geldenhuys concludes that this implies that Christ will provide a written authority for his church the way God did for his people in the Old Testament:

> The fact *as such* that Jesus possesses supreme divine authority is, even apart from its being acknowledged by all New Testament authors and by the whole of the Early Church, of the greatest significance for the study of the making of the New Testament. For it gives us the assurance that the Lord of all authority would have seen to it that, through the working of his power, an adequate and completely reliable account of and an authentic proclamation concerning the significance of His life and work were written and preserved for the ages to come. Because the revelation of God in Christ was complete and *ephapax* . . . (once for all), it follows logically that the Lord to whom all authority in heaven and on earth is given would have regulated the history of the Early Church in such a way that the canon of the New Testament would be genuine and all sufficient.[2]

This logical deduction that Geldenhuys makes is, in fact, what the New Testament reveals. From the beginning of his ministry, Jesus was preparing for the transmission of his truth and authority to his church through authorized spokesmen who would teach with his authority, commit their teachings to writing, and leave a body of inspired writings through which Christ would govern his church until his return. Christ did this by calling, commissioning, and then sending the Spirit to guide the apostles.

Jesus Chose and Prepared the Apostles

The term *apostle* is not a synonym of *disciple*. *Disciple* means "follower" or "learner," and *apostle* means "authorized representative." Listen to the transition from disciples to apostles in Luke 6:12–13: "In these days he went out to the mountain to pray, and all night he continued in prayer to God. And when day came, he called his *disciples* and chose from them twelve, whom he named *apostles*." So all apostles are disciples. But not all disciples are apostles. All Christians are disciples

---

[2] J. Norval Geldenhuys, *Supreme Authority: The Authority of the Lord, His Apostles, and the New Testament* (Grand Rapids, MI: Eerdmans, 1953), 43.

(Acts 11:26). But the twelve apostles are a group of disciples to whom Jesus gave a share in his authority. Notice in Matthew 10:1–2 that the Twelve are first called "disciples," but after being given authority they are called "apostles":

> He called to him his twelve *disciples* and gave them authority over unclean spirits, to cast them out, and to heal every disease and every affliction. The names of the twelve *apostles* are these: first, Simon . . . (Matt. 10:1–2)

In the beginning, Jesus prepared them for their authorized, representative ministry by overseeing their work personally:

> He called the twelve together and gave them power and authority over all demons and to cure diseases, and he sent them out to proclaim the kingdom of God and to heal. . . . And they departed and went through the villages, preaching the gospel and healing everywhere. . . . On their return the apostles told him all that they had done. And he took them and withdrew apart to a town called Bethsaida. (Luke 9:1–2, 6, 10)

They were his emissaries. As he was completing his earthly ministry, Jesus prayed to God the Father and confirmed that what the Father had given him to do, he had done: "I glorified you on earth, having accomplished the work that you gave me to do" (John 17:4). Included in that mission from the Father was this: "I have given them your word" (v. 14). He says it again: "I have given them the words that you gave me" (v. 8). This was the heart of the apostolic authorization. God had words that he wanted his people on earth to know. Therefore, he sent his Son on this mission—to transmit truth from God to man in words given by the Father: "For this purpose I was born and for this purpose I have come into the world—to bear witness to the truth" (John 18:37).

Their Words Were His Words

In choosing twelve apostles, Jesus put in place the continuation of that authoritative transfer of truth from God to man. They became his authorized ambassadors of God's word. What happened to them happened to him; their reception was his reception (Matt. 10:40). Their words were his words (John 15:7). They began to be his voice while he was still here (Matt. 10:27). They became his voice (Acts 8:25) and his miracle-working hands (Acts 5:12) when he had ascended to the Father. This is why Luke begins his second volume, the book of Acts, by saying, "In the first book [the Gospel of Luke], O Theophilus, I have dealt with all that Jesus *began* to do and teach" (Acts 1:1). In other words, the point is that while on earth Jesus "began" to do and to teach his church; and now that he has ascended, he continues to "do and teach"—namely, by his Spirit through his inspired spokesmen.

That is what happened through the apostles in a unique way, because that kind of authorized representation is what it means to be an apostle.

> By calling the twelve men whom He chose out of the wider circle of disciples by the name "apostles" (*sheluhim*) and not merely "messengers" or "heralds," Jesus thus made it clear that they were to be His delegates whom He would send with the commission to teach and to act in His name and on His authority. That this was indeed what He meant is shown by the whole history of His dealings with the Twelve.[3]

As we saw in chapter 3, the way Jesus secured the reliability of the apostles' representative work was to promise them the special help of the Holy Spirit, the Spirit of truth (John 14:25–26; 16:12–14). Therefore, when Jesus had ascended to heaven, the apostles had a profound sense of God-given responsibility to serve as completely submitted to the authority of the risen Christ. They knew that they had unique authority. And they knew that it was not absolute. They were men under authority.

"In the Sight of God We Speak in Christ"

Paul (Rom. 1:1), James (1:1), Peter (2 Pet. 1:1) and Jude (Jude 1) all called themselves "slaves" of Jesus Christ. That is, they did not belong to themselves and did not teach the church as though they could speak

---

[3] Ibid., 54. "Applied to a person, *apostolos* denotes more than *aggelos*. The 'apostle' is not only the messenger but the delegate of the person who sends him. He is entrusted with a mission, has powers conferred upon him." J. B. Lightfoot, *Epistle to the Galatians* (New York: Macmillan, 1865), 89.

for themselves or from themselves (1 Cor. 15:10; Matt. 10:20); they spoke as men under authority.

> We are not, like so many, peddlers of God's word, but as men of sincerity, as commissioned by God, in the sight of God we speak in Christ. (2 Cor. 2:17)

> We have renounced disgraceful, underhanded ways. We refuse to practice cunning or to tamper with God's word, but by the open statement of the truth we would commend ourselves to everyone's conscience in the sight of God. (2 Cor. 4:2)

On earth Jesus had established himself as their supreme Lord and authority. His word was absolute. The band of apostles was not a democracy. Jesus was the King. His word was law. As James Denny puts it,

> Nothing is more unlike Jesus than to do violence to anyone's liberty, or to invade the sacredness of conscience and of personal responsibility; but the broad fact is unquestionable that, without breaking their wills, He imposed His own will upon them, and became for them a supreme moral authority to which they submitted absolutely and by which they were inspired.[4]

Twelve Foundations

Thus when Judas, one of the Twelve, needed to be replaced, the eleven apostles knew that the Lord himself would rightfully make this choice. He had made clear that the criteria for belonging to the Twelve were

> men who have accompanied us during all the time that the Lord Jesus went in and out among us, beginning from the baptism of John until the day when he was taken up from us—one of these men must become with us a witness to his resurrection. (Acts 1:21–22)

With those Jesus-given criteria, the eleven put forward two candidates and prayed for Jesus to choose, and they cast lots:

> They prayed and said, "You, Lord, who know the hearts of all, show which one of these two you have chosen to take the place in this

---

[4] James Denny, in *Dictionary of Christ in the Gospels*, ed. James Hastings (Edinburgh: T&T Clark, 1906), s.v. "authority."

ministry and apostleship from which Judas turned aside to go to his own place." And they cast lots for them, and the lot fell on Matthias, and he was numbered with the eleven apostles. (Acts 1:24–26)

Once the Twelve were established for their foundational ministry, there was no plan or provision to be replaced. Paul referred to the new and growing church as "the household of God, built on the *foundation of the apostles and prophets*, Christ Jesus himself being the cornerstone" (Eph. 2:19–20); and John described the church in Revelation as a city coming down from heaven whose wall had "*twelve foundations, and on them were the twelve names of the twelve apostles of the Lamb*" (Rev. 21:14). The point of Paul and John is that foundations that Christ puts in place are unshakeable and once for all. They are not replaced in every generation. The apostles were once for all.

Alfred Plummer clarifies this point on the basis of the intrinsic purpose of the apostolate as Jesus created it:

> The absence from Christ's teaching of any statement respecting the priesthood of the Twelve, or respecting the transmission of the powers of the Twelve to others, is remarkable. As the primary function of the Twelve was to be witnesses of what Christ had taught and done, especially in rising from the dead, no transmission of so exceptional an office was possible.[5]

Paul, an Apostle, by the Command of God

We will have much more to say about the great apostle Paul in chapter 17. And, of course, he is worthy of all the attention we can give him. Under Jesus, no man has been more influential in the history of the world than Paul. That is a gigantic claim, but such is my estimate of how his letters have worked their way into the psyche of the human race wherever Christianity has spread. Certainly in my case, it would be true that, after Jesus, no one has shaped me more than Paul. My esteem of him and my affection for him are almost boundless. It will become evident why as we go on, especially in chapter 17.

Paul's calling as an apostle was as astonishing to him as it was to the

---

[5] A. Plummer, in *Dictionary of the Apostolic Church*, ed. James Hastings (New York: Charles Scribner's Sons, 1916), s.v. "apostle."

Twelve. We saw the process of his approval in chapter 3. But once the risen Christ had called and confirmed him as an apostle (Gal. 1:1), and the Twelve had recognized him as an equal (Gal. 2:7–10), Paul's witness to the inspiration and authority of the apostles was unparalleled. He was unwavering in the affirmation of his own apostleship (1 Tim. 2:7; 1 Cor. 9:1–2; 15:8–10; 2 Cor. 12:12). He knew that Jesus had given him unique authority for building up the church (2 Cor. 10:8; 13:10). He knew that the gospel he preached was foundational and would be the touchstone for all other contenders (Gal. 1:8–10). He knew that when he preached in the name of Christ, what he delivered was truly the word of God (1 Thess. 2:13). He knew that his preaching came not from his own will but that he had been entrusted with his message "by the command of God" (Titus 1:3).

Therefore, Paul knew that he was not inferior to any pretending super-apostles, even if they came from Jerusalem: "I was not at all inferior to these super-apostles, even though I am nothing. The signs of a true apostle were performed among you with utmost patience, with signs and wonders and mighty works" (2 Cor. 12:11–12). And he pointed out, with astonishing forcefulness, that his authority was higher than any prophetic claim to authority among the charismatics at Corinth: "If anyone thinks that he is a prophet, or spiritual, he should acknowledge that the things I am writing to you are a command of the Lord. If anyone does not recognize this, he is not recognized" (1 Cor. 14:37–38).

It is not surprising, then, that Paul puts the Thessalonians under oath to make sure his letter is read to the church (see 1 Thess. 5:27). Paul saw his letters as no ordinary Christian preaching. They were foundational. They are what Christian preaching would be based on till Jesus comes again. Paul knew that God had given him the role of speaking by the Holy Spirit: "We impart this [wisdom] in words not taught by human wisdom but taught by the Spirit, interpreting spiritual truths to those who are spiritual" (1 Cor. 2:12–13).

In other words, Paul claims that in fulfillment of Jesus's promise to send his Spirit to guide the apostles into truth (John 14:25–26; 16:12–14), he was inspired by the Spirit to write truth that was essentially on a par with the inspired and authoritative Old Testament Scriptures. As we've seen before, this is what Peter said about Paul's writings:

And count the patience of our Lord as salvation, just as our beloved brother Paul also wrote to you according to the wisdom given him, as he does in all his letters when he speaks in them of these matters. There are some things in them that are hard to understand, which the ignorant and unstable twist to their own destruction, as they do the *other Scriptures*. (2 Pet. 3:15–16)

Their Authority Stands with His

The claim of the apostles to speak with unerring truthfulness in Christ by the Holy Spirit is the organic outgrowth of the Old Testament hope and of the incarnation of the Son of God as Jesus the Messiah. The apostles did not thrust themselves on the church with imaginary claims of prophetic inspiration. They were called and appointed by the Old Testament–fulfilling, divinely sent Messiah. Their truthfulness and authority stands or falls with his.

He came to bear witness to the truth (John 18:37) with all the authority of God (John 17:2; Matt. 28:18). He planned and prepared for that truth and authority to be preserved through a band of apostles whom he would guide by his own Spirit into all the truth needed for the foundation and preservation of his church (John 14:25–26; 16:12–14; Eph. 2:20; 1 Cor. 2:13). In perfect harmony with God's will for Christ and Christ's will for this church, those spokesmen put their teachings into writing with a sober, conscious sense that what they wrote for the church would be her infallible charter till Jesus comes again.

Therefore, in the coming chapters we turn to the question of whether the Bible's claims for itself (which we have seen in chapters 5–7) are true. Is the Christian Bible the word of God in the full sense of inspired, inerrant Scripture? My answer to that question is yes. And the rest of this book is my effort to show how we can have well-grounded conviction that this is so.

PART 4

How Can We Know the Christian Scriptures Are True?

". . . by a sight of its glory"

All things have been handed over to me by my Father, and no one knows who the Son is except the Father, or who the Father is except the Son and anyone to whom the Son chooses to reveal him.

LUKE 10:22

8

A Shared Concern with Jonathan Edwards

Is the Bible true? Completely true? All of it. Is it so trustworthy in all it teaches that it can function as the test of all other claims to truth? Since I have argued that the Bible's own view of itself is that it is the word of God, not just the word of man, that question now includes: Is this claim true? Is the Bible the true word of God? When rightly understood, does it teach anything that is untrue? And, of course, when we ask that question, we are keeping in mind that much of the teaching in the Old Testament (such as laws pertaining to food and circumcision and sacrifices and purification rituals that set Israel off from the nations) has been fulfilled and brought to an end by Christ and does not apply to us today the way it applied to Israel in Old Testament times.

Verbally Inspired, Infallible, without Error

Keeping all that in mind, we are asking, *Is the Bible, as an expression of God's truth, infallible? Is it inerrant?* Which leads to the related question, *Does the Bible have final authority in our lives?* Should we try to bring all our thinking and feeling and acting into line with what the Bible teaches?

My answer goes like this, which is from the affirmation of faith that governs Bethlehem College and Seminary and the desiringGod.org website, as well as the church I pastored for thirty-three years and other sister churches:

> 1.1 We believe that the Bible, consisting of the sixty-six books of the Old and New Testaments, is the infallible Word of God, verbally inspired by God, and without error in the original manuscripts.

> 1.2 We believe that God's intentions, revealed in the Bible, are the supreme and final authority in testing all claims about what is true and what is right. In matters not addressed by the Bible, what is true and right is assessed by criteria consistent with the teachings of Scripture.

In other words, yes, the Bible is completely true. Yes, its claim to be the word of God is true. Yes, when rightly understood, it teaches nothing untrue. It is thus without error. Therefore, as God's true, inerrant word, it has full authority over our lives. And so, yes, we should endeavor to bring all our thinking and feeling and acting into line with what the Bible teaches.

The Most Urgent Question

How do we know this? It is an urgent question. It's not like saying, "How can I know the moon goes around the earth?" Or, "How can I know Abraham Lincoln existed?" The reason those questions are not urgent is that whether you believe them or not has almost no effect on the way you live. The answers to those questions do not determine where you will spend eternity—in heaven or in hell. But according to the Bible, Jesus said, "Whoever believes in the Son has eternal life; whoever does not obey the Son shall not see life, but the wrath of God remains on him" (John 3:36). And the apostle Paul said, "Believe in the Lord Jesus, and you will be saved" (Acts 16:31; cf. Rom. 10:9). This is why a record of Jesus's deeds and words was written down: "These are written so that you may believe that Jesus is the Christ, the Son of God, and that by believing you may have life in his name" (John 20:31).

In other words, the Bible teaches things vastly more important than the moon's revolutions or the existence of Abraham Lincoln. It teaches the way to escape the wrath of God and enter into eternal life. And it claims to teach the only way. It depicts a totally authoritative Jesus who says, "I am the way, and the truth, and the life. No one comes to the Father except through me" (John 14:6). And it makes the radical claim that "there is salvation in no one else, for there is no other name under heaven given among men by which we must be saved" (Acts 4:12).

So the question of whether the Bible is true is urgent—for everyone. Our eternal destinies depend on whether we believe the good news of this book. And our way of life depends on it as well. In a rare moment of public disapproval, the apostle Paul reprimanded the apostle Peter for not acting in accord with his own teaching: "I opposed him to his face . . . when I saw that their conduct was not in step with the truth of the gospel" (Gal. 2:11, 14). In other words there is "conduct" that is "in step with the truth." This is what the Bible teaches (see 1 Thess. 4:1). The teaching of this Book shows the way to eternal life and shapes the way we live in this life. Therefore, knowing whether the Bible teaches the truth is of ultimate importance.

The Place of Historical Reasoning

There was a season in my life when I spent much of my mental energy on demonstrating, with historical reasoning, that Christ rose from the dead, and that his claims are true, and that the Bible is true.[1] I was, and am, deeply thankful for the scholars who helped me see the historical credibility of the New Testament in those days. Those scholars are being faithful to the words of Luke that tell us Jesus gave visible, historical evidences for his bodily resurrection: "He presented himself alive to them after his suffering *by many proofs,* appearing to them during forty days and speaking about the kingdom of God" (Acts 1:3). They are following in the steps of the apostle Paul, who argued for the truth of the gospel by pointing out to those who were not eyewitnesses of Jesus's

---

[1] I will devote an entire chapter to the place of historical reasoning (chap. 17) and the proper place it has in our study of Scripture. See Daniel P. Fuller, *Easter Faith and History* (Grand Rapids, MI: Eerdmans, 1965); Wolfhart Pannenberg, *Jesus, God and Man* (Philadelphia: Westminster Press, 1968); John Piper, *Desiring God: Meditations of a Christian Hedonist,* rev. ed. (Colorado Springs, CO: Multnomah, 2011), 332–39; William Lane Craig, *The Son Rises: The Historical Evidence of the Resurrection of Jesus* (Eugene, OR: Wipf & Stock, 2001); Gary R. Habermas and Michael Licona, *The Case for the Resurrection of Jesus* (Grand Rapids, MI: Kregel, 2004); Lee Strobel, *The Case for the Resurrection: A First-Century Investigative Reporter Probes History's Pivotal Event* (Grand Rapids, MI: Zondervan, 2010); N. T. Wright, *The Resurrection of the Son of God* (Minneapolis, MN: Fortress Press, 2003); Michael R. Licona, *The Resurrection of Jesus: A New Historiographical Approach* (Carol Stream, IL: IVP Academic, 2010); Craig S. Keener, *The Historical Jesus of the Gospels* (Grand Rapids, MI: Eerdmans, 2012).

resurrection that some five hundred eyewitnesses were still living, if any should care to confirm the truth in that way. He said

> that [Jesus] was buried, that he was raised on the third day in ac- cordance with the Scriptures, and that he appeared to Cephas, then to the twelve. Then he appeared to more than five hundred brothers at one time, most of whom are still alive, though some have fallen asleep. Then he appeared to James, then to all the apostles. Last of all, as to one untimely born, he appeared also to me. (1 Cor. 15:4–8)

What turned my focus (not my approval or my interest) away from historical reasoning as a support for faith was the realization that most people in the world—especially in the less-educated, developing world—have neither the training nor the time to pursue such detailed arguments in support of their faith. And yet the Bible assumes that those who hear the gospel may know the truth of it and may stake their lives on it—indeed must stake their lives on it. "Whoever loves his life loses it, and whoever hates his life in this world will keep it for eternal life" (John 12:25).

The Bible assumes that through the written word of the apostles, a person may come to know that he has eternal life. "I write these things to you who believe in the name of the Son of God that you may *know* that you have eternal life" (1 John 5:13). And the apostles themselves *knew* this about others as well: "We *know*, brothers loved by God, that he has chosen you, because our gospel came to you not only in word, but also in power and in the Holy Spirit and with full conviction" (1 Thess. 1:4–5). The truth of Christ's teachings may be known by those whose will is submissive to God's will: "If anyone's will is to do God's will, he will know whether the teaching is from God or whether I am speaking on my own authority" (John 7:17).

This means that the Bible assumes there is a basis for firm and justi- fied knowledge that what it teaches is true. It assumes that everyone who hears a faithful narration of the gospel is responsible to believe it—not by leaping into the dark, but by seeing real and compelling grounds for faith. According to Scripture, people don't have to be edu- cated historians to know the historical truth of Scripture. This is utterly crucial, since the vast majority of the people in the world who will hear the gospel are in no position to comprehend the complexity of the (legitimate!) historical reasoning that supports the resurrection of Jesus and the reliability of the Bible.

The Insufficiency of Historical Reasoning

As I worked my way though the historical-critical method, which dominated the scholarly world in the six years of my formal theological education (1968–1974), it became increasingly clear that the results of such study would not provide a sure foundation for faith that you could stake your life on. In 1975 Edgar Krentz published *The Historical-Critical Method* in which he states, "Historical criticism produces only probable results. It relativizes everything. But faith needs certainty."[2]

Some have tried to make a virtue out of this crisis by arguing that faith, by its very nature, far from needing certainty, takes a risk and leaps into uncertainty. They say, "Criticism frees us from the tyranny of history and makes the vulnerability of faith clear."[3] They might quote 2 Corinthians 5:7, "We walk by faith, not by sight." But this passage is referring to the future hope that we can't see, not to the past basis for hope that we may be able to see: "We are always of good courage. We know that while we are at home in the body we are away from the Lord" (2 Cor. 5:6). Indeed, "faith is the assurance of things hoped for, the conviction of *things not seen*" (Heb. 11:1). Yes, the *things believed* are unseen. But the New Testament does not say that the *foundations* of faith are unseen.

When I entered my theological studies, one of the most prominent German theologians was Wolfhart Pannenberg. Pannenberg deplored what he called the flight "into a harbor supposedly safe from the historical-critical flood tide."[4] He argued that the separation of faith from its real, historical grounds is "injurious to the essence of faith" and leads "into blind credulity."[5] I think Pannenberg is right, as far as he goes. My way of saying it is that faith cannot glorify its object by leaping into the dark. Instead, such faith glorifies its own risk-taking boldness when it

---

[2] Edgar Krentz, *The Historical-Critical Method* (Philadelphia: Fortress Press, 1975), 67.
[3] Ibid., 67.
[4] Wolfhart Pannenberg, "Redemptive Event and History," in *Basic Questions in Theology*, vol. 1, trans. George H. Kehm (Philadelphia: Fortress Press, 1970), 16.
[5] Ibid., 28.

leaps into it-knows-not-what. That is not New Testament faith, as we will see in a moment.

But Pannenberg did not offer an adequate solution to the problem of the average nonhistorian who needs solid ground under the feet of his faith if he is going to venture all on Christ. No doubt one of the reasons I was sensitive to the inadequacy of Pannenberg's position is that Daniel Fuller, the most influential teacher I had in seminary, brought it to my attention. Three years before I became his student, he had written in *Easter Faith and History,*

> If historical reasoning is the only way by which men can attain faith, then faith becomes the possibility for only the few who can think historically, and faith for the common man is possible only if he is willing to commit himself to the authority of a priesthood of historians.
>
> Pannenberg, it will be remembered, wants to make faith the possibility for all men by having what is, virtually, a priesthood of historians. Theology's task as he sees it, is to assert the credibility of the Christian proclamation, so that laymen can believe it because of the authority that the theologian, with special historical skills, can provide.[6]

Pannenberg puts it like this:

> Believing trust can also arise in such a way that the believer does not always have to prove on his own the trustworthiness of the knowledge presupposed therein. It is the special task of theology to do this. Not every individual Christian needs to undertake this task. He can trust on the assumption that things are in order with respect to the ground of his trust. This point of view presupposes, of course, an atmosphere of confidence in the reliability of the Christian tradition.[7]

This seemed to me an inadequate response to the problem the average layman faces in coming to faith in what the Bible teaches. His eternal life is at stake. It will not do to say, "He can trust *on the assumption that things are in order* with respect to the ground of his trust." Given the vast and numerous disagreements in the scholarly world about the

---

historicity and meaning of what the Bible teaches, it seems facile to say we can all just trust that "things are in order."

Nonhistorians Are Not Expected to Leap into the Dark

It seemed to me that there had to be another way for the average layperson with little time and little historical training to have a basis for firm and justified knowledge that the Bible is true. The Bible does not teach or assume that we come to faith by leaping into the dark. It assumes that we embrace Christ and his Scripture by seeing real and compelling grounds for faith.

I found help at this point from a surprising source. At least it surprised me at the time. While I was wrestling with these things in Germany, I was reading Jonathan Edwards for my own personal spiritual enrichment amid all the critical studies. Little did I expect to find him addressing this problem with such amazing insight and relevance. I was so helped by Edwards that I wrote two articles about it.[8]

Edwards's starting point is not, *What kind of certainty is possible for historical reasoning?* but rather, *What is possible for the ordinary members of the church?* In his *Treatise Concerning Religious Affections*, Edwards says ordinary people cannot come to well-grounded faith the way a trained historian might:

> It is impossible that men, who have not something of a general view of the historical world, or the series of history from age to age, should come at the force of arguments for the truth of Christianity, drawn from history to that degree, as effectually to induce them to venture their all upon it.[9]

The voice of the missionary[10] can be heard when he adds,

> Miserable is the condition of the Houssatunnuck Indians and others, who have lately manifested a desire to be instructed in Christianity,

---

[8] John Piper, "Jonathan Edwards on the Problem of Faith and History," *Scottish Journal of Theology* 31 (1978): 217–28; "The Glory of God and the Ground of Faith," *Reformed Journal* 26 (November 1976): 17–20. The following comments about Edwards are based largely on these two articles.

[9] Jonathan Edwards, *A Treatise Concerning Religious Affections*, vol. 2, *The Works of Jonathan Edwards*, ed. John Smith (New Haven, CT: Yale University Press, 1957), 303.

[10] From 1751 to 1758, Edwards was pastor of the church in the frontier town of Stockbridge, MA, and missionary to the Indians. His concern for Indian evangelization extends back into his pastorate at Northampton, as is shown by these comments in *Religious Affections*, which were written between 1742 and 1746.

if they can come at no evidence of the truth of Christianity, sufficient to induce them to sell all for Christ, in any other way but this [path of historical reasoning].[11]

You might think that Edwards is leading us to say that faith in the message of the Bible is a leap in the dark rather than a valid sight of real, objective foundations that provide a basis for firm and justified knowledge. But, no, that is not where he is leading us. To be sure, he insists that historical argumentation cannot provide the deepest and surest ground of faith for the nonhistorian (or for the historian either, as we shall see). Nevertheless, he still maintains that ordinary people can have a "certainty of divine things" founded on "real evidence" and "good reason."[12]

Unwarranted Trust Is No Honor to the Trusted One

Edwards is deeply persuaded, as I think we all should be, that the fruit of Christian faith is no better than nonsupernatural virtue unless this faith is rooted in "a reasonable persuasion or conviction."[13]

Before I let him explain, think of it this way: suppose you meet a man on the street whom you do not recognize, and he gives you a bag with $50,000 in cash and asks you to deposit it in the bank for him. He says that his account number is in the bag. You are surprised because you do not know him at all. You ask, "Why do you trust me with this?" Suppose he says, "No reason; I'm just taking a risk." What is the effect of that faith in you? Does it honor you? No, it does not. It shows the man is a fool.

But suppose he said, "I know that you don't know me, but I work in the same building you do, and I have watched you for the last year. I have seen your integrity in a dozen ways. I have spoken to people who know you. The reason I am trusting you with this money is that I have *good reason* to believe you are honest and reliable." Now, what is the effect of that faith? It truly honors you. Why? Because it is based on real evidence that you *are* honorable. The fruit of such faith is not folly. The fruit of such faith is wisdom, and that faith and wisdom honor the person who is trusted.

---

[11] Edwards, *Religious Affections*, 304.
[12] Ibid., 291, 295.
[13] Ibid., 295.

So it is with God. If God says, "Why did you trust my word?" and we say, "No reason, I'm just taking a risk," God is not honored and we are fools. So Edwards is right to say that the fruit of Christian faith is no better than merely natural virtue unless this faith is rooted in "a reasonable persuasion or conviction."[14] But what is that? How can our faith in the Bible find this firm foundation?

Now we let Edwards explain:

> By a reasonable conviction, I mean a conviction founded on real evidence, or upon that which is a good reason, or just ground of conviction. Men may have a strong persuasion that the Christian religion is true, when their persuasion is not at all built on evidence, but altogether on education, and the opinion of others; as many Mahometans are strongly persuaded of the truth of the Mahometan religion, because their fathers, and neighbors, and nation believe it. That belief of the truth of the Christian religion which is built on the very same grounds, with Mahometans' belief of the Mahometan religion, is the same sort of belief. And though the thing believed happens to be better; yet that [doesn't] make the belief itself, to be of a better sort: for though the thing believed happens to be true; yet the belief of it is not owing to this truth, but to education. So that as the conviction is no better than the Mahometans' conviction; so the affections that flow from it, are no better, in themselves, than the religious affections of Mahometans.[15]

So Edwards believes it is essential for genuine, saving faith to be based on "real evidence, or upon that which is a good reason, or just ground of conviction."

Scripture Encourages Us to Have Good Grounds of Faith

Surely this is where the Scripture leads us. For example, the apostle John says, "Beloved, do not believe every spirit, but *test* the spirits to see whether they are from God" (1 John 4:1). In other words, don't be gullible. Look for "real evidence" and "good reason" and "just grounds."

---

[14] Ibid.
[15] Ibid.

Similarly, it would have been illuminating to hear some of Paul's missionary preaching, because, according to Luke, he had an interesting custom: "Paul went in, as was his custom, and on three Sabbath days he *reasoned* with them from the Scriptures, *explaining and proving* that it was necessary for the Christ to suffer and to rise from the dead, and saying, 'This Jesus, whom I proclaim to you, is the Christ'" (Acts 17:2–3). So Paul believed that "reasoning" and "explaining and proving" were legitimate and fitting ways to lead a person to well-founded faith.

Luke explicitly praises the Jews in Berea because when Paul taught them new things, they tested them: "Now these Jews were more noble than those in Thessalonica; they received the word with all eagerness, examining the Scriptures daily to see if these things were so" (Acts 17:11). They believed they had good grounds for trusting the Scripture. So other claims to truth had to be in line with that truth.

One might ask, "Well, are you saying, then, that *knowing* and *believing* are the same thing?" No. Believing, in the saving sense, always includes the heartfelt embrace of what is believed; knowing doesn't always include that. Nevertheless, it is important to see that believing and knowing are not alternatives in the New Testament. Belief is based on knowledge and leads to deeper knowledge. Jesus prays concerning his disciples, "Now they *know* that everything that you have given me is from you. For I have given them the words that you gave me, and they have received them and have come to *know* in truth that I came from you; and they have *believed* that you sent me" (John 17:7–8).

Pointing in the same direction, Paul writes to the Corinthians, "We *believe*, and so we also speak, *knowing* that he who raised the Lord Jesus will raise us also with Jesus" (2 Cor. 4:13–14; cf. 5:1). And in John's first epistle, he bears witness to "that which we have seen with our eyes, which we looked upon and have touched with our hands, concerning the word of life" (1 John 1:1). So we can see that his faith is grounded in real evidence, and he can say, "We have come to *know* and to *believe* the love that God has for us" (1 John 4:16).

So, when Jonathan Edwards says that saving faith must be based on "real evidence, or upon that which is a good reason, or just ground of conviction," he is saying what the Scriptures themselves say.

The Object of Faith Is More Than Facts

Before we ask what that "real evidence" is, we need to clarify more precisely what Edwards thinks the object of faith is. The reason for this is that the nature of the object of faith dictates the nature of the "real evidence" for its reality. For example, if the object of the faith were honey, then one real evidence that it is, in fact, honey would be taste. But if the object of faith were ammonia, then a better real evidence would be smell. The nature of what we are trying to know determines how we can know it. Honey says, know me with taste. Ammonia says, know me with smell.

According to Edwards, the object of true saving conviction is "the great things of the gospel."[16] By "the gospel," he means "the doctrines there taught, the word there spoken, and the divine counsels, acts, and works there revealed."[17] He refers to the gospel as "the glorious doctrine the word of God contains, concerning God, Jesus Christ, the way of salvation by him, and the world of glory that he has entered into, and purchased for all them who believe."[18]

But here's a crucial fact for Edwards: the object of our faith is not merely the factuality of the gospel, but also the "holy beauty and amiableness [the old meaning of *lovely*] that is in divine things."[19] It is the glory of God's moral perfections. It is the beauty, or glory, of these perfections that are the proper object of our conviction. It is the "supreme and holy excellency and beauty of those things."[20] Beauty, excellency, perfection, amiableness [loveliness], divinity, holiness—these are the qualities of the gospel of which saving faith must be certain. Not just historical facts or doctrinal propositions.

Even though some of this vocabulary may be new to modern people, what Edwards is saying is not new to most thoughtful Christians. Most of us have, at some point, realized that there is a kind of faith that the devils have that is of no saving benefit. Edwards is making sure that our faith is of a saving kind. For example, James, Jesus's brother, wrote, "You believe that God is one; you do well. Even *the demons*

---

[16] Ibid., 291.
[17] Ibid., 300.
[18] Ibid., 294.
[19] Ibid., 301.
[20] Ibid., 297.

believe—and shudder!" (James 2:19). What Edwards is getting at is that believing in the existence of divine reality—even the divine reality of the gospel or the Bible—does not mean you believe in a way that will do you any good. The demons know there is a gospel, and they know that the Bible is God's word. But what they do not see, as Edwards says, is the beauty, excellency, perfection, loveliness, and holiness of the truth. "Seeing they do not see" (Matt. 13:13). That is the lot of all of us until God gives us eyes to see (Eph. 1:17–18).

The Known Determines the Way of Knowing

So the nature of what we need to know determines how we can know it. If the glory of God in the gospel is what we must know—if this is where our faith must rest—then the eyes to see this glory are not merely the eyes of our head, but what Paul calls the "eyes of our heart" (Eph. 1:18). This is why Edwards says, "The gospel of the blessed God does not go abroad a-begging for its evidence, so much as some think: it has its highest and most proper evidence in itself."[21] Specifically,

> The mind ascends to the truth of the gospel but by one step, and that is its divine glory. . . . Unless men may come to a reasonable solid persuasion and conviction of the truth of the gospel, by the internal evidences of it, in the way that has been spoken, viz. by a sight of its glory; 'tis impossible that those who are illiterate, and unacquainted with history, should have any thorough and effectual conviction of it at all.[22]

Therefore, well-grounded faith is not only *reasonable* faith (based on real evidence and good grounds), but also *spiritual* faith, that is, it is enabled by the Holy *Spirit* and mediated through *spiritual* perception of divine glory in the truth of the gospel. Not all reasonable conviction is saving conviction. "Some natural men [with no spiritual life] yield a kind of assent of their judgments to the truth of the Christian religion from the rational proofs or arguments that are offered to evince it."[23] But that kind of persuasion is of no saving use. Edwards cites as

---

[21] Ibid., 307.
[22] Ibid., 299, 303.
[23] Ibid., 295.

examples Judas and many Jews who heard Jesus (John 2:23–25) and Simon the sorcerer (Acts 8:13, 23).

What is needed is the kind of spiritual sight that Simon Peter was given: "Simon Peter replied, 'You are the Christ, the Son of the living God.' And Jesus answered him, 'Blessed are you, Simon Bar-Jonah! For flesh and blood has not revealed this to you, but my Father who is in heaven'" (Matt. 16:16–17). In other words, there is a glory in the person of Jesus that is really there but which we are blind to apart from God's gift. Jesus described it like this:

> I thank you, Father, Lord of heaven and earth, that you have hidden these things from the wise and understanding and revealed them to little children; yes, Father, for such was your gracious will. All things have been handed over to me by my Father, and no one knows who the Son is except the Father, or who the Father is except the Son and anyone to whom the Son chooses to reveal him. (Luke 10:21–22)

Spiritual perception or understanding "consists in a sense and taste of the divine, supreme, and holy excellency and beauty of those things."[24] In other words, there is a difference between mere intellectual knowledge and knowledge that is rooted in the God-given spiritual sight of divine glory that is really there. In spiritual knowledge, we not only exercise our rational capacity but also "taste" with our spiritual capacity. "Oh, *taste* and *see* that the LORD is good! Blessed is the man who takes refuge in him!" (Ps. 34:8). "Like newborn infants, long for the pure spiritual milk . . . if indeed you have *tasted* that the Lord is good" (1 Pet. 2:2–3). "He that has perceived the sweet taste of honey, knows much more about it than he who has only looked upon and felt it."[25] Thus "spiritual understanding primarily consists in this sense, or taste of the moral beauty of divine things."[26]

The Biblical Text That Turned the Lights On

I admit that when I first read these things in Jonathan Edwards, the language was new to me. This way of thinking was new to me. This way

---

[24] Ibid., 297.
[25] Ibid., 272.
[26] Ibid., 273.

of describing how I came to believe and to know the truth was new to me. But paradoxically, it did not feel foreign. That is, it seemed to me that he was describing reality—my reality. He was putting words and descriptions on the mystery of my faith. It is possible to experience true divine wonders in your conversion but never to be taught a true description of what your experience is. Then someone starts to describe your experience in words you have never heard, and in ways you have never understood, and suddenly the strange words all sound exactly right. They may be new words, but they are describing a deep, real, personal experience. That is the way it was for me.

The passage of Scripture that made the lights go on for me was 2 Corinthians 4:4–6. When Edwards used this passage to support what he was saying, it was as though God himself put the stamp of approval on it. For in the end, it is not Edwards or Piper or any other man who compels true faith, but God himself. "My speech and my message were not in plausible words of wisdom, but in demonstration of the Spirit and of power, *so that your faith might not rest in the wisdom of men but in the power of God*" (1 Cor. 2:4–5). Here is the key passage.

> Even if our gospel is veiled, it is veiled to those who are perishing. In their case the god of this world has blinded the minds of the unbelievers, to keep them from seeing the light of the gospel of the glory of Christ, who is the image of God. For what we proclaim is not ourselves, but Jesus Christ as Lord, with ourselves as your servants for Jesus' sake. For God, who said, "Let light shine out of darkness," has shone in our hearts to give the light of the knowledge of the glory of God in the face of Jesus Christ. (2 Cor. 4:3–6)

Notice how similar the wording of verse 4 is to the wording of verse 6. There are some very close parallels. In verse 4 Satan blinds; in verse 6 God enlightens. The thing Satan hides from men in verse 4 is what God enables us to see in verse 6. Notice the other parallels as we put the verses beside each other:

Verse 4	Verse 6
the light	the light
of the gospel	of the knowledge

Verse 4	Verse 6
of the glory	of the glory
of Christ	of God
who is the image of God	in the face of Jesus Christ

The parallels help explain the terms. "Gospel" and "knowledge" are parallel because the *gospel* is the true story of events about Christ and what he accomplished that can be *known*. In the gospel there are facts to be known: "Now I would remind you, brothers, of the *gospel*. . . . Christ *died* for our sins in accordance with the Scriptures, that he was *buried*, that he was *raised* on the third day in accordance with the Scriptures" (1 Cor. 15:1–4). There is no gospel without historical facts that can be known.

But the focus of this text is that the gospel is the good news of the "glory of Christ." The devil has kept us from seeing "the light of the gospel of the *glory* of Christ." So when the historical facts are known rightly they are known as glorious, beautiful. At first glance, we might think that the "glory of Christ" (v. 4) and the "glory of God" (v. 6) are different glories. But if we look carefully, we notice that as soon as Paul mentions the "glory of Christ" (v. 4), he describes Christ as "who is the image of God." And as soon as he mentions the "glory of God" (v. 6), he describes this glory as "in the face of Jesus Christ." In other words, Paul is making sure that we see the glory of Christ and the glory of God as one glory. Christ is the image of God, and God's glory shines in the face of Christ.

So the mark of the unbeliever referred to in verse 4 ("the god of this world has blinded the minds of the *unbelievers*") is blindness to this divine glory in the gospel. The unbeliever "knows" the facts of the gospel, perhaps, but he does not see "the light of the gospel of the *glory* of Christ." The Christ of the gospel does not shine in the eyes of the unbeliever's heart. The unbeliever does not see the glory of Christ as divine beauty and thus as his supreme treasure. When the gospel is preached, or the Scriptures are read, he sees facts but not glory.

Faith Arises from Seeing What Is Really There

It is crucial to emphasize here that this glory of Christ in the gospel is an objective reality. The glory is in Christ and in the gospel. It is not in us. It is not subjective, but objective. This is why it can function as "real evidence" and "good grounds" for our faith. We do not make it up. We do not bring it to the gospel or to the Scripture. It is there. And if it is there, it is meant to be seen, but for the spiritual blindness that makes us so dull. Edwards stresses the reality of this glory:

> Now this distinguishing glory of the Divine Being has its brightest appearance and manifestation, in the things proposed and exhibited to us in the gospel, the doctrines there taught, the word there spoken, and the divine counsels, acts and works there revealed. These things have the clearest, most admirable, and distinguishing representations and exhibitions of the glory of God's moral perfections, that ever were made to the world. And if there be such a distinguishing, evidential manifestation of divine glory in the gospel, 'tis reasonable to suppose that there may be such a thing as seeing it: what should hinder but that it may be seen? 'Tis no argument that it can't be seen, that some don't see it; though they may be discerning men in temporal matters. If there be such ineffable, distinguishing, evidential excellencies in the gospel, 'tis reasonable to suppose that they are such as are not to be discerned, but by the special influence and enlightenings of the Spirit of God.[27]

Edwards asks, *What is the basis for firm and justified knowledge of the truth of the gospel?* He answers, "The glory of God's moral perfections" shining truly and objectively "in the face of Jesus Christ" in the gospel—"the doctrines there taught, the word there spoken, and the divine counsels, acts and works there revealed."

Commenting on 2 Corinthians 4:4–6, together with 3:18 ("We all, with unveiled face, *beholding the glory of the Lord*, are being transformed into the same image from one degree of glory to another"), Edwards says, "Nothing can be more evident than that a saving belief of the gospel is here spoken of by the apostle as arising from the mind being enlightened to behold the divine glory of the things it exhibits."[28] In other words, the "real evidence" and "just ground" on which saving faith rests is the glory of God manifested in the gospel.

---

[27] Ibid., 300.
[28] Ibid., 298.

The Beauty of Christ Proclaimed

We have not said anything about verse 5, which is sandwiched between the two parallel verses (4 and 6) that describe the gospel of the glory of Christ. Paul writes, "For what we proclaim is not ourselves, but Jesus Christ as Lord, with ourselves as your servants for Jesus' sake." There are two focal points in this verse: first, Christ, the Lord, and, second, the lowly position of Christ's preacher as a slave. Both of these focal points are important for understanding how Paul helped people see the glory of God so that they could have well-grounded faith in the truth of his word.

First, he proclaimed Jesus Christ as Lord. If the true ground of faith is "the glory of God in the face of Jesus Christ," then proclamation that aims at faith should be a vivid and true portrayal of the glorious Christ. People must come face-to-face with Christ in what they hear or read. People should be able to say with the apostle John, "We have seen his glory, glory as of the only Son from the Father, full of grace and truth" (John 1:14). John wrote his Gospel so that we might see, through his own inspired portrait of the Christ, the glory he saw firsthand.

The glory that the disciples saw in Jesus, and that we see when he is faithfully portrayed, was the moral beauty of a man whose food was to do the will of his Father in heaven (John 4:34). He never desired to seek his own glory at anyone's innocent expense but always sought his Father's glory, even to the point of death. Precisely in his last hour of betrayal, his glory became most visible: "For this purpose I have come to this hour. Father, glorify your name. . . . Now is the Son of Man glorified, and God is glorified in him" (John 12:27–28; 13:31). It is this beautiful, self-emptying allegiance of Jesus to the Father's glory that stamps him as true and confirms our faith: "The one who speaks on his own authority seeks his own glory; but the one who seeks the glory of him who sent him is true, and in him there is no falsehood" (John 7:18).

This is the beautiful Christ whom Paul proclaimed as Lord. Even though Paul did not focus on the earthly life of Jesus the way John and the other Gospel writers did, yet the same character of Christ is presented. He set aside his rights as God to take on the form of a slave and humbly die in obedience to his Father (Phil. 2:6–8). Though he was rich, yet for our sakes he became poor (2 Cor. 8:9). He did not please himself but took the reproaches of men that he might accept us into his fellowship to the glory of God (Rom. 15:2, 7). When Paul proclaimed the glory of this crucified Christ, in the fullness of the gospel, he believed that he had given an adequate ground of saving faith.

The Beauty of Christ Embodied

The second focal point of 2 Corinthians 4:5 is this: the person who proclaims the Lord of glory is a slave for Jesus's sake of those he is seeking to persuade: "For what we proclaim is not ourselves, but Jesus Christ as Lord, *with ourselves as your servants for Jesus' sake.*" In other words, the proclaimer embodies the beauty of the proclaimed. He freely lays down his God-given freedom and takes up the role of slave and puts himself at the disposal of others for their good (Phil. 2:5). There is a clear cause and a precise purpose of this behavior.

The cause of this self-giving behavior is found five verses earlier in 2 Corinthians 3:18: "We all, with unveiled face, beholding the glory of the Lord, are being transformed into the same image from one degree of glory to another. For this comes from the Lord who is the Spirit." The one who proclaims the glory of Christ as Lord must have *seen* that glory. And according to Paul, you cannot see the glory of Christ and remain unchanged. Beholding the glory of the Lord we are being transformed.

The promise that the apostle John gives in his first letter, that "when Christ appears we shall *be like him*, because we shall *see* him as he is" (1 John 3:2), is already being fulfilled, as we behold the glory of Christ in the gospel. That is what Paul is saying in 2 Corinthians 3:18. We tend to become like those we admire. This means that we, like him, set aside our rights and do not seek to please merely ourselves, but rather we become servants for the benefit of others. Beholding the beauty of Christ's character, we begin to share it.

The purpose of this transformation into a self-giving servant role is to provide another display of the glory of God as the ground of faith—an embodied display. So we present the glory of Christ not only in our gospel but also in our lives. While proclaiming the light of the knowledge of the glory of God in the face of Christ, we also become the light of the world, so that men may see our good deeds and glorify our Father who is in heaven (Matt. 5:16). If we see and love the glory of God in Christ and are being transformed by it, we become a mirror of that glory and a means to the well-grounded faith of others. This is why 2 Corinthians 4:5 stands between verses 4 and 6. The proclamation of the glory of the Lord, and the embodiment of the glory of the Lord, are the occasion for the miracle of verse 6 or the blindness of verse 4 (cf. 2 Cor. 2:15–16).

Liberation from the Devil's Blindness by God and Man

What is plain from the relationship between 2 Corinthians 4:5 and its bookends, verses 4 and 6, is that people come to a well-grounded, saving knowledge of the truth by a combination of human communication, and divine illumination, of God's glory. Verse 5 is human communication: "What we proclaim is not ourselves, but Jesus Christ as Lord, with ourselves as your servants for Jesus' sake." And verse 6 is supernatural divine illumination: "God, who said, 'Let light shine out of darkness,' has shone in our hearts to give the light of the knowledge of the glory of God in the face of Jesus Christ." The glory of Christ is proclaimed and embodied in human language and life, and the glory of Christ is illuminated by God as he enables the heart to see.

There is a remarkable confirmation of this pattern in 2 Timothy 2:24–26. Here is both human proclamation and embodiment, on the one hand, and divine illumination, on the other hand:

> The Lord's servant must not be quarrelsome but kind to everyone, able to teach, patiently enduring evil, correcting his opponents with gentleness. God may perhaps grant them repentance leading to a knowledge of the truth, and they may come to their senses and escape from the snare of the devil, after being captured by him to do his will.

Notice that the "Lord's servant" ("slave," as in 2 Cor. 4:5) is supposed to deliver both clear content and humble example. Content: "able to teach, correcting his opponents." Example: "not quarrelsome but kind to everyone, patiently enduring evil, with gentleness." Will that open the hearts of the "opponents" and reveal to them the beauty of Christ that the Lord's servant is proclaiming and embodying? Not automatically. Paul would say this human witness is *essential* but in-sufficient by itself.

The risen Lord Jesus had commissioned Paul with these words: "I am sending you to open their eyes, so that they may turn from dark-ness to light and from the power of Satan to God" (Acts 26:17–18). Paul knew (as 2 Cor. 4:6; 2 Tim. 2:25; and Eph. 1:17 show) that God is the decisive power in giving spiritual sight. But here was Jesus tell-ing him to go do what only God could do. That is because God has chosen to make the human witness essential in bringing people to well-grounded faith.

What is Paul's answer in 2 Timothy 2:25 to the question, *Does the work of "the Lord's servant" in teaching and loving open the hearts of those he is teaching and loving?* Paul says, "God *may perhaps grant them repentance* leading to a knowledge of the truth, and they may come to their senses and escape from the snare of the devil, after being captured by him to do his will." We do not have final control or final say in how effective our teaching and loving is. But there is great hope, because God does have final say, and no power of human resistance can stand when God decides to "grant repentance."

As in 2 Corinthians 4:4, here in 2 Timothy 2:26 we meet Satan again, the "god of this world." In 2 Corinthians 4:4, he is blinding peo-ple to the truth. In 2 Timothy 2:26, he has them in his snare, captured to do his will. And here in 2 Timothy 2:25, we also meet the sovereign God of 2 Corinthians 4:6. There he does what he did on the first day of creation. He says, "Let light shine," so that the person trapped in dark-ness suddenly sees the glory of God. Here this sovereign God "grants repentance." The effect of this supernatural work is that the captive of Satan is freed from his stupor—his blindness. He comes to his senses and sees the truth and beauty of what was before boring and untrue. He comes to a knowledge of the truth.

It is real knowledge. It is based on real evidence and good grounds. The liberated captive realizes that his ignorance of the truth of this knowledge was not because there were no grounds for the truth, but because he was blind. He was in a demonic stupor. Now, by God's sovereign grace, he has "come to his senses" and sees the truth. He has knowledge of the truth.

From the Gospel to the Scriptures

Up to this point in the present chapter, we have focused mainly on the way a person comes to a well-grounded conviction of the truth of the *gospel*. We have not drawn the connection explicitly from this argument to the same well-grounded conviction of the truth of the *Scriptures*. But the implications for Edwards are easy to see. He has been thinking of the gospel in the widest terms. Recall that by "gospel" he means "the doctrines there taught, the word there spoken, and the divine counsels, acts, and works there revealed."[29] Or again: "the glorious doctrine the word of God contains, concerning God, Jesus Christ, the way of salvation by him, and the world of glory that he has entered into, and purchased for all them who believe."[30]

These, of course, are enormous ranges of truth—the divine counsels, acts, and works revealed in the gospel, the way of salvation by Christ, and the world of glory. In other words, the word "gospel" has been shorthand for the "whole counsel of God" (Acts 20:27) that provides the foundations, explanations, and implications of the saving work of Christ. This is not something distinct from the Scriptures. Rather, it is what the Scriptures are. The Scriptures are the writings that God saw as necessary to provide the foundations, explanations, and implications of his saving work in the world.

Therefore, the path we have been describing toward a well-grounded conviction of the truth of the gospel is the same path that leads to a well-grounded conviction of the truth of the Scriptures. As the gospel carries in it a real, objective, self-authenticating divine glory, so, in the same way, "the Scriptures themselves are an evidence of their own divine authority."[31]

That Same Glory

Authentic faith is based on "good reason or just ground." While historical reasoning can demonstrate with high probability to the eye of the scholar that Jesus rose from the dead, yet the mass of ordinary people do not have the time or the tools to pursue such disciplined study. If

---

[29] Ibid., 300.
[30] Ibid., 294.
[31] Jonathan Edwards, *The "Miscellanies"* (Entries Nos. a-z, 1-500), vol. 13, *The Works of Jonathan Edwards*, ed. Thomas Schafer (New Haven, CT: Yale University Press, 1994), 410 (#333).

well-grounded, saving faith is to be available to all, it must be found in a more direct way than through detailed historical arguments.

Jonathan Edwards points us to 2 Corinthians 4:3–6, which proves to be a watershed of insight. Here the presence or absence of saving faith is shown to depend on whether one is blind or has been granted by God to see the light of the knowledge of the glory of God in Christ. Edwards calls this glory an "ineffable, distinguishing, evidential excellency in the gospel," which can be seen by those who are not blind and which is a "just ground" for saving faith. I think he is right.

This divine glory, as we will see, pervades the Bible. It proves to be a warrant for believing not only that part of Scripture called "the gospel" but all of God's word, which is, in fact, organically connected to the gospel and bears the marks of that same glory that shines most brightly in Christ and his saving work.

For many people, this kind of argument for the truth of Scripture— indeed this kind of vocabulary—is new and foreign. For that reason, the next chapter tries to remove unnecessary bewilderment. I hope to give four analogies of what it is like to see the glory of God through his word. I say, "unnecessary" bewilderment because it may be that the realities we are dealing with are genuinely so foreign to you that you must start in a bewildered condition.

For example, if you have never been in any vehicle that accelerates rapidly and so have never felt the g-force pushing you back against your seat, you may be utterly bewildered when it happens the first time. It is a new experience of reality. But then you learn what it is, and you make it part of your understanding and your vocabulary. That is the way it is with all experiences of new reality. The language of God's glory and of spiritual sight must sound bewildering to those who have no experience of it. So in the next chapter, I will try to at least remove unnecessary bewilderment.

How precious is your steadfast love, O God!
 The children of mankind take refuge in
  the shadow of your wings.
They feast on the abundance of your house,
 and you give them drink from the river of
  your delights.
For with you is the fountain of life;
 in your light do we see light.

PSALM 36:7–9

9

What It Is Like to See
the Glory of God

I am arguing that "the mind ascends to the truth of the gospel [and the Scriptures] but by one step, and that is its divine glory."[1] More than anyone else, outside the Scriptures themselves, Jonathan Edwards helped me understand this experience. But even in his day (1703–1758), the argument sounded strange to many. Even though his culture was more at home with religious language than our own, his descriptions of seeing divine glory in the Scriptures were not only bewildering to many Christians, but offensive. Here is the way Edwards exhorted his church and the way I would exhort us:

> Let all prejudices against spiritual knowledge be cast away. There are many who entertain prejudices against all spiritual experiences that are talked of. They hear ministers of the gospel speak much of saving illumination, of light let in, of discoveries, of conviction, of a sense of our own vileness, or a sight of God's glory, etc. and they are prejudiced against it all. Such talk is not pleasing in their ears. They hardly believe there are any such things; yea, some are prejudiced against the very expressions whereby those things are signified. . . . This is a very great hindrance to salutary illumination and spiritual

[1] Jonathan Edwards, *A Treatise Concerning Religious Affections*, vol. 2, *The Works of Jonathan Edwards*, ed. John Smith (New Haven, CT: Yale University Press, 1957), 299.

knowledge. Wherefore let none thus entertain prejudices of this nature.[2]

In other words, if the language I am using to talk about how the Bible reveals its complete truthfulness is new or strange or even off-putting, don't let this become a great hindrance to spiritual knowledge. Of course, don't believe anything just because it's new—or old! Believe it because it is biblical and true.

What I have learned over the years is that our grasp of reality itself can be hindered by having inadequate language to name the reality. If you can't name it, it's hard to receive or pass on. For example, if you have no word for chivalry, will you know it when you see it? Will you be able to help your child have it?

One of the great gifts of Scripture is that it creates for us categories of thought that help us grasp more truth. And it gives us terms to talk about those categories that we would not have without the Bible. So, Edwards would say, and I say, test the categories and the terms of this book by Scripture, not just by your experience. We are all learners. And there is always more to see and know about God and his ways than we can imagine.

Four Analogies for Divine Illumination

My aim in this chapter is to shed as much light on the process of divine illumination as I can by means of four analogies or illustrations. In other words, I am asking, what is it *like* to experience the miracle of 2 Corinthians 4:6? "God, who said, 'Let light shine out of darkness,' has shone in our hearts to give the light of the knowledge of the glory of God in the face of Jesus Christ." No analogy is a one-for-one likeness. These illustrations are only pointers. The actual sight of divine glory remains a supernatural experience with no natural counterpart.

The Rational Soul and the Word of God

First, there is an analogy that Edwards himself offers. Keep in mind it is an analogy, not an exact duplicate, of the experience of knowing the

---

[2] Jonathan Edwards, "A Spiritual Understanding of Divine Things Denied to the Unregenerate," in *Sermons and Discourses, 1723–1729*, vol. 14, *The Works of Jonathan Edwards*, ed. Harry S. Stout and Kenneth P. Minkema (New Haven, CT: Yale University Press, 1997), 91.

divine reality of Scripture. I recommend a slow and careful reading. The phraseology is complex, but it is not unintelligible; and it repays what you put into it.

> The being of God is evident by the Scriptures, and the Scriptures themselves are an evidence of their own divine authority, after the same manner as the existence of a human thinking being is evident by the motions, behavior and speech of a body of a human form and contexture, or that that body is animated by a rational mind. For we know this no otherwise than by the consistency, harmony and concurrence of the train of actions and sounds, and their agreement to all that we can suppose to be in a rational mind. These are a clear evidence of an understanding and design that is the original of those actions.
>
> So there is that wondrous universal harmony and consent and concurrence in the aim and drift [of the Scriptures], such an universal appearance of a wonderful glorious design, such stamps everywhere of exalted and divine wisdom, majesty and holiness in matter, manner, contexture and aim; that the evidence is the same that the Scriptures are the word and work of a divine mind, to one that is thoroughly acquainted with them, as 'tis that the words and actions of an understanding man are from a rational mind, to one that has of a long time been his familiar acquaintance.[3]

Most of us overlook the wonders that surround us. Not Edwards. It is a wonder that we can watch a human body move (eyes, lips, forehead, shoulders), listen to human vocal cords make sounds, and follow the interplay of these motions and sounds with the surrounding people and things, and—from all of this physical, sensory data—draw the well-grounded conviction that somehow connected with this physical body of motion and sound is a human thinking being—a rational soul.

We can't see a soul, or personhood, or personality, or rationality. So how do we know there is more than body? Edwards says, "The consistency, harmony and concurrence of the train of actions and sounds" agree with "all that we can suppose to be in a rational mind." Most of the time, we do not consciously make an inference from what we

---

[3] Jonathan Edwards, *The "Miscellanies"* (Entries Nos. a-z, 1-500), vol. 13, *The Works of Jonathan Edwards*, ed. Thomas Schafer (New Haven, CT: Yale University Press, 1994), 410–11 (Miscellany 333).

see to what we believe about persons. The awareness of personhood is immediate, because the union between personhood (soul) and body is so profound.

Then Edwards draws the analogy to the Scriptures and the God whose being they express. In the analogy, the Scriptures correspond to the human body, and God corresponds to the soul. When we construe the meaning of Scripture, we see in the meaning a "wondrous universal harmony and consent and concurrence in the aim and drift." We see the pervasive presence of "a wonderful glorious design." We see abundant "stamps of exalted and divine wisdom, majesty and holiness in matter, manner, contexture, and aim." And in this meaning of Scripture, we discern the "word and work of a divine mind."

Just as we seldom pause and consciously think of the fact that we infer a soul behind the actions and words of our human friend, so we seldom pause and recognize that we infer a divine mind behind the Scriptures. The reason is that, in a sense, "behind" is the wrong word. The soul is not merely *behind* the body, and the word of *God* is not merely *behind* the human Scriptures. The union in both cases is so profound that when we see the acting human body as we ought, and we see the meaning of the Scriptures as we ought, there is no conscious inferring. There is immediate sight. This is a rational person, not just a body. This is the word of God, not just of man.

The Painter and the God Who Speaks

In the next illustration, consider the analogy between knowing that God is the author of Scripture and knowing that Rembrandt painted "The Storm on the Sea of Galilee." The question I am raising here is this: How much of the painting must you see to know that it is Rembrandt's? And how much of the Scripture must you read to know it is God's word? The reason this question matters is that it helps us clarify in what sense the self-authenticating glory of God is visible through the Scriptures.

Most would agree that if you covered Rembrandt's painting with black paper, and then made a pinhole in the paper that revealed a tiny speck of the painting, we would not be able to have a well-grounded knowledge that the painting is by Rembrandt. We would not even know what we are looking at. Similarly, the distinguishing glory of God in Scripture is not in the shape of the letters. Looking through a pinhole at the Scriptures, you might see one letter. That would not reveal the distinguishing glory of the divine author.

The Meaning of Texts Is Where the Glory Shines

Rather, the glory of God that marks the Scriptures as divine is manifested through the *meaning* of the writings. I emphasize this because, among other reasons, it seems to be one of the implications of Paul's words in 2 Corinthians 4:4, when he refers to "the light of the *gospel* of the glory of Christ." The "glory of Christ" shines its "light" into our hearts (v. 6) as the "light of the *gospel*." But this is not the light of the Greek letter epsilon, upsilon, or any other isolated letters or isolated words. The "gospel" stands for a historical complex of events and the meaning those events have in the purpose of God. Therefore, the glory of the gospel will shine not through unintelligible, isolated fragments of those events, or through fragments of that divine meaning, but rather through a sufficient verbal account of that historical reality and that divine meaning.

How much of the Scripture is a "sufficient verbal account"? That is similar to the question, how large does the pinhole have to become before we can recognize the distinguishing traits of Rembrandt's inimitable style—especially the way he uses light? The answer to that question will depend on two things: where on the painting the pinhole is focused and what artistic sensibilities the beholder brings to the painting.

There are parts of Scripture where God's meaning requires a great enlargement of the pinhole. For example, if the pinhole were positioned over the middle of the book of Job, it would need to be enlarged to encompass most of the book, because the lengthy dialogues between Job and his friends don't find their divinely appointed resolution and point without the beginning and the ending of the book. On the other hand, if the pinhole were positioned over the Gospel of John or the epistle to the Romans, the enlargement to a sufficient verbal account of God's distinguishing glory may be much smaller. God's self-authenticating meaning is sufficiently present in shorter portions of the writing.

The Artistic Sensitivities of the Beholder Make a Difference

How much the pinhole over the painting must be enlarged before the beholder can see that this painting is a Rembrandt also depends on the artistic sensibilities of the person who is beholding. A person with extensive engagement with Rembrandt through his paintings may be able to see the marks of the master much earlier than someone like me. I know a few things about Rembrandt's style, but not much. And my engagement with him through his paintings is about as much as you would get in a college art-appreciation class.

Similarly, a person with extensive engagement with God, through his word, will probably more readily see the traits of his glory in the Scriptures than someone who has little experience with the Scriptures. This is not because the seeing is a merely natural affair, or that the person who sees more readily has merely natural gifts. It's because of two things. One is that the glory shines in the *meaning*, not through the isolated words or phrases. We saw above why this is. It implies that a person with more experience in the Scriptures will usually be able to construe the true meaning of a passage more readily than someone with little experience.

The other reason that a seasoned lover of the Scriptures will usually see the glory of God in it more readily is that he has been changed by it. "Beholding the glory of the Lord, we are being transformed into the same image from one degree of glory to another" (2 Cor. 3:18). The glory of God revealed in the Scriptures transforms our mind and heart so that there is a more ready harmony with the glory of God in the word. And thus we see it and approve it more readily. This has large implications for the correlation between our practice of the Scriptures and our understanding of the Scriptures. Thus Edwards says, "Spiritual knowledge is increased only by the practice of virtue and holiness."[4]

God Does Not Sign His Masterpiece

What if the pinhole of the paper covering the painting were just above the author's signature? Then anyone who can read (with no knowledge

---

[4] Ibid., 287 (Miscellany 123). "Spiritual knowledge is increased only by the practice of virtue and holiness. For we cannot have the idea without the adapted disposition of mind, and the more suitable the disposition, the more clear and intense the idea; but the more we practice, the more is the disposition increased."

of the artist's excellencies at all) could know it was by Rembrandt. I mention this to draw attention to the fact that at this point the analogy fails. God does not sign his masterpiece. The reason he doesn't is that such knowledge would do us no good. The only knowledge of God's authorship that has any eternal, saving value is a knowledge discovered by the sight of his glory in the word.

The Devil knows that the Bible is God's word. He saw him do it. But this knowledge does him no good. Why? Because it is a knowledge based on external awareness of God's involvement (like reading a signature), not on the internal sight of the self-authenticating beauty of God in the meaning of the Scriptures. The glory of God is not like a signature on the painting of Scripture. It is not like a lantern hung in the window of the right house telling us where to enter. The glory of God is not an add-on to the meaning of Scripture. It is *in* the meaning.

The analogy of Christ's incarnation may be helpful here. Jesus Christ is human the way the Scripture is human writing. And Jesus is also divine, as the Scriptures are also the word of God.

In order to be known as God incarnate, Jesus did not depend on an external voice from heaven saying, "This is my beloved Son" (Matt. 3:17; 17:5). To be sure, God gave him this endorsement. But Jesus never appealed to it as the proof of who he was. Instead he asked, "Have I been with you so long, and you still do not know me, Philip? Whoever has seen me has seen the Father" (John 14:9). In other words, watching and listening to Jesus should have been enough. So when John wrote his Gospel, after spending three years with Jesus, he said, "The Word became flesh and dwelt among us, and we have seen his glory, glory as of the only Son from the Father, full of grace and truth" (John 1:14).

The point here is that God was discernible in Jesus not because God put a signature on the painting, or hung a lantern in his house, or shouted Christ's divinity from heaven, but because God was in Jesus. God was who Jesus was. They were united. The marks of divinity were in Jesus—the whole, acting, thinking, feeling, speaking person. So it is with the Scriptures. They do not have a signature, or a lantern, or a voice spoken over them. The word of man itself is united with the word of God. The marks of divinity are in the meaning of the writing.

What this meant for Jesus is that you could not discern the divine glory of Jesus by looking at his bare feet or at a single moment of his body sleeping. You had to see him acting, and hear his word, and watch his demeanor. So it is with the Scripture. You can't see the divine glory of Christ in the Scripture by merely looking at a letter of the alphabet in one of its sentences, or by a random glance at a "sleeping sentence" with no connection with other sentences to make the meaning plain. As with a Rembrandt, the marks of the master's distinguishing greatness are in the composition—the meaning of the God-breathed writing.

The Light of God Brings All Truth to Light

In the third illustration, we pursue some thoughts triggered by Psalm 36:9: "In your light do we see light." And these thoughts are provoked further by the catalyst of a famous quote from C. S. Lewis: "I believe in Christianity as I believe that the Sun has risen, not only because I see it, but because by it I see everything else."[5]

Ordinarily when we seek to have a well-grounded conviction about some claim to truth in this world, we bring all our experience to bear on the claim and try to make sense out of it. What we know from experience before we hear the claim, we apply to the claim to see if it measures up. Does it cohere with what we know to be true? Does it make sense in the light of what we already know? What we know from experience is the standard, the arbiter, the measure of truth.

But what happens when we encounter a claim that says, "I am the Standard, the Arbiter, the Truth"? This claim is unique. It is not like other claims to truth in this world. When the ultimate Measure of all reality speaks, you don't subject this Measure to the measure of your mind or your experience of the world. He created all that. When the ultimate Standard of all truth and beauty appears, he is not put in the dock to be judged by the prior perceptions of truth and beauty that we bring to the courtroom.

The eternal, absolute original is seen as true and beautiful not because he coheres with what we know but because all the truth and beauty we know coheres in him. It is measured by him, and it is seen flowing from him. He does not make sense, and thus have plausibility,

[5] C. S. Lewis, "Is Theology Poetry?," in *C. S. Lewis, Essay Collection and Other Short Pieces* (London: HarperCollins, 2000), 21.

in the light of this world. He brings sense to the world. He is sense. The light that we have in the world does not shine on him and reveal his truth. He is the light of the world, and in his light we see light.

"In Your Light Do We See Light"

Psalm 36:9 says, "With you is the fountain of life; in your light do we see light." What does it mean that in God's light we see light? Consider the context. The first four verses of the psalm describe the condition of those who have "no fear of God" (v. 1). Instead, "transgression speaks to the wicked deep in his heart" (v. 1). What does it say? He "flatters himself . . . that his iniquity cannot be found out" (v. 2). The denial of God and the power of sin put the man in a dream world of illusion. He thinks he is self-sufficient and safe. So he gives himself over to words of deceit and acts of evil (vv. 3–4). He is like an ant denying the existence of earth, or a bird denying the existence of air, or a fish denying the existence of water.

Then the psalmist (David) puts the majesty of God over against this illusion. "Your steadfast love, O Lord, extends to the heavens, your faithfulness to the clouds. Your righteousness is like the mountains of God; your judgments are like the great deep; man and beast you save, O Lord" (vv. 5–6). God-denying man and beasts who do not know God are both sustained by the God they do not know. Mountains and great deeps do not vanish because man and beast are blind to their glory.

But David knows how all-encompassing is the love of God holding all things in being. He sings its preciousness: "How precious is your steadfast love, O God!" (v. 7). Whether they see it or not, he confesses that all mankind live in the sustaining care of God. They have their life and breath and everything from God. "The children of mankind take refuge in the shadow of your wings. They feast on the abundance of your house, and you give them drink from the river of your delights" (vv. 7–8). The people—the children of mankind—who "have no fear of God" and who "flatter themselves" that they are self-sufficient and safe apart from God—these very people live on the abundance of God's house without knowing it. They drink from his river of delights. They are sustained by the God they deny.

How can this be? Verse 9 begins with "for" (Heb. *kiy*), which gives the reason: "For with you is the fountain of life; in your light do we see light." The reason even those who have no fear of God can live and drink from the life of God is that God is the source of all life. There is no life apart from God. And God is the source of all light. There is no light, no knowledge, no wisdom, apart from God. All existence and all knowledge depend on God. If we have life, we live by him. "In him we live and move and have our being" (Acts 17:28). If we have any knowledge, we know by him. "From him and through him and to him are all things" (Rom. 11:36). We do not shed light on him by the light we see. He is the origin, the source. If we have any measure of light, it is he who is shedding light on what we see, not we.

Thus when the Son of God came into the world—when the Word became flesh (John 1:14)—"the true light, which gives light to everyone, was coming into the world" (John 1:9). The original, the source, became part of the stream of creation that flows from him. The light entered the light that he created. Jesus Christ is unique. He is really creature, and really Creator—one person in two natures. He is one who can be known and the one who makes all knowing possible. He is a point of light—a point of truth and knowledge—that enters our minds, and he is the light by which we see all points of light. Thus we know him to be true, not because our light shows him to be so, but because his divine light shines with its own, all-enlightening, all-explaining glory.

And so it is with his word, the Scriptures, which are organically related to the incarnate Word. As the light of the world, Christ is the sum and brightness of all Old Testament truth. And he willed that the light he brought into the world be preserved again as the sum and brightness of the New Testament. As Herman Bavinck puts it, Scripture "is the product of God's incarnation in Christ and in a sense its continuation."[6] Thus we know the Scriptures to be true, not because our light shows them to be so, but because their divine light shines with its own unique, all-enlightening, all-explaining glory.

What Did Peter See That Judas Did Not?

In our fourth illustration, I would like to reflect with you on the difference between what the apostles Peter and Judas saw when they looked at

---

[6] Herman Bavinck, *Reformed Dogmatics, vol. 1: Prolegomena* (Grand Rapids, MI: Baker Academic, 2003), 380.

Jesus. Even calling Judas an "apostle" is shocking. But there it is: "The names of the twelve apostles are these: first, Simon, who is called Peter . . . and Judas Iscariot" (Matt. 10:2–4). He would not fulfill the purpose of an apostle to speak the truth on Jesus's behalf, and so he was taken out of the Twelve before the apostles were entrusted with the mission at Jesus's departure. Jesus knew Judas would fail when he chose him. "Jesus knew from the beginning . . . who it was who would betray him" (John 6:64). So Judas is chosen so that we can learn from his failure.

Peter was different. For all his stumbling, Peter saw Christ as compellingly true and great. To know him was supremely rewarding. When others were leaving Jesus because his teachings were becoming increasingly controversial, Jesus asked the Twelve, "Do you want to go away as well?" And Peter answered, "Lord, to whom shall we go? You have the words of eternal life" (John 6:67–68). And when Jesus asked his disciples, "Who do you say that I am?" Peter answered, "You are the Christ, the Son of the living God" (Matt. 16:16). In other words, Peter saw the person and the teachings of Jesus as irresistibly true, great, and satisfying. You are the greatest person. Your teachings are unsurpassed. There is no other person we prefer to you. You are the Messiah. You are the Son of God. Our quest is over.

"Flesh and Blood Has Not Revealed This to You"

How did Peter, who was manifestly an imperfect and sinful man (Luke 5:8), see Christ for who he really was? Jesus answers, using Peter's original name, "Blessed are you, Simon Bar-Jonah! For flesh and blood has not revealed this to you, but my Father who is in heaven" (Matt. 16:17). This was Jesus's way of saying what Paul said in 2 Corinthians 4:6 and 2 Timothy 2:25 and Ephesians 1:17—namely, that God must open the eyes of our hearts before the glory of God in Christ and his word can be seen for what it is.

Peter was not unique in this regard. Jesus said to his disciples, "To you it has been given to know the secrets of the kingdom of God, but for others they are in parables, so that 'seeing they may not see, and hearing they may not understand'" (Luke 8:10). All the true followers of Jesus had experienced what Peter did. God had "given them to know." This is the way anyone comes to know the truth and beauty of Christ.

> Jesus declared, "I thank you, Father, Lord of heaven and earth, that you have hidden these things from the wise and understanding and revealed them to little children; yes, Father, for such was your gracious will. All things have been handed over to me by my Father, and no one knows the Son except the Father, and no one knows the Father except the Son and anyone to whom the Son chooses to reveal him. (Matt. 11:25–27)

No one knows the Father or the Son apart from this supernatural gift of sight. The reason Peter saw Jesus as true and great and supremely rewarding was that God, in free and sovereign mercy, chose to open his eyes to see what Paul called "the glory of God in the face of Jesus Christ."

Withholding Healing Does Not Cause Blindness

But for Judas and others like him, "Seeing they do not see, and hearing they do not hear" (Matt. 13:13). Judas saw the same physical Jesus that Peter saw. He was part of the circle of apostles. He was with Jesus almost nonstop for three years. Why did he not see? It is not fitting to say that he didn't see because God did not open his eyes. God's gracious gift of sight is why people see. Its absence is not properly why they don't see. God's withholding of healing is not the cause of their blindness.

The story of Judas reveals why he could not see the glory of God in Christ. Judas was a lover of money (Matt. 26:15), a liar (Luke 22:48), a thief (John 12:6), and a traitor (Mark 14:10). This was his blindness. When Jesus visited Martha and Mary's home, Mary anointed Jesus with expensive ointment. Judas objected, "'Why was this ointment not sold for three hundred denarii and given to the poor?' He said this, not because he cared about the poor, but because he was a thief, and having charge of the moneybag he used to help himself to what was put into it" (John 12:4–6).

There it is: lover of money, thief, liar. That is what loving God's creation more than God does to the human soul. He helped himself to what was put into the apostles' treasury. He was a thief. And he covered his stealing by hypocritical protests about loving the poor. He was a liar. He asked Jesus at the Last Supper, "Is it I, Rabbi [who will betray you?]" (Matt. 26:25), although he knew perfectly well he was the one. He was a deceiver through and through. He betrayed Jesus with a kiss—a lying kiss (Luke 22:47). Loving money turns people into liars and thieves who cannot see the glory of Christ.

Covetousness Causes Blindness to Glory

Why does loving money make you blind to the glory of Jesus? Because the glory of Jesus lays claim on our hearts as the greatest treasure in the world. "The kingdom of heaven is like treasure hidden in a field, which a man found and covered up. Then in his joy he goes and sells all that he has and buys that field" (Matt. 13:44). As the king of Israel, whose kingdom would never end (Luke 1:32–33), Jesus was the embodiment of the kingdom of God. Where he worked, the kingly rule of God was working (Luke 11:20). Therefore, this one-verse parable about the kingdom of God (Matt. 13:44) is about finding Jesus as our supreme treasure. When we see him for who he is—infinitely beautiful, valuable, and satisfying—our love for money is neutralized. We see this because, in the parable, the man who found the treasure *joyfully* sells all that he has to possess it. This signifies a radical replacement of money with Christ as our supreme treasure.

It is either-or. Money or Christ. "No one can serve two masters, for either he will hate the one and love the other, or he will be devoted to the one and despise the other. You cannot serve God and money" (Matt. 6:24; cf. Matt. 10:37–39; Luke 8:14; Mark 10:21–22). Nor can you serve Christ and money. Judas is the proof. The love of money blinds the mind to the superior worth of Jesus. Even before we reason it out, our hearts are rebelling against the claim of Jesus to replace money as the supreme treasure of our lives.

So Judas saw the same Jesus whom Peter saw, but he did not see him as compellingly glorious, beautiful, and all-satisfying. He was not blind to the human being. He was blind to the infinite beauty and value of divine glory.

And the reason for the blindness was not that he was a helpless pawn in the hands of Satan but that he joined Satan in hating the broad daylight of Christ's glory. His blindness—our blindness—is rooted in his rebellion. Here's what Jesus said in John 3:19–20 about our blindness to his glory:

Light has come into the world, and people *loved* the darkness rather than the light because their works were evil. For everyone who does wicked things *hates* the light and does not come to the light, lest his works should be exposed.

The root of our blindness is not that we are *victims* of darkness, but *lovers* of darkness. The root of our blindness is not that we are *hindered* from the light, but that we are *haters* of the light. We love the darkness of doing things our way, and we hate the light of the surpassing beauty of the all-authoritative, all-satisfying, sovereign Christ. And, therefore, our blindness is blameworthy—not, as the lawyers say, exculpatory. It does not remove our guilt. It *is* our guilt.

In this analogy, Judas represents people who approach the Christian Scriptures with a mind and a heart that are so out of tune with the music of its meaning that they cannot hear it for what it is. There is such a dissonance that the heart repels the revelation of God as undesirable and untrue. Peter represents the people who come to the Scriptures with a mind and a heart humbled by the Holy Spirit and open to the beauty and truth of God's glory shining through the meaning of the text. What the analogy brings to light is that two people can be looking at the very same person (Jesus Christ) or the very same book (the Bible) and miss what is really there. It shows that the pathway to seeing includes the purification of our hearts. "Blessed are the pure in heart, for they shall see God" (Matt. 5:8).

The Scriptures Reveal the Glory

The point of these four analogies has been to illustrate how the Scriptures are manifested as the word of God by revealing his glory. What is it like to experience a well-grounded conviction of the truth of Scripture by the sight of its God-given glory?

The path we have been describing toward a well-grounded conviction of the truth of Scripture is rooted in Paul's teaching in 2 Corinthians 4:4–6, where he says that through the hearing (or reading) of the gospel, God imparts to our hearts "the light of the knowledge of the glory of God in the face of Jesus Christ." This pathway to certainty in the gospel is the same path that leads to a well-grounded conviction of the truth of all of Scripture. As the gospel carries in it a real, objective, self-authenticating divine glory, so, in the same way, "the Scriptures themselves are an evidence of their own divine authority."[7]

One of the implications of this pathway to certainty is that other paths that offer probabilities and risk become problematic. There have been some famous examples of these other paths. Dealing with one of them will clarify the different path I am following. So we turn in the next chapter to Pascal's Wager.

---

[7] Edwards, "*Miscellanies*," 410 (Miscellany 333).

I do not cease . . . remembering you in my prayers, that the God of our Lord Jesus Christ, the Father of glory, may give you the Spirit of wisdom and of revelation in the knowledge of him, having the eyes of your hearts enlightened, that you may know what is the hope to which he has called you, what are the riches of his glorious inheritance in the saints.

EPHESIANS 1:16–18

10

Pondering Pascal's Wager

As I wrote the previous two chapters, I was moved by the concern that a complex historical argument for the truth of the Bible is out of reach for most people in the world. Most people don't have the tools or the time to work out such an argument. Not only that, but such arguments yield only probable results and leave a person with the sense that his confidence in the Bible is only as firm as his grasp of the present state of historical studies. My concern, therefore, has been to find a way to have a well-grounded confidence in the truth of the Bible based on evidence that a person can see, even if he has no historical training and little time to devote to rigorous study.

How Do I Have Confidence in My Wife?

One way to think about this approach is to compare it to the confidence I have that my wife is faithful to me—that she is not having an affair with another man. How can I have a well-grounded confidence that she is faithful? One approach would be to hire a private detective and assign him to do the necessary surveillance to prove she is not having a secret rendezvous. But that approach leaves me worried that the private detective may not be thorough. Maybe he missed something. Maybe she suspects he is there and has found a way to send him on a wild-goose chase while she carries on her affair. This approach is going to leave me worried and unconvinced.

The only way to have the kind of well-grounded confidence in my wife that leaves me with complete peace of mind is to base it on a direct awareness of the kind of person she is. Over time I come to know her very deeply. I see the profound marks of integrity and holiness and the fear of God and devotion to Christ and to me. These are realities that no private detective can prove to me. I know them firsthand. I cannot quantify them. If I could, they would lose their force, because then I would always be wondering if I need a little more "quantity" to establish her character. It's not like that. It is more immediate. More intuitive. But not merely subjective. It is based on countless hours and experiences together. This way of knowing the faithfulness of my wife produces a well-grounded confidence that I would stake my life on. I sleep peacefully without fretting.

If this is possible in the case of a wife who is merely human and is imperfect and sinful, how much more is it possible to know in a direct way the truth and faithfulness of God's word, as the divine glory of his character appears through the Scriptures he inspired. In this chapter, I want to pursue this way of knowing the truth of Scripture by relating it to Pascal's Wager. The reason I think this will shed more light on how we gain a well-grounded confidence in Scripture is that the inadequacy of Pascal's Wager sends us to the Scriptures themselves with insights that deepen and strengthen our understanding of how we know the Bible is true.

Pascal's Wager

Pascal was a French mathematician and philosopher who died in 1662. His most famous work is *Pensées* (which means *Thoughts*). In thought 233, he proposed his wager, which has to do with how you decide whether to believe in God or not. In its popular form, it is, I think, quite misleading. That is why I deal with it here. In showing how it is misleading, we shed light on the process of coming to well-grounded belief in God and his word, not belief based on a venture.

The gist of the wager is that venturing to believe in God involves little risk and great possible gain. Or to put it another way: betting that God does not exist and finding yourself wrong results in eternal loss. But betting that God does exist and finding yourself wrong results in little loss. So venture on God. In Pascal's own words, the wager goes like this:[1]

> God is, or He is not. But to which side shall we incline? Reason can decide nothing here. . . . A game is being played at the extremity of this infinite distance where heads or tails will turn up. What will you wager? According to reason . . . you can defend neither of the propositions. . . .
>
> You must wager. It is not optional. You are embarked. Which will you choose then? . . . Your reason is no more shocked in choosing one rather than the other, since you must of necessity choose. . . . But your happiness? Let us weigh the gain and the loss in wagering that God is. . . .
>
> If you gain, you gain all; if you lose, you lose nothing. Wager, then, without hesitation that He is. . . . There is here an infinity of an infinitely happy life to gain, a chance of gain against a finite number of chances of loss. . . . Wherever the infinite is, and there is not an infinity of chances of loss against that of gain, there is no time to hesitate, you must give all. . . .
>
> And so our proposition is of infinite force, when there is the finite at stake in a game where there are equal risks of gain and of loss, and the infinite to gain. This is demonstrable; and if men are capable of any truths, this is one. (*Pensées*, 233)

The Wager as Simple and Misleading

Here is where the popular (and misleading) understanding of Pascal's Wager ends. Why is it misleading?

It is misleading because it gives the impression that saving faith in God is a choice we make without seeing God as true and compellingly beautiful. The wager says, "You do not know if God is really there. God himself is not a reality to you. He is a possibility. When you look at nature, or at the gospel story of Christ crucified and risen, you do not see a divine glory that is convincing and beautiful to you." Nevertheless, the wager says, "You must choose." And it says, "Choose him. But when you do, the choice you make is not owing to a sight of glory that convinces and enthralls."

---

[1] Some of these thoughts were first published in an article on Pascal's Wager at http://www.desiringGod.org.

But according to the Scriptures, such a choice is of no eternal value. It is not saving faith. It is a purely natural thing, not a supernatural thing. We are drawn to something that we do not know. We are hoping for an eternal extension and improvement of the happiness we have here in the things of this world (since we do not know God). But saving faith is not like that. It is rooted in the sight and foretaste of happiness in supernatural reality—God himself. According to the Scriptures, living faith is created in the dead soul by the miracle of new birth. "Everyone who believes that Jesus is the Christ has been born of God" (1 John 5:1). That's how faith happens.

Without this new birth, we are merely flesh—merely human, merely natural. "That which is born of the flesh is flesh, and that which is born of the Spirit is spirit" (John 3:6). And the mind of the flesh cannot submit to God (Rom. 8:7); it cannot please God (Rom. 8:8); and it cannot see the things of God as anything but folly (1 Cor. 2:14). "The god of this world has blinded the minds of the unbelievers, to keep them from seeing the light of the gospel of the glory of Christ, who is the image of God" (2 Cor. 4:4).

In order, therefore, for saving faith to come into being, God must grant repentance. "God may perhaps grant them repentance leading to a knowledge of the truth" (2 Tim. 2:25). That is, he must make the spiritually dead come to life. "When we were dead in our trespasses, God made us alive together with Christ" (Eph. 2:5). This new birth, "through the living and abiding word of God" (1 Pet. 1:23), gives the light of the knowledge of the glory of God. "God, who said, 'Let light shine out of darkness,' has shone in our hearts to give the light of the knowledge of the glory of God in the face of Jesus Christ" (2 Cor. 4:6).

This supernaturally given, spiritual sight of the glory of God in Christ is the ground of saving faith. God is seen with the eyes of the heart as truly as the eyes of our head see the sun in the sky. And this sight of the glory of God in Christ compels us. It is no more resistible than the enjoyment of your favorite food is resistible when it is in your mouth. And so it is when God becomes your favorite, by the opening of your eyes to see his convincing and enthralling beauty. To see him as supreme in beauty is to desire him above all.

Therefore, the popular and simple view of Pascal's Wager is misleading. It gives the impression that you might actually have an eternal happiness in God by simply choosing to believe he exists, when you have neither tasted nor seen his convincing and enthralling glory. But according to the Scriptures, that is not saving faith. As we saw in chapter 8, groundless faith does not display the trustworthiness of the one trusted. The "faith" of the wager does not embrace God as true or beautiful. God is an unknown risk. But that is no honor to God and, therefore, is no saving faith, because saving faith glorifies the reliability of God to keep his promises (Rom. 4:20). The only faith of eternal value is well-grounded faith. But Pascal's Wager, in its popular form, gives the impression that one can have eternal life on a venture.

The Wager as Complex and Challenging

But, in fact, Pascal was aware of this problem with his wager, though most popular uses of the wager do not take note of this. To be fair to him, we need to make this clear. He pictures his listener responding to the wager,

> "I confess it, I admit it. But, still, is there no means of seeing the faces of the cards?"—Yes, Scripture and the rest, etc. "Yes, but I have my hands tied and my mouth closed; I am forced to wager, and am not free. *I am not released, and am so made that I cannot believe. What, then, would you have me do?*" (emphasis added)

Pascal answers,

> True. But at least learn your inability to believe, since reason brings you to this, and yet you cannot believe. Endeavour then to convince yourself, not by increase of proofs of God, but by the abatement of your passions. You would like to attain faith, and do not know the way; you would like to cure yourself of unbelief, and ask the remedy for it. Learn of those who have been bound like you, and who now stake all their possessions. These are people who know the way which you would follow, and who are cured of an ill of which you would be cured.

It is not easy to know from the brevity of *Pensées* precisely how Pascal conceives of this "cure" for unbelief. His basic answer is: Set out on the road of faith as if you believed, and you will soon have eyes to see the certainty of it all.

> I will tell you that . . . at each step you take on this road, you will see so great certainty of gain, so much nothingness in what you risk, that you will at last recognize that you have wagered for something certain and infinite, for which you have given nothing.

I would like to think that Pascal means: Pursue the miracle of new birth by immersing yourself in the word of God through which the miracle of sight and certainty comes (1 Pet. 1:23). But I am afraid that is not what he means. His Roman Catholic sacramentalism laid out a different path. He counsels the seeker: Follow those who have acted "as if they believed, taking the holy water, having masses said, etc. Even this will naturally make you believe."

I think that is not good counsel. But the wager, in its true complexity, is a wise and sobering challenge. The challenge is not to seek faith through holy water and masses. The challenge is to realize that infinite things are at stake. Saving faith is essential, and it is not a wager. Rather, it is an entering through the door of Christ, irresistibly drawn by the convincing and compelling foretaste of the enthralling beauty of God in the gospel.

Pascal's Wager applies not only to faith in God but also to faith in the word of God. Venturing on the Bible, with no good ground for doing so, is no honor to the Scriptures. God's word is not esteemed if one believes it by the toss of a coin. Indeed, such "belief," as we have seen, would not be a belief of any value. It would be like a man's choosing which of two women to marry by tossing a coin. The chosen one would know she was not chosen because of any good reasons. The faith in God's word that honors God has foundations. We have seen its divine glory. We have seen "the glory of God in the face of Jesus Christ." And we cannot turn away to another. In this way, Christ and his word are honored.

Unnamable Experiences and Serious Doubts

However, this does not mean that there are no doubts along the way. Nor does it mean that the conscious experiences of all who embrace the Bible as God's word are the same. One may come to a well-grounded confidence in God's word and never have even heard the term "glory of God." One may never have heard of terms such as "self-authenticating" or "internal testimony" or "compelling and irresistible evidence" or the like. The experience of seeing God's self-attesting reality in Scripture is vastly different from being able to explain that experience. They are not the same.

Millions of people have come to a well-grounded confidence in the Bible and have not been able to find sufficient words to describe that experience. I do not even claim that the words I am using here are sufficient to do it justice. So let it be clear: the miracle of seeing "the glory of God in the face of Jesus Christ" through the Scriptures can happen to a person who never will be able to explain sufficiently why he trusts the Bible. His trust may be well-grounded without his knowing how it is.

The Conversion and Execution of Tokichi Ishii

For example, take the story of the conversion and execution of Tokichi Ishii—a man who was hanged for murder in Tokyo in 1918.[2] He had been sent to prison more than twenty times and was known for being as cruel as a tiger. On one occasion, after attacking a prison official, he was gagged and bound and his body suspended in such a way that his toes barely reached the ground. But he stubbornly refused to say he was sorry for what he had done.

Just before being sentenced to death, Tokichi was sent a New Testament by two Christian missionaries, Miss West and Miss McDonald. After a visit from Miss West, he began to read the story of Jesus's trial and execution. His attention was riveted by the sentence, "And Jesus said, 'Father, forgive them, for they know not what they do'" (Luke 23:34). This sentence transformed his life.

> I stopped: I was stabbed to the heart, as if by a five-inch nail. What did the verse reveal to me? Shall I call it the love of the heart of Christ? Shall I call it His compassion? I do not know what to call it. I only know that with an unspeakably grateful heart I believed.[3]

---

[2] This story is taken from John Piper, *Desiring God: Meditations of a Christian Hedonist*, rev. ed. (Colorado Springs: Multnomah, 2011), 147–48. It is recounted in Norman Anderson, *God's Word for God's World* (London: Hodder & Stoughton, 1981), 25.
[3] Ibid.

That is what I mean by the power of God's word to awaken well-grounded faith, even if the believer does not know how to describe what has happened. In the context of Jesus's life, one sentence ("Father, forgive them, for they know not what they do") was a true and compelling lightning bolt of divine beauty. It was enough. Faith was born. And the foundation was solid.

Tokichi was sentenced to death and accepted it as "the fair, impartial judgment of God." Now the word that brought him to faith also sustained his faith in an amazing way. Near the end, Miss West directed him to the words of 2 Corinthians 6:8–10 concerning the suffering of the righteous. The words moved him very deeply, and he wrote,

> "As sorrowing, yet always rejoicing." People will say that I must have a very sorrowful heart because I am daily awaiting the execution of the death sentence. This is not the case. I feel neither sorrow nor distress nor any pain. Locked up in a prison cell six feet by nine in size I am infinitely happier than I was in the days of my sinning when I did not know God. Day and night . . . I am talking with Jesus Christ.

Here is the key: Through the word of God, Tokichi Ishii had truly met the living God. He had seen the glory of God in the face of Christ. He now knows God. "I am infinitely happier than I was . . . when I did not know God." This was real knowledge with a real basis in the divine beauty of Christ as he prayed for his enemies when they were killing him, and as he died for them. The authenticity of Tokichi's experience did not depend on his ability to put it into words, though he did this with remarkable effectiveness.

The Doubts of Billy Graham

Not only may one's authentic experience of God's glory in Scripture be clouded with the inadequacy of human language, but it may also be clouded by doubts and still be real. The resolution of these doubts may at times look like the resolution of Pascal's Wager—just ventured on the Bible. I say it may look like this. But in genuine faith—well-grounded faith—there is always more going on.

Billy Graham's crisis of confidence in the Bible that came to a head in 1949 is a good example. In 1948, Graham's friend Charles Templeton was having doubts about the integrity of the Scriptures. He left his pastorate in Toronto and entered Princeton Seminary. Billy commended Templeton and said that if he had chosen Oxford, he would have gone with him. Billy "hankered for post graduate study."[4] And doubts were brewing in his own mind, though he felt he and Templeton were moving in different directions—Templeton toward bolstering his doubts, Graham toward resolving them.

Billy's doubts were not in a vacuum. He had seen God's mighty hand through Scripture. He knew that "when he took the Bible as God's Word and used it, his preaching had power. Already he had seen men and women weighted by cares and morally bankrupt made alive and radiant."[5] In subsequent years he would say, "When I preach the Bible straight—no questions, no doubts, no hesitations—then God gives me a power that's beyond me. When I say, 'The Bible says,' God gives me this incredible power. It's something I don't completely understand. . . . When I pick up the Bible, I feel as though I have a rapier in my hands."[6]

But in 1949, the battle raged in his soul. In the words of his biographer, John Pollock,

> He must soon decide once and for all either to spend his life studying whether or not God had spoken, or to spend it as God's ambassador, bringing a message which he might not fully comprehend in all details until after death. Must an intellectually honest man know everything about the Bible's origins before he could use it? Were theological professors the only ones qualified to speak of religion, or might a simple American, or an ignorant jungle villager, or even a child, lead another to Christ?[7]

The crisis came to a head in August 1949 at Forest Home retreat center near San Bernardino, California:

> Billy was deeply disturbed. . . . After supper, instead of attending evening service, he retired to his log cabin and read again the Bible passage concerning its authority. . . . He meditated on the attitude

---

[4] John Pollock, *Billy Graham: The Authorized Biography* (Grand Rapids, MI: Zondervan, 1966), 50.
[5] Ibid., 51.
[6] http://www.ccel.us/billy.ch3.html; accessed March 5, 2015.
[7] Pollock, *Billy Graham*, 52.

of Christ, who fulfilled the law. . . . "He loved the Scriptures, quoted from them constantly, and never once intimated that they might be wrong."

Billy went out in the forest and wandered up the mountain, praying as he walked. . . . He knew he had reached what he believed to be a crisis.

He saw that intellect alone could not resolve the question of authority. He must go beyond intellect. . . . "So I went back and I got my Bible, and I went out in the moonlight. And I got to a stump and put the Bible on the stump. And I knelt down, and I said, 'Oh, God; I cannot prove certain things. I cannot answer some of the questions Chuck [Templeton] is raising and some of the other people are raising, but I accept this Book by faith as the Word of God.'"[8]

Was Billy Graham's conviction from that point on based on a guess? Was he making Pascal's Wager? Was the statement, "I accept this Book by faith as the Word of God," well-grounded? Of course, I cannot know Billy Graham's heart at that moment. My point here is that such a resolution of doubts does not *have* to be a leap in the dark. He was not leaping into the dark. The thirty-year-old Graham had seen much of God in the Scriptures. He had tasted the power of God's word in his own preaching. What his experience—and the experience of thousands—teaches us is that the sight of God's self-authenticating glory in Scripture is often an embattled sight. What we have seen and tasted and known with justified certainty one day may be clouded the next day.

Embattled Sight

Jonathan Edwards described such experiences like this:

[It] is remarkable, that the same persons reading the same portion of Scripture, at one time shall be greatly affected with it, and see what is astonishingly glorious in it, . . . the pertinency and pithiness of the expression, admirable majesty, coherence, and harmony; and at another time [to those same persons it] shall seem insipid, mean, impertinent, and inconsistent.[9]

---

[8] Ibid., 53.
[9] Jonathan Edwards, *The "Miscellanies" (Entries Nos. a-z, 1-500)*, vol. 13, *The Works of Jonathan Edwards*, ed. Thomas Schafer (New Haven, CT: Yale University Press, 1994), 289 (Miscellany 126).

In other words, God does not ordain that his illumining work in the human mind triumph without warfare. God could, if he willed, make himself so consistently clear and compelling that such experiences of clouded sight would never happen. But we know from Scripture, as well as from our own experience, that this is not the way he works. Paul would not pray for the Ephesians the way he does if God sustained unbroken the clearest views of his glory in all the saints. He prays

> that the God of our Lord Jesus Christ, the Father of glory, may give you the Spirit of wisdom and of revelation in the knowledge of him, having the eyes of your hearts enlightened, that you may know what is the hope to which he has called you, what are the riches of the glory of his inheritance in the saints. (Eph. 1:17–18)

Paul is asking that God would cause the believers to see, with the "eyes of your hearts," the compelling glory that God has promised them in his word—the hope of their calling and the glory of his inheritance. The spiritual sight of these things is real, but it is embattled. We fight by prayer, and by a steady gaze at the word of God, for the sight of his glory that sustains our well-grounded hope.

Again Paul prays that the Ephesians

> may have strength to comprehend with all the saints what is the breadth and length and height and depth, and to know the love of Christ that surpasses knowledge, that you may be filled with all the fullness of God. (Eph. 3:18–19)

There is a kind of "strength" that is not muscular but spiritual. It is strength "to comprehend . . . and to know the love of Christ" revealed in the word of God. The love of Christ has a "breadth and length and height and depth" that makes it an inimitable, self-authenticating reality. This can be seen by the eyes of the heart when God's "strength" of sight is given. And when it is seen for what it is, we know it is real. No mere human can produce it. But this conviction is an embattled conviction. That's why Paul is praying for them.

Suppose someone should ask, "Well, if the sight of God's divine reality in the Scriptures can be bright one day and clouded the next, how are we to know which day is to be believed?" My answer is this: If you have truly seen the holiness of God through the Scriptures—the pure, transcendent, supreme worth and beauty of God through his word—this sight will hold you during embattled seasons. There is an infinite qualitative difference between the witness of God through his word and the witness of clouded darkness. The battle may be so severe that in your own mind you cannot, at a given time, distinguish between the divine light and human darkness. But God has promised to hold on to those who are born of God, and who possess the Holy Spirit, and have seen his glory (1 Cor. 1:8–9; 1 Thess. 3:13; Jude 24–25). He will assert himself in due time and break through the clouds so that you see clearly again (Ps. 42:5).

Jesus taught us through his prayer in John 17 that while he was on the earth, he had begun a ministry of illumination in the minds of his disciples that he intended for his Father to preserve when Jesus was no longer in the world. He had revealed the Father's glory to his disciples: "I glorified you on earth. . . . The glory that you have given me I have given to them" (John 17:4, 22). Jesus's point was that he had revealed to his disciples the glory of the Father so that they could know that he is real. And now, as he prepares for his absence, he asks the Father to preserve that illumination in the disciples:

> I have manifested your name to the people whom you gave me out
> of the world. . . . Holy Father, keep them in your name, which you
> have given me. . . . While I was with them, I kept them in your name,
> which you have given me. I have guarded them, and not one of them
> has been lost except the son of destruction, that the Scripture might
> be fulfilled. . . . I do not ask that you take them out of the world,
> but that you keep them from the evil one. . . . Sanctify them in the
> truth; your word is truth. (John 17:6–17)

The aim of this prayer is to give us the joyful confidence (v. 13) that the manifestation of the Father's glory, once it is given, will never be lost. And we may be sure of this: Jesus was not praying for those disciples only, but, as he says, for twenty-first-century believers as well: "I do not ask for these only, but also for those who will believe in me through their word" (John 17:20).

So, even though the supernatural gift of seeing God's glory in the word is an embattled experience, it is not an uncertain one. God does not cause people to be born again with new eyes, only to let them die and go blind for eternity. He "will sustain you to the end. . . . God is faithful, by whom you were called into the fellowship of his Son, Jesus Christ our Lord" (1 Cor. 1:8–9). "He who began a good work in you will bring it to completion at the day of Jesus Christ" (Phil. 1:6). "Who shall separate us from the love of Christ?" (Rom. 8:35).

Authentic Faith Is Not a Wager

We have now moved into the subject matter of the next chapter, namely, the new birth and its relationship to the work of God in giving us a well-grounded confidence in the Bible as the word of God. What we have seen here, with the help of Pascal's Wager, is that there is no authentic faith—no saving faith that honors God—based on a guess. Embracing the reality of God in Christ, revealed in Scripture, is not a wager. The only kind of trust that honors the one who is trusted is a well-grounded trust.

The experience of Tokishi Ichii illustrated that a person may come to that kind of well-grounded trust even if one lacks sufficient words to describe it. And the experience of Billy Graham illustrated that a genuine sight of the divine truth of Scripture is an embattled sight. In the end, the victory of the believer in that battle is the work of God, not man. That is the truth that lies behind the historic teaching about the "internal testimony of the Holy Spirit," which is what we turn to now.

The Spirit is the one who testifies, because the Spirit is the truth. . . . If we receive the testimony of men, the testimony of God is greater, for this is the testimony of God that he has borne concerning his Son. . . . And this is the testimony, that God gave us eternal life, and this life is in his Son.

1 JOHN 5:6, 9, 11

11

John Calvin and the
Internal Testimony
of the Holy Spirit

In the previous chapter, we saw that Billy Graham passed through a crisis of doubt about the truth of the Bible. His biographer, John Pollock, revealed that some of his questions were the same as the ones that have shaped the approach of this book. According to Pollock, Graham was asking,

> Must an intellectually honest man know everything about the Bible's origins before he could use it? Were theological professors the only ones qualified to speak of religion, or might a simple American, or an ignorant jungle villager, or even a child, lead another to Christ?[1]

I am profoundly thankful for rigorous biblical scholarship. I am thankful that all through the history of the church God has raised up brilliant academic servants of Christ who have turned over every stone in gathering rational and historical evidences that the Bible is a reliable record of God's acts in history and of God's interpretation of those acts. In my own pilgrimage, these scholars have been very helpful.

---

[1] John Pollock, *Billy Graham: The Authorized Biography* (Grand Rapids, MI: Zondervan, 1966), 52.

Sharing Billy Graham's Burden

But ever since my seminary days, I have carried the burden of the non-scholar. To use Billy Graham's words, how will the "simple American, or an ignorant jungle villager, or even a child" know that the Bible is the word of God? Or, when some part of the Bible is used to preach the gospel, how will the nonscholar discern that this is the very truth of God? I have argued that God is not honored, and the soul is not saved, by so-called faith that has no good evidence or solid ground. Saving faith in the gospel, and the "whole counsel of God" in the Scripture that supports and explains and applies it, is a well-grounded conviction, not a wager or a venture or a guess. It is a contradiction in terms to say, "I embrace and depend on and am enthralled by the glory of God that I guess is there." If we don't see it, we don't honor it. And if we see it, we know it is there.

So my question for fifty years has been this: How can average people, with no scholarly training and little time to invest in historical studies, know for sure that the Bible is the reliable word of God in all that it teaches?

Historically and biblically, one answer that has been given is: We can know the Bible is the word of God by "the internal testimony of the Spirit." What is that? I find it both enlightening and inspiring to follow the life and thought of John Calvin on this matter. This will lead us, then, into the crucial parts of Scripture that describe what I mean by the witness of the Spirit.

Calvin's Conversion[2]

Calvin was born July 10, 1509, in Noyon, France, when Martin Luther was twenty-five years old and had just begun to teach the Bible in Wittenberg. We know almost nothing of Calvin's early home life. When he was fourteen, his father sent him to study theology at the University of Paris, which at that time was untouched by the Reformation in Germany and steeped in Medieval theology. But five years later (when Calvin was nineteen), his father ran afoul of the church and told his son to leave theology and study law, which he did for the next three years at Orleans and Bourges.

---

[2] Some of what follows is adapted from John Piper, *John Calvin and His Passion for the Majesty of God* (Wheaton, IL: Crossway, 2009), 21–23.

His father died in May 1531, when Calvin was twenty-one. Calvin felt free then to turn from law to his first love, which had become the classics. Sometime during these years, he came into contact with the message and the spirit of the Reformation, and by 1533 something dramatic had happened in his life.

In November 1533, Nicholas Cop, a friend of Calvin, preached at the opening of the winter term at the University of Paris and was called to account by the Parliament for his Lutheran-like doctrines. He fled the city, and a general persecution broke out against what King Francis I called "the cursed Lutheran sect." Calvin was among those who escaped. The connection with Cop was so close that some suspect Calvin actually wrote the message that Cop delivered. So by 1533, Calvin had crossed the line. He was wholly devoted to Christ and to the cause of the Reformation.

What had happened? Calvin recounts, seven years later, how his conversion came about. He describes how he had been struggling to live out the Catholic faith with zeal,

> when, lo, a very different form of doctrine started up, not one which led us away from the Christian profession, but one which brought it back to its fountain . . . to its original purity. Offended by the novelty, I lent an unwilling ear, and at first, I confess, strenuously and passionately resisted . . . to confess that I had all my life long been in ignorance and error. . . .
>
> I at length perceived, as if light had broken in upon me, [a very key phrase, in view of what we will see], in what a sty of error I had wallowed, and how much pollution and impurity I had thereby contracted. Being exceedingly alarmed at the misery into which I had fallen . . . as in duty bound, [I] made it my first business to betake myself to thy way [O God], condemning my past life, not without groans and tears.[3]
>
> God, by a sudden conversion subdued and brought my mind to a teachable frame. . . . Having thus received some taste and knowledge of true godliness, I was immediately inflamed with [an] intense desire to make progress.[4]

[3] John Dillenberger, *John Calvin, Selections from His Writings* (Saarbrücken, Germany: Scholars Press, 1975), 114–15.
[4] Ibid., 26.

How did God bring Calvin to faith? Calvin mentions two key things. One was the inbreaking of light: "I at length perceived, *as if light had broken in upon me*, in what a sty of error I had wallowed." The other was the creation of humility: "God, by a sudden conversion subdued and brought my mind to a teachable frame." By this Spirit-wrought illumination and humiliation God created in Calvin a profound confidence in God and his word.

How this happened is extremely important, and we need to let Calvin himself describe it in his most famous work, the *Institutes*, especially book 1, chapters 7 and 8. Here he wrestles with how we can come to a saving knowledge of God through the Scriptures. His answer is the famous phrase "the internal testimony of the Holy Spirit."

The Internal Testimony of the Spirit, Not the Testimony of the Church

This was Calvin's answer to the claim of the Roman Catholic Church that ordinary Christians were dependent on the church to decide for them concerning the authority of the church:

> A most pernicious error widely prevails that Scripture has only so much weight as is conceded to it by the consent of the church. As if the eternal and inviolable truth of God depended upon the decision of men! . . . Yet, if this is so, what will happen to miserable consciences seeking firm assurance of eternal life if all promises of it consist in and depend solely upon the judgment of men?[5]

In the place of the church, Calvin saw the majesty of God's word itself, which carries its own self-authenticating brightness and sweetness:

> How can we be assured that this has sprung from God unless we have recourse to the decree of the church? It is as if someone asked: Whence will we learn to distinguish light from darkness, white from black, sweet from bitter? Indeed, Scripture exhibits fully as clear evidence of its own truth as white and black things do of their color, or sweet and bitter things do of their taste. (*Institutes*, I, vvii, 2)[6]

---

[5] John Calvin, *Institutes of the Christian Religion*, trans. F. L. Battles, ed. J. T. McNeill (Philadelphia: Westminster Press, 1960), 1.7.1.

[6] A hundred years after Calvin, the Reformed scholastic Francis Turretin echoed Calvin's insight: "Light is immediately most certainly known to us by its own brightness; food by its peculiar sweetness; an odor

Yet it would be a mistake to describe the self-authenticating power of the word itself without the role of the Holy Spirit:

> The testimony of the Spirit is more excellent than all reason. For as God alone is a fit witness of himself in his word, the Word will not find acceptance in men's hearts before it is sealed by the inward testimony of the Spirit. The same Spirit therefore who has spoken through the mouths of the prophets must penetrate into our hearts to persuade us that they faithfully proclaimed what had been divinely commanded . . . because until he illumines their minds, they ever waver among many doubts![7]

What about the role of historical augments and other efforts of apologetics to confirm the truth of God's word? Do they have a place? Calvin answers:

> Of themselves these [proofs] are not strong enough to provide a firm faith until our Heavenly Father, revealing his majesty there, lifts reverence for Scripture beyond the realm of controversy. Therefore Scripture will ultimately suffice for a saving knowledge of God only when its certainty is founded upon the inward persuasion of the Holy Spirit. Indeed, these human testimonies which exist to confirm it will not be vain if, as secondary aids to our feebleness, they follow that chief and highest testimony.[8]

We saw in the preceding chapter that the spiritual sight of the majesty of God in the word is an embattled sight. It can be clouded. In God's wisdom and providence, he has ordained that "human testimonies" and "secondary aids" are used from time to time to push these clouds aside and serve the sight of God's glory in Scripture. That, I think, is what Calvin meant.

---

by its peculiar fragrance without any additional testimony. Thus the Scripture, which is set forth to us in respect to the new man and spiritual senses, now under the symbol of a clear light (Ps. 119:105), then of the most sweetest food (Ps. 19:10; Is. 55:1, 2; Heb. 5:14) and again of the sweetest smelling savor (Cant. 1:3), may easily be distinguished of itself by the senses of the new man as soon as it is presented to them and makes itself known by its own light, sweetness and fragrance (*euōdia*); so that there is no need to seek elsewhere for proof that this is light, food or a sweet smelling savor." Francis Turretin, *Institutes of Elenctic Theology*, ed. James T. Dennison Jr., trans. George Musgrave Giger, vol. 1 (Phillipsburg, NJ: P&R, 1992–1997), 89–90.

[7] Calvin, *Institutes*, 1.7.4.

[8] Ibid., 1.8.13.

How Does It Work?

So for Calvin, "Scripture will ultimately suffice for a saving knowledge of God only when its certainty is founded upon the inward persuasion of the Holy Spirit." So two things came together for Calvin to give him a saving knowledge of God: Scripture itself and the inward persuasion of the Holy Spirit. Neither alone suffices to save.

But how does this actually work? What does the Spirit do? The answer is not that the Spirit gives us added revelation to what is in Scripture, but that he awakens us, as from the dead, to see and taste the divine reality of God in Scripture, which authenticates it as God's own word. He says, "Our Heavenly Father, revealing his majesty [in Scripture], lifts reverence for Scripture beyond the realm of controversy." There's the key for Calvin: the witness of God to Scripture is the immediate, unassailable, life-giving revelation to the mind of the majesty of God manifest in the Scriptures themselves.

Over and over again in his description of what happens in coming to faith, we see his references to the majesty of God revealed in Scripture and vindicating Scripture. So already in the dynamics of his conversion, the central passion of his life was being ignited.

We are almost at the bottom of this experience now. If we go just a bit deeper, we will see more clearly why his conversion resulted in such an "invincible constancy" in Calvin's lifelong allegiance to the majesty of God and the truth of God's word. Here are the words that will take us deeper:

> Therefore illumined by [the Spirit's] power, we believe neither by our own [note this!] nor by anyone else's judgment that Scripture is from God; but above human judgment we affirm with utter certainty (just as if we were gazing upon the majesty of God himself) that it has flowed to us from the very mouth of God by the ministry of men.[9]

This is almost baffling. Not by our own "judgment" do we believe that Scripture is from God—what does that mean? Must we not form judgments about such things? Yes, we must. But beneath a spiritually vital

---

[9] Ibid., 1.7.5.

judgment—a judgment that signifies that true eternal life is present—is a Spirit-given illumination of the majesty of God himself. The sight of God's glory precedes and grounds the formation of rational judgments about its truth.

When Calvin says, in the above quote, that our certainty about the Scriptures comes from a sight of God's glory, as if we were gazing upon the majesty of God himself, the words "as if" are simply meant to distinguish the "gazing upon the majesty of God himself" immediately, without Scripture as the prism in between, from gazing upon the majesty of God in Scripture. We really do see the majesty of God with the eyes of the heart (Eph. 1:18); but we see it in the Scripture, not *as if* in the unmediated presence of God.

The Witness Is Not Added to Scripture

Thus the internal testimony of the Spirit is not an *added* revelation to what we see in Scripture. It is not the voice of the Spirit saying to our mind, "What you are now looking at in the Bible is the majesty of God; so start seeing it." Seeing doesn't work that way. You can't see what you don't see. And if you see, you don't need to be told to see. The testimony of the Spirit, therefore, is not added information that is not given in the Scripture itself. John Frame points out that this is the common understanding of the testimony of the Spirit:

> Does the Spirit tell us what books belong in the canon? Does He help us decide between rival interpretations? Does He help us with scholarly questions about literary genre, variant readings, and the like? Not in the sense of whispering in our ears the solutions to these problems. On that question, the Reformers, the orthodox, and Berkouwer are agreed: Scripture never represents the Spirit's work as the giving of new information *about* the Bible.
>
> No one, for example, ought to claim that the Spirit has given him a list of canonical books. The actual list comes through historical and theological investigation of the contents of these books. Yet the Spirit has certainly played an important role in the history of the canon. By illumining and persuading the church concerning the true canonical books, He has helped the church to distinguish between

false and true. He has motivated the church to seek out reasons for what He was teaching them in their hearts.[10]

So even though the expression "testimony of the Spirit" might mislead us into thinking it means added information to what we have in the Scripture, Calvin meant that the work of the Spirit was to open the eyes of our hearts to see the majesty of God in the Scriptures. In this sense, then—though it sounds paradoxical—the "testimony of the Spirit" is the work of God to give us the sight of the *self*-testimony of Scripture. "Let this point therefore stand: that those whom the Holy Spirit has inwardly taught truly rest upon Scripture, and that Scripture indeed is self-authenticated."[11]

The Westminster Confession puts it like this:

> The . . . incomparable excellencies, and the entire perfection [of the Scriptures], are arguments whereby it does abundantly evidence it-self to be the Word of God: yet notwithstanding, our full persuasion and assurance of the infallible truth and divine authority thereof, is from the inward work of the Holy Spirit bearing witness by and with the Word in our hearts. (Article 1.5)

The testimony of the Spirit is "by and with" the word. I am not sure what "with" is supposed to add to "by" in this phrase. But the focus, as with Calvin, is not on added information, but on how the Spirit enables us to see what the Scripture itself reveals.

The Testimony Is That God Gave Us Life

As always, the crucial step now is to turn to the Scriptures themselves to see what (and if) they teach about the testimony of the Spirit. In my effort to test these things by the Scriptures, the key text has proved to be 1 John 5:6–11:

> The Spirit is the one who testifies, because the Spirit is the truth. . . .
> If we receive the testimony of men, the testimony of God is greater,
> for this is the testimony of God that he has borne concerning his

---

[10] Cited in *Hermeneutics, Authority, and Canon*, ed. D. A. Carson and John D. Woodbridge (Grand Rapids, MI: Zondervan, 1986), 229.
[11] Calvin, *Institutes*, 1.7.4.

Son. . . . And this is the testimony, that God gave us eternal life, and this life is in his Son.

John begins in verse 6, "The Spirit is the one who testifies." This is the "testimony of God" (v. 9). And it is "greater" than any human testimony (v. 9)—including, I think John would say in this context, as we saw above, the testimony of our own judgment. And what is that testimony of God? It is not merely a word delivered to our judgment for reflection, for then our conviction would rely on that reflection. What is it then?

Verse 11 is the key: "And this is the testimony, that God gave us eternal life." I take that to mean that God testifies to us of his reality and the reality of his Son and his word by giving us life from the dead so that we come alive to his majesty and see him for who he is in his word. In that instant of coming to life, we do not reason from premises to conclusions; we see light because we are awake—alive from the dead—and there is no prior human judgment that persuades us we are alive and awake and seeing. God's testimony to his word is *life from the dead that immediately sees.*

Calvin had described his conversion experience with God's word "as if light had broken in upon me, . . . [I] thus received some taste and knowledge of true godliness." What brought him to a well-grounded conviction of the majesty of God in his word was the immediate experience of light and taste. Before, he was dead to the brightness and sweetness of the majesty of God in his word. But God gave him life. And that life is God's testimony to his word.

We were dead and blind to spiritual majesty. Then the Spirit "testifies." He makes us alive. He gives us life. "This is the testimony, that God gave us eternal life" (v. 11). When Lazarus was raised from the dead by the call, or the "testimony," of Christ, he knew, without a process of reasoning, that he was alive. He heard the majestic word. That was the testimony. He was alive.

By the Testimony We See What Is Really There

Similarly, according to Paul, we were all blinded to the glory of Christ in the gospel. What needed to happen for us to see this self-authenticating "light of the gospel of the glory of Christ" (2 Cor. 4:4)? What needed to happen was the work of God described in verse 6: "For God, who said, 'Let light shine out of darkness,' has shone in our hearts to give the light of the knowledge of the glory of God in the face of Jesus Christ" (2 Cor. 4:6). God's word of creation—his word of testimony!—brought life and light to our souls. We saw—in the word—"the light of the knowledge of the glory of God."

That is the "internal testimony of the Spirit." The word has its own glory—the glory of God in Christ with all its traces. And that glory convinces us, when, by the work of the Spirit, we are granted to see what is really there. J. I. Packer confirms that for Calvin the self-attestation of Scripture and the internal testimony of the Holy Spirit work together:

> Calvin affirms Scripture to be self-authenticating through the inner witness of the Holy Spirit. What is this "inner witness"? Not a special quality of experience, nor a new, private revelation, nor an existential "decision," but a work of enlightenment whereby, through the medium of verbal testimony, the blind eyes of the spirit are opened, and divine realities come to be recognized and embraced for what they are. This recognition, Calvin says, is as immediate and unanalysable as the perceiving of a color, or a taste, by physical sense—an event about which no more can be said than that when appropriate stimuli were present it happened, and when it happened we know it had happened.[12]

The Spirit Gives Life

The apostle John has confirmed that Calvin was on the right track in teaching the necessity of the Holy Spirit in bringing us to a well-grounded confidence in the Bible as the word of God. This testimony is not an addition to what is revealed in the word itself. As we saw in chapter 9, God does not hang a lantern on the house of Scripture so that we will know it is his house. He does not certify his masterpiece with a distinguishing, Rembrandt-like signature. He does not give a voice from heaven: "This is my book, listen to it." That is not what the word

---

[12] J. I. Packer, "Calvin the Theologian," in *John Calvin, A Collection of Essays* (Grand Rapids, MI: Eerdmans, 1966), 166.

"testimony" or "witness" means in the phrase "testimony [or witness] of the Holy Spirit."

Rather, the testimony of the Spirit is the work of the Spirit to give us new life and, with this life, eyes to see what is really there in the self-attesting divine glories of Scripture—the meaning of Scripture. In other words, this chapter has confirmed what we saw already from the apostle Paul in 2 Corinthians 4:4–6 and 2 Timothy 2:24–26. The light of the knowledge of the glory of God in the face of Christ is visible in the word of God only to those into whose hearts the Creator of the universe says, "Let there be light." This is virtually the same as the life-giving witness of 1 John 5:11.

Knowing that our ability to see the self-authenticating glory of God in Scripture depends on the sovereign work of the Holy Spirit should make us humbly and joyfully prayerful that the Spirit would come with his life-giving, light-giving power and cause the truth and beauty of God's word to shine in our minds and hearts.

What has emerged over the course of our study is that the glory of God is of supreme importance in the process of seeing the Scriptures as the word of God. We turn now to focus on this central reality as the "scope of the whole"—the whole of God's *world* and the whole of God's *word*. The comparison between seeing God's glory in his world, and seeing it in his word will confirm and clarify the importance of that glory in convincing us of God as creator of the world and inspirer of the word.

PART 5

How Are the Christian Scriptures Confirmed by the Peculiar Glory of God?

"... the light of the gospel of the glory of Christ"

Men . . . by their unrighteousness suppress the truth. For what can be known about God is plain to them, because God has shown it to them. For his invisible attributes, namely, his eternal power and divine nature, have been clearly perceived, ever since the creation of the world, in the things that have been made. So they are without excuse. For although they knew God, they did not honor him as God or give thanks to him, but they became futile in their thinking, and their foolish hearts were darkened. Claiming to be wise, they became fools, and exchanged the glory of the immortal God for images.

ROMANS 1:18–23

12

The Glory of God
as the Scope of the
World and the Word

The whole Bible, properly understood, has this divine purpose: to communicate or display the glory of God. And this pervasive aim of the Scriptures to glorify God, in what they teach and how they teach it, reveals the handiwork of God in the writing of the Bible. That is the point of this chapter. But let me put it in the wider context of the book.

Here and in the following chapters (12–17), my aim is to flesh out the experience of seeing the self-authenticating glory of God in his word and clarify how it actually produces a well-grounded confidence in the complete truthfulness of Scripture. In a sense, these chapters will be an extension of chapter 9, where I gave four illustrations or analogies of what it is like to see the glory of God in Scripture. But those were only analogies; here we turn to the actual experience of seeing the glory.

The point of this chapter is to show why the glory of God is playing such a central role in confirming the truth of God's word. What we are going to see is that the glory of God in his *world* and in his *word* is the central reality of both. This is the unrivaled divine radiance that we are responsible to see, whether we are looking at God's works in nature or God's words in the Bible. By comparing the sight of glory in nature with the sight of glory in Scripture, we will see how central the glory of God is in the process of knowing God; we will see that the supernatural is known through the natural; and we will see that we are responsible to have this knowledge—both through the world and through the word.

Well-Grounded Knowledge of Truth for Everyone

But before we focus on this comparison of the world and the word, let's clarify further why we are taking this approach—to pursue well-grounded confidence in God's word through a sight of his glory.

In chapters 8–11, I argued that ordinary people with little or no education can have a well-grounded conviction in the truth of Scripture. There are strong, compelling, scholarly, historical arguments for the authenticity of the biblical writings.[1] But most people in the world, many of whom are preliterate, have little access to such arguments. They meet the gospel in some limited portion of God's word or in the oral transmission of the biblical message. My concern is to show that all of us, including these people, may come to a well-grounded confidence in the truth of the gospel, and as the knowledge of Scripture grows, that same confidence can extend to all of the Bible.

One reason for taking this approach, which I have not mentioned yet, is that the New Testament teaches that people are accountable to respond to the gospel with well-grounded belief when it is faithfully preached in accordance with God's word. Another reason, which we have touched on, is that the gospel has in it a self-authenticating light, or glory, that makes such well-grounded belief possible.

We Will Be Judged for What We Have Access to Knowing

The apostle Paul does not assume that people who never had an opportunity to hear the gospel are responsible for believing it. Rather, their judgment will come for other reasons. "All who have sinned without the law will also perish without the law, and all who have sinned under the law will be judged by the law" (Rom. 2:12). The reason, he

---

[1] See chap. 8n1.

says, that those without the law (or, by implication, without the gospel) will perish is that they will be judged only on the basis of the revelation they had access to but suppressed:

> The wrath of God is revealed from heaven against all ungodliness and unrighteousness of men, who by their unrighteousness suppress the truth. For what can be known about God is plain to them, because God has shown it to them. . . . So they are without excuse. For although they knew God, they did not honor him as God or give thanks to him. (Rom. 1:18–21)

But Paul does assume that if people hear a true rendering of the word of Christ, they are responsible to believe it and are liable to judgment for not believing it. That conviction is what lies behind these words in Romans 10:

> "Everyone who calls on the name of the Lord will be saved." How then will they call on him in whom they have not believed? And how are they to believe in him of whom they have never heard? And how are they to hear without someone preaching? . . . So faith comes from hearing, and hearing through the word of Christ. (vv. 13–17)

So when such preaching of the word of Christ is rejected, Paul warns us that rejecting the gospel means rejecting eternal life: "It was necessary that the word of God be spoken first to you. Since you thrust it aside and judge yourselves unworthy of eternal life, behold, we are turning to the Gentiles" (Acts 13:46). He warns that refusing the truth of the gospel will expose a person to a final deception and judgment "because they refused to love the truth and so be saved" and because they "did not believe the truth but had pleasure in unrighteousness" (2 Thess. 2:10, 12).

On the other hand, Paul rejoices and thanks God when the faithful preaching of the gospel leads people to believe. "We thank God constantly for this, that when you received the word of God, which you heard from us, you accepted it not as the word of men but as what it really is, the word of God" (1 Thess. 2:13). So I conclude from the Scriptures that people are accountable to believe the gospel when it is faithfully preached in accordance with God's word.

This Well-Grounded Faith Is Possible through the Gospel

Second, I conclude that the gospel has in it a self-authenticating light, or glory, that makes such well-grounded belief possible. We saw this, most clearly where Paul speaks of "the light of the gospel of the glory of Christ" and "the light of the knowledge of the glory of God in the face of Jesus Christ" (2 Cor. 4:4–6). In other words, Paul teaches that the gospel—a faithful rendering of the "word of Christ" (Rom. 10:17) that reveals the person and work of Christ in the way he saves sinners—has in it a "glory" that can be seen by the eyes of the heart (Eph. 1:17; 2 Cor. 4:6). Thus we have agreed with Jonathan Edwards when he says about this passage,

> Nothing can be more evident, than that a saving belief of the gospel is here spoken of, by the Apostle, as arising from the mind's being enlightened to behold the divine glory of the things it exhibits. . . .
>
> Unless men may come to a reasonable solid persuasion and conviction of the truth of the gospel, by the internal evidences of it, in the way that has been spoken, viz. by a sight of its glory; 'tis impossible that those who are illiterate, and unacquainted with history, should have any thorough and effectual conviction of it at all.[2]

That is what drives the approach we are taking. First, people must hear the gospel to be saved and are responsible to believe the truth when they hear it. Second, the gospel has in it a self-authenticating light, or glory, that makes such well-grounded belief possible. And as a believer's knowledge of the Scripture grows, that same divine glory confirms all of it.

Now we turn to the main burden of this chapter—a comparison between seeing God's glory through his world and seeing it through his word.

What Can Be Known about God Is Plain to Them

First, consider with me the way God expects human beings to see his glory in the natural world. This will shed significant light on how he expects us to see his glory in his written word. The key passage of

---

[2] Jonathan Edwards, *A Treatise Concerning Religious Affections*, vol. 2, *The Works of Jonathan Edwards*, ed. John Smith (New Haven, CT: Yale University Press, 1957), 299, 303.

Scripture is Romans 1:19–21, where Paul is speaking of human beings in general everywhere in the world:

> What can be known about God is *plain to them*, because God has shown it to them. For his invisible attributes, namely, his eternal power and divine nature, have been *clearly perceived*, ever since the creation of the world, in the things that have been made. So they are without excuse. For although *they knew God*, they did not honor him as God or give thanks to him, but they became futile in their thinking, and their foolish hearts were darkened.

This passage reveals how God makes himself knowable and holds all human beings accountable to know him, glorify him, and thank him. Notice the phrase "invisible attributes" (literally "invisibles" or "invisible things") in verse 20. This is what God is revealing. He is making the "invisible" knowable. He is making himself—his glory and beneficence (which call for glorification and thanks)—knowable.

What specifically is he making knowable? He mentions two "invisibles": "his eternal power and divine nature [his Godness; his deity]" (v. 20). We know there are other invisible attributes God reveals in the natural world, such as his generous goodness to undeserving people (Acts 14:16–17), his wisdom (Ps. 104:24), and his splendor and majesty (Ps. 104:1). So God expects human beings to know and respond worshipfully to the invisible things he has revealed.

How are they revealed? Paul's answer is remarkably forceful. They are "clearly perceived . . . in the things that have been made [τοῖς ποιήμασιν νοούμενα καθορᾶται]." Literally: "They are clearly seen, being understood, in the things that are made." There are three steps here: (1) God made the universe (τοῖς ποιήμασιν); (2) our minds grasp something of God by the things made (τοῖς ποιήμασιν νοούμενα); (3) by that mental grasp, we see clearly the unseen (καθορᾶται). Note carefully: the objects that are seen are not the things that are made (τοῖς ποιήμασιν). The dative case means that we see clearly "*by* the things that are made." So Paul is saying that (1) *by* the created things visible to the physical eye (τοῖς ποιήμασιν), and (2) *by* the mental grasp of these things as we think about them (νοούμενα), we "clearly perceive" or "see" the invisible attributes of God's power and deity.

Admit It or Not, the Glory of God Is Plain

If someone says, "Well, I don't see them," Paul answers, "Yes, you do." He says this twice. Verse 19: "What can be known about God is *plain to them* [τὸ γνωστὸν τοῦ θεοῦ φανερόν ἐστιν ἐν αὐτοῖς]." And verse 21: "Although *they knew* God, they did not honor him as God [γνόντες τὸν θεὸν οὐχ ὡς θεὸν ἐδόξασαν]." So even if we protest that we do not see or know God from the natural world, Paul disagrees and says we do. We *all* do. And what we may call "not knowing," Paul calls *suppressing* the known. People "by their unrighteousness suppress the truth" (Rom. 1:18).

The things that are known about God from nature are things that make us accountable to "honor him as God [and] give thanks" (v. 21). So this must include his existence, his glorious majesty, and his generosity to give us "life and breath and everything" (Acts 17:25).

"The heavens declare the glory of God" (Ps. 19:1). This is why God made them—to put his majestic glory on display. The Hubble Space Telescope sends back infrared images of faint galaxies perhaps twelve billion light-years away (twelve billion times six trillion miles). Even within our Milky Way, there are stars so great as to defy description, like Eta Carinae, which is five million times brighter than our sun.

If you stumble over this vastness, thinking that it seems disproportionately large compared to the infinitesimally small man and his habitation, remember that the meaning of this magnitude is not mainly about us. It's about God. "The heavens declare the glory of *God*." The reason for "wasting" so much space on a universe to house a speck of humanity is to make a point about our Maker, not us. "Lift up your eyes on high and see: who created these? He who brings out their host by number, calling them all by name, by the greatness of his might, and because he is strong in power not one is missing" (Isa. 40:26).

God intends for the created world to communicate his majesty. As the poet Gerard Manley Hopkins puts it in his most famous poem,

> The world is charged with the grandeur of God.
> 　It will flame out, like shining from shook foil. . . .
> 　There lives the dearest freshness deep down things;
> And though the last lights off the black West went

Oh, morning, at the brown brink eastward, springs—
Because the Holy Ghost over the bent
World broods with warm breast and with ah! bright wings.

The words "dearest freshness deep down things" points to the other fact, besides revealing the majesty of God, that the world reveals the beneficence of God. God expects us not only to glorify him, but to thank him (Rom. 1:21). Whatever sustains and pleases us comes ultimately from his hand (even if we have made a God-replacing idol of it, Ps. 36:7–9).

But the effect of sin is to make us resist glorifying and thanking God (v. 21). Deep down in our souls, there is a rebellion against the majesty of God and his all-sufficiency. We do not like to be utterly subject to his power or utterly dependent on his mercy. Deep down we also perceive that our resistance to God is so damning that we cannot live with the consciousness of it. The result is that we "suppress the truth" (v. 18) and become futile in our thinking and dark in our hearts (v. 21). We either deny the existence of God, or distort his majesty to make him tolerable.

What Do I Know from the Natural World?

What Paul teaches in Romans 1:18–23 is profoundly relevant to how we know the truth of the Scriptures. Let me take you with me on the path that I have walked in my own experience of the world and the word.

When I come to Romans 1, I am confronted with the stunning truths that what can be known about God is plain to John Piper, and that God has manifested himself to John Piper (v. 19); and that John Piper has clearly perceived, by the workings of his mind and by the things that are made, the power and deity of God (v. 20); and that therefore, at the root of his being, John Piper knows God (v. 21) but has failed to glorify God and thank him in anything like the measure God deserves.

Confronted with these staggering truths about myself, I have tried to honestly take stock of what I know of God from the natural world. Here is my best effort to discern the knowledge of God in my own mind and heart that is an immediate effect of my consciousness in the world as a human being.

I do not mean I would have seen all this without the special grace of new birth and the transformation of the mind that comes by the Holy Spirit. But neither do I mean that I see these things because the Bible tells me they are there—which would, of course, settle the matter. The things I see involve reasoning about what I have seen, not just sheer observation. I do not know how much of these things I would see without the enabling grace of the Spirit. My point is that these things are really there to see in nature, not just in the Bible. And I suspect that our Creator will find fault with the world for not seeing even more than this.

- God exists. This is the most basic meaning of the world, and it is known to all.

- God is the single originator of all spiritual and material reality that is not God, for two absolute originators of all things is a contradiction.

- God is totally self-sufficient with no dependence on anything outside himself to be all that he is, for that is implied in being the Creator of absolutely everything.

- God is without beginning or ending or progress from worse to better, and therefore absolute and perfect, for God cannot be improved by what is absolutely dependent on him for its being and excellence.

- God is the one on whom I am dependent moment by moment for all things, none of which I deserve, and who is therefore beneficent. This follows from God's absoluteness as the Creator and sustainer of all things, together with the countless riches around me, and my own guilty conscience, which comes from my failing to live up to my own innate standards.

- God is personal and confronts me as the person who gave me a personhood that is not merely physical. For the existence of my own personhood and my innate sense of its moral significance can only be explained by a personal God.

- God accounts for the intelligent design manifest in the macro (galaxies) and micro (molecules and cells) universe—a fact as manifest as the automobile testifying to the existence of man.

- God knows all. For he made and sustains all.

- God deserves to be reverenced and admired and thanked and looked to for guidance and help. This follows from my innate sense of moral judgment in view of everything seen so far.

- God sees me as guilty for failing to give him the glory and thanks he deserves, and he thus gives ultimate explanation to the universal, bad conscience in the world. This follows from the perfect personal dimension in God and the defective moral dimension in me, which my conscience reveals with unwavering constancy.

- God might save me from my guilt but would need to do it in a way that overcomes my evil impulse to resist him and would have to make a way for his glory to be sustained, while not punishing me for treason. For it is manifested that I have belittled his glory, and I cannot pay a debt as large as I owe, since I have offended infinite goodness.

Again, the point here is not that anyone sees all this without the special help of God's Spirit. The point is: it is really there to see, and we are responsible to see it.

Stunning, Self-Evident Things That I Cannot Not Know

All of this amounts to the deep and inescapable realization that God made the world to communicate his glory—that is, the greatness and beauty of his manifold perfections. And he made me to experience his glory, and through this experience to glorify and thank him. I am created to *magnify* the glory of God—not the way a *microscope* magnifies (making small things look bigger than they are), but the way a *telescope* magnifies (making things that appear small to the world look as gigantic as they really are). And I know intuitively that thanking God is a way of glorifying him. God's glorious beneficence is magnified in my humble, dependent, thankful witness to his goodness to me. This is confirmed in Psalm 50:23: "The one who offers thanksgiving as his sacrifice glorifies me."

It is also intuitively obvious to me that if God's self-revelation obliges me to *thank* him, then the revelation of God's glory is for my good, that is, for my enjoyment. This is what I sense intuitively. Paul expects us to discern this in the things that are made. And this is what I do discern: if there rises in my heart a profound indebtedness to God for the revelation of his glory, then I am a witness to the truth that this revelation is good for me.

It is also self-evident to me that a gratitude to God that finds his gifts pleasing but his person displeasing is not a gratitude that glorifies him. Therefore, it is evident that in creation the goodness of God's gifts are meant to give us a taste of the goodness of God himself. In this way, our thankfulness is a form of glorifying *him*, not just his gifts.

Therefore, I also know intuitively that if I find God displeasing, I do not glorify him. Or to put it another way, if I fail to find God supremely satisfying to my soul, then I do not glorify him as I ought. Or to put it positively, if I do find God to be my supreme satisfaction, by that very satisfaction God is put on display as the all-satisfying, all-glorious one. Therefore, I know intuitively that the revelation of his glory is for my ultimate joy, and that by finding this joy in him, he will be glorified. This knowledge is given in the way I and the world have been created. And it is confirmed in Psalm 19:1–5:

> The heavens declare the glory of God,
>> and the sky above proclaims his handiwork. . . .
> In them he has set a tent for the sun,
>> which comes out like a bridegroom leaving his chamber,
> and, like a strong man, runs its course with joy.

In this way, the created universe declares the glory of God. That is, the sun rises in its glorious, blazing supremacy over the day. And what does that signify about the glory of God? It is "like a strong man, [who] runs its course *with joy*." The glory of the sun is meant to be experienced as the revelation of joy in God whose glory it is.

As best I know my own heart and mind, these things are known by me from the very fact that the natural world exists and from the fact that I exist as a conscious, knowing, valuing person in such a world.

"By the Scope of the Whole"

Now what is the connection between, on the one hand, knowing God through nature in this way and, on the other hand, the self-authenticating nature of the Holy Scriptures? The Westminster Larger Catechism provides the link—and explains why the word "scope" is in the title of this chapter. Question 4 of this historic catechism, which was completed in 1647, reads, "How doth it appear that the Scriptures are the word of God?" In other words, how can we know that the Bible is God's word and, therefore, true? Part of the answer is crucial to our line of thinking in this chapter—and this book! "Answer: The Scriptures manifest themselves to be the word of God, by . . . the scope of the whole, *which is to give all glory to God.*"[3]

What does that mean? Turning the phrases around, it says, "The aim or the purpose of the Scriptures, namely, to give all glory to God, is the scope of the whole Bible." I take the phrase "scope of the whole" to mean "all that the Bible takes into view in the totality of its writings." In other words, the whole Bible, properly understood, has this divine purpose—to communicate or display the glory of God.

Now you can see immediately how this relates to the purpose of the natural world in Romans 1:18–23. If the catechism is right, the whole of God's *word* is declaring the glory of God. And that, Paul says, is what the whole of God's *world* is doing also: "The heavens declare the glory of God" (Ps. 19:1). What this means, then, is that if God holds us accountable to see his glory by means of the created world, how much more will he hold us accountable to see his glory by means of his inspired word.

This is true, if indeed the pervasive, God-given design of Scripture is to reveal God's glory. The men who wrote the Westminster Larger Catechism believed that was indeed the design of the whole Bible. Jonathan

---

[3] Emphasis added. The whole answer reads: "The Scriptures manifest themselves to be the word of God, by their majesty and purity; by the consent of all the parts, and the scope of the whole, which is to give all glory to God; by their light and power to convince and convert sinners, to comfort and build up believers unto salvation. But the Spirit of God, bearing witness by and with the Scriptures in the heart of man, is alone able fully to persuade it that they are the very word of God."

Edwards put it like this, in the book that has shaped my thinking more than any other book outside the Bible, the *End for Which God Created the World*:

> All that is ever spoken of in the Scripture as an ultimate end of God's works is included in that one phrase, *the glory of God*. . . . The refulgence shines upon and into the creature, and is reflected back to the luminary. The beams of glory come from God, and are something of God and are refunded back again to their original. So that the whole is *of* God, and *in* God, and *to* God, and God is the beginning, middle and end in this affair.[4]

In other words, the Scripture bears uniform and pervasive witness to the truth that everything that happens is ultimately for the glory of God. This is God's design for his *world*, and this is God's design for his *word*. And because it is God's design for the world and the word, the glory of God is central in how ordinary people come to know God through the world and through the word.

We Were Made to Know God's Glory through the World and the Word

Return for a moment to Romans 1. Paul said that all human beings, deep down in their souls, "know God" (v. 21). "What can be known about God is plain to them" (v. 19). Specifically, Paul says, all humans know the *glory* of God, because that is the truth we suppress and the treasure we exchange. "They . . . exchanged the *glory* of the immortal God for images" (v. 23).

I do not take Paul to mean that all humans have a spiritual, saving knowledge of God's glory, since he says we are under God's wrath and without excuse (vv. 18–21). Rather, I take him to mean that because we are all created in God's image, with the original destiny of imaging forth God's glory, there are traces of this design in our souls. Sin has dethroned the glory of God as our supreme treasure and pleasure, but it has not destroyed the God-shaped template that this dethronement left behind.

We were made for the glory of God. Our minds are designed to

---

[4] Jonathan Edwards, *The Dissertation Concerning the End for Which God Created the World*, vol. 8, *The Works of Jonathan Edwards*, ed. Paul Ramsey (New Haven, CT: Yale University Press, 1989), 526, 531.

know the glory of God, and our hearts are designed to *love* the glory of God. The deepest longing of the human soul is to know and enjoy the glory of God. We were made for this. "Bring my sons from afar and my daughters from the ends of the earth . . . whom I have created *for my glory*"—says the Lord (Isa. 43:6–7). To see it, to savor it, and to show it—that is why we exist.

The untracked, unimaginable stretches of the created universe are a parable about the inexhaustible riches of the glory of God (Rom. 9:23). The physical eye is meant to say to the spiritual eye, "Not this, but the Maker of this, is the desire of your soul." Paul says, "We rejoice in hope of the glory of God" (Rom. 5:2). Or, even more precisely, he says that we were "prepared beforehand for glory" (Rom. 9:23). This is why we were created—that he might "make known the riches of his glory for vessels of mercy" (Rom. 9:23).

This is what Paul meant when he said that every human being knows God (Rom. 1:21). There is in every human heart a true witness to the reality of the glory of God in the world and in the word. It is the witness of a residual template (as a jigsaw puzzle piece is cut so that only one special piece fits). The template in our heart is waiting for the perfect fit of its divine counterpart—the glory of God. This is why seeing the glory of God is the healing of our disordered lives. "We all, with unveiled face, *beholding the glory of the Lord, are being changed* into his likeness from one degree of glory to another" (2 Cor. 3:18). There is in every soul a witness, however obscured, that we were made for the glory of God.

This witness is of such a nature, therefore, that when the glory of God breaks through our blindness, which is caused by sin (1 John 2:11), and compounded by Satan (2 Cor. 4:4), the knowledge of this glory is immediate, compelling, and justified. It is a well-grounded knowledge. It sees and knows with a well-grounded certainty that this world is God's world and this Scripture is God's word.

The Difference between Knowing God by the World and by the Word

There is a difference in the way God reveals his glory in the creation of nature and the way he reveals his glory in the inspiration of Scripture.

There is a difference between the way the sun reveals the glory of God and the way the book of Romans reveals the glory of God. In Romans, what reveals the glory of God is the *meaning* of the writing, not the material parchment and ink and letters. God's aim is not that anyone would look at Paul's original letter and say, "What a glorious and good God must lie behind such penmanship!" Rather, the words that God guided Paul to write are revelatory because these are the chosen instruments of God's *meaning*. The sun, on the other hand, is not like the parchment and ink and letters. Only they have such blazing magnitude and beauty that they reveal the glory of God directly, and that *is* its meaning. God *does* expect us to look at the "solar writing" and say, "What a glorious and good God writes with such fire!"

God's World and Word Reveal His Glory

In spite of the differences between God's revelation in nature and his revelation in Scripture, the comparison is important and illuminating. That is what this chapter has been about—the way God's world and God's word both reveal the glory of God. There are three reasons why the comparison is illuminating.

First, the comparison shows that the "scope of the whole" in both cases—the natural world and the inspired word—is the glory of God. The Larger Catechism says, "The Scriptures manifest themselves to be the word of God, by . . . the scope of the whole, which is to give all glory to God." This points to the link between Scripture and nature. Both carry the same self-authenticating message: All things exist for the glory of God. This makes the world and the word self-authenticating (as *God's* world and *God's* word), because it corresponds to the deep-seated knowledge of our souls (Rom. 1:21).

Second, the comparison shows that the glory of God is meant to be seen by means of things that are *not* his glory. A cloud, a star, a galaxy are not the glory of God. God manifested his glory in them (Rom. 1:19). We see the glory of God "*by* the things that are made" (Rom. 1:20 NKJV). This is possible because we ourselves know God (Rom. 1:19, 21). We have suppressed this knowledge. But deeper than all our suppressing is a primordial template designed to fit perfectly with the glory of God. We know from this template—this design—that we were made to see and savor the glory of God. In sin we have exchanged that glory for images. But they do not fit the template. They are bogus counterparts. Therefore, we have a constant witness in the world and in our own souls that we were made to worship God for his glory.

Similarly (though not in precisely the same way) the glory of God shines through the Scriptures that he inspired. In this way, God confirms that these writings are his. Yet these writings are not the glory of God, and even their meaning is not identical with the glory of God. We are meant to see the glory of God *by means of* the writing and its meaning. Neither the natural world nor the inspired word are identical with the glory of God, but they were designed by God to reveal his glory.

Third, we are all accountable, therefore, to see the glory of God in the world and in the word. There is sufficient glory in the world and the word, and there is sufficient knowledge in our souls, to make us responsible to see the glory of God. And we are, therefore, accountable to glorify and thank God in response to his creation and to trust God in response to his word. The creation of incomparable galaxies obliges us to worship his power. The creation of verbal meaning obliges us to believe its truth.

In the following chapters, we turn to the peculiar essence of the self-authenticating glory of God revealed in this meaning of Scripture. My hope is to show that it is not only glory in general that authenticates the Scripture but also the particular way God reveals his glory that makes his word supremely compelling.

Thus says the One who is high and lifted up,
   who inhabits eternity, whose name is Holy:
"I dwell in the high and holy place,
      and also with him who is of a contrite
         and lowly spirit,
to revive the spirit of the lowly,
      and to revive the heart of the contrite."

ISAIAH 57:15

13

Majesty in Meekness:
The Peculiar Glory in Jesus Christ

In the preceding chapter, we saw that the answer of the Westminster Larger Catechism touched on something profound. When asked, "How doth it appear that the Scriptures are the word of God?" it answers, "The Scriptures manifest themselves to be the word of God, by . . . *the scope of the whole, which is to give all glory to God.*" Among all the evidences for the divine origin of Scripture that the catechism mentions,[1] this part of the answer is crucial in the argument we are pursuing. The catechism is saying, as we saw, that the whole Bible, properly understood, has this divine purpose—to communicate or display the glory of God. And this pervasive aim of the Scriptures to glorify God, in what they teach and how they teach it, reveals the handiwork of God in the writing of the Bible.

The Self-Attesting Scripture, Gospel, and Universe
We know we are onto something profound here, not only because this links the self-attestation of Scripture with the self-attestation of the whole creation (Rom. 1:18–21, the theme of chapter 12), but also because it links the self-attestation of Scripture with the self-attestation

---
[1] See chap. 12n3 for the catechism's whole answer.

of the gospel. This is most clearly seen in 2 Corinthians 4:4–6 (which we unfolded in chapter 8). Paul refers to "the light of the *gospel* of the *glory* of Christ, who is the image of God." In other words, the gospel is summed up as the gospel of the *glory of Christ*. And this glory is said to stream out from the gospel with a *light*. In verse 4, "the god of this world" (Satan) blinds people from seeing that light. In verse 6, God reverses that blindness: He "gives the *light* of the knowledge of the glory of God in the face of Jesus Christ."

In other words, the way the gospel wins the well-grounded confidence of its hearers is by shining into the heart with "the light of the gospel of the *glory of Christ*." Don't miss how amazing this is. The gospel is a verbal narration of the events of Christ's death and resurrection and the meaning of those events (1 Cor. 15:1–4). And this verbal narration is the prism through which God causes spiritual glory to shine into the human heart. In this way, divine glory becomes the self-attesting power of the gospel to win our heart's embrace.

So when the catechism says that "the Scriptures manifest themselves to be the word of God by the scope of the whole, which is to give all glory to God," it is linking the self-attestation of Scripture to the self-attestation of the gospel (2 Cor. 4:4–6) and the self-attestation of the whole created world (Rom. 1:18–21). One of the most important implications is to show that this way of thinking about a well-grounded confidence in the Bible is not only biblical but is at the heart of the Bible—the pervasive exaltation of the glory of God, reaching its apex in the person and work of Jesus Christ.

That God Is Glorious and How God Is Glorious

One question remaining from the last chapter is whether the Larger Catechism is actually correct in saying that the "scope of the whole" of Scripture is in fact "to give all glory to God." So what I aim to do in this chapter is show that the answer to that question is yes. In doing so, we find that there are two ways that the Bible aims to give all the glory to God. One is that the Bible says repeatedly, from beginning to end, that God does all that he does for his own glory and that we should do the same. The other is that the Bible describes what it is about God's ways that actually make them glorious. In other words, what we find is that the Bible "gives all glory to God" not only by showing *that* God does all for his glory but also *how*—both *that* God is glorious and the *way* he is glorious in all he does.

That the Scriptures do both of these (that and how) is a great and merciful service to us. God is going to great lengths, in his self-revelation, to help us see the self-authenticating display of his glory. It's as though, time after time, he pauses in the very act of shining, and tells us why this is, in fact, a self-evident and compelling shining. It's as though a husband should be standing at the locked door of his home, calling out to his wife to open, and yet she says, "How can I know it's you?" And instead of turning away in anger because she doesn't recognize his voice, he reminds her, through the door, of the distinguishing traits of his own voice, until she says, "Oh, yes, now I hear it," and opens the door. God is very patient with our slowness to hear his voice. And we should be deeply thankful. For Jesus said, "My sheep hear my voice, and I know them, and they follow me" (John 10:27).

God Displays His Glory from Beginning to End

First, we focus briefly on the fact that the Bible, from beginning to end, declares and shows that God does everything for his glory. I say we will do this *briefly*, even though it is a vast theme in Scripture. The reason is that I (and others) have devoted so much space in other books to showing that this is so.[2] Let a summary of the history of redemption suffice here. From eternity past to eternity future, God's actions are described as self-exalting. God is aiming in all he does to communicate his glory. Take six critical points in redemptive history.

Predestination

> He predestined us for adoption as sons through Jesus Christ, according to the purpose of his will, *to the praise of his glorious grace.* (Eph. 1:5–6)

---

[2] This theme is woven throughout John Piper, *The Pleasures of God: Meditations on God's Delight in Being God* (Colorado Springs: Multnomah, 2012), esp. chaps. 2 and 4. Also John Piper, *Let the Nations Be Glad!: The Supremacy of God in Missions* (Grand Rapids, MI: Baker Academic, 2010), esp. pp. 40–46. Two others who have shown this theme extensively are Jonathan Edwards in his *The End for Which God Created the World*, which I published alongside my appreciation of it in John Piper, *God's Passion for His Glory* (Wheaton, IL: Crossway, 1998); and James M. Hamilton, *God's Glory in Salvation through Judgment: A Biblical Theology* (Wheaton, IL: Crossway, 2010). A concise list of texts highlighting this theme is found at Desiring God: http://www.desiringgod.org/articles/biblical-texts-to-show-gods-zeal-for-his-own-glory.

Creation

> Bring my sons from afar
> > and my daughters from the end of the earth,
> everyone who is called by my name,
> > whom *I created for my glory*,
> > whom I formed and made. (Isa. 43:6–7)

Incarnation

> Christ became a servant to the circumcised to show God's truthfulness, . . . and in order *that the Gentiles might glorify God for his mercy.* (Rom. 15:8–9)

Propitiation

> God put [Christ] forward as a propitiation by his blood, to be received by faith. *This was to show God's righteousness*, because in his divine forbearance he had passed over former sins. *It was to show his righteousness* at the present time, so that he might be just and the justifier of the one who has faith in Jesus. (Rom. 3:25–26)

Sanctification

> It is my prayer that your love may abound more and more, with knowledge and all discernment, so that you may approve what is excellent, and so be pure and blameless for the day of Christ, filled with the fruit of righteousness that comes through Jesus Christ, *to the glory and praise of God.* (Phil. 1:9–11)

Consummation

> They will suffer the punishment of eternal destruction, away from the presence of the Lord and from the glory of his might, when he comes on that day *to be glorified in his saints, and to be marveled at among all who have believed.* (2 Thess. 1:9–10)

From predestination in eternity past to consummation at the end of history, God's ultimate aim in all his works has been the praise of his glory. This summary is a small taste of the fruit that grows everywhere in the Bible. The "scope of the whole" is indeed to give all glory to God. The catechism is correct. Indeed, to be more precise, the scope of

Scripture is to show that God *himself* upholds and displays his glory, and that he calls us to join him by making this the aim of our lives down to its smallest details. "Whether you eat or drink, or whatever you do, do all to the glory of God" (1 Cor. 10:31).

Is Divine Self-Exaltation Glorious?

It is a great sadness that this theme of God's self-exaltation—his doing all things to communicate his own glory—has driven many people away from the Scriptures.

- Oprah Winfrey walked away from orthodox Christianity when she was about twenty-seven years old because of the biblical teaching that God is jealous—he demands that he and no one else get our highest allegiance and affection. It didn't sound loving to her.[3]

- Brad Pitt turned away from his boyhood faith, he says, because God says, "You have to say that I'm the best. . . . It seemed to be about ego."[4]

- Erik Reece, professor and the writer of *An American Gospel*, rejected the Jesus of the Gospels because only an egomaniac would demand that we love him more than we love our parents and children.[5]

- Michael Prowse, a columnist for the *London Financial Times*, turned away because only "tyrants, puffed up with pride, crave adulation."[6]

People see God's exaltation and communication of his own glory as a problem. They don't like it. They think such self-exaltation is immoral and loveless, even pathological. But there is another way to look at it.

Suppose your heart is a template made for its counterpart, the glory of God (see chapter 12). Suppose you were created to know and love and be satisfied by the majesty and beauty of God. Suppose the glory of

---

[3] https://www.youtube.com/watch?v=n2SrZJlPnjk; accessed March 10, 2015.
[4] http://parade.com/50120/parade/interview-with-brad-pitt/; accessed March 10, 2015.
[5] http://www.npr.org/templates/story/story.php?storyId=104067081; accessed March 10, 2015.
[6] Michael Prowse, "God the Lover, Not God the Father, Offers Hope," *London Financial Times*, March 30, 2002.

God was the most beautiful reality in the universe to you and therefore the most satisfying to your soul. Suppose you hungered and thirsted for the presence of the greatness of God more than for anything in the world. And suppose this God, in spite of all your sin, had made a way for the glory of his holiness and righteousness to be maintained and exalted, while still giving himself in friendship to you for your enjoyment forever.

If that were true, then God's unwavering commitment to uphold and display his glory would not be a mark of selfish pride but a mark of self-giving love. He would be upholding and communicating the very thing for which your soul longs. This would not be the pattern of an old woman wanting compliments, or an egomaniac, or a needy tyrant, or an insecure, jealous lover. Rather, it would be the pattern of the true and living and gracious God. You would see that there is no other God like this and no other book like the Bible, which presents him so faithfully. You would see a self-authenticating divine glory. No other person, no other god, no other book bears these marks of holy, divine self-exaltation echoing in the everlasting, God-centered joy of his people.

He Is Glorious as Many Ways as the Diamond Has Facets

We have already made the turn, with those last two paragraphs, from the truth that the Bible shows *that* God does all for his glory to the even more remarkable truth that the Bible shows *how* God acts for this glory.

When we think about *how* the glory of God is glorious, or why one particular *way* of revealing the glory of God is glorious, we need to acknowledge that we are way over our heads. And that is a good thing. If I could see, let alone describe, all the ways God makes his glory appear glorious to different people and to different peoples or cultures, I would indeed be God. Remember that one of my driving concerns is that God intends that all people, no matter how educated or primitive, be able to have a well-grounded confidence in the truth of God's word, when it is presented to them accurately and sufficiently. What this means is that for millions of individuals and for thousands of cultures, God has designed a way, in the inspired Scriptures, for the light of the glory of Christ to be seen and known with profound certainty.

Therefore, it would be presumptuous of me to suppose I could point out all the ways the Scriptures can do this. Think of the Scriptures as a diamond that God has cut with innumerable facets—innumerable, perfectly reflecting surfaces. As the Scriptures are read by countless persons and in thousands of cultures, that diamond is turned in ways that suddenly catch and release a beam of God's self-authenticating glory that I have never noticed. For example, a certain culture may have insight into the divine purpose of the biblical genealogies that reveals a dimension of his glory that I, in my individualistic culture, may have been blind to.[7] This is happening every day around the world. Indeed, it happens in my life over and over again, as some new facet of the diamond sends a new ray of God's glory into the retina of the eyes of my heart.

So the aim of what we are turning to now, in this and the following chapters, is not to describe all the ways that God makes his glory appear glorious to our minds and hearts, but to show some examples—some facets of the diamond—that I think are close to the heart of what makes the glory of God so compelling among all the competing religious claims of the world.

The Heart of His Glory: Majesty in Meekness

Close to the heart of what makes the glory of God glorious is the way his majesty and his meekness combine. Or another way to put it would be that God is more glorious because he is a paradoxical juxtaposition of seemingly opposite traits rather than being a manifestation of only majestic strengths. And the unifying mark of these paradoxical juxtapositions is that the majestic heights of God are glorified especially through the way they serve or stoop in lowliness to save the weak. In other words, what is distinctly stunning—indeed self-authenticating—about the Christian God (and his Scriptures) is that he wins the praise of his majesty not by amassing slave labor to serve him but by becoming a servant to free the slaves of sin.

---

[7]There is a remarkable instance of this from the Binumarien tribe of Papua New Guinea, whose grasp of the genealogy of Jesus opened their eyes to the reality of Christ as a real person, not a mere spirit. The story is told in Lynette Oates, *Hidden People: How a Remote New Guinea Culture Was Brought Back from the Brink of Extinction* (Sutherland, NSW: Albatross, 1992), 205–7. The story is also recorded at http://creation.com/binumarien-people-find-bible-true; accessed March 11, 2015.

The Glory of Isaiah's God

The prophet Isaiah marvels at the uniqueness of God among all the gods of the peoples: "From of old no one has heard or perceived by the ear, no eye has seen a God besides you, who acts for those who wait for him" (Isa. 64:4). Isaiah says there is no God like him. He is unique. Then he describes what it is that sets God apart as amazing from all the other gods. "He acts for those who wait for him." In other words, other gods demand that people join their labor force. But the true God becomes a labor force for those who wait for him. If we will humble ourselves and cease defaulting to human self-reliance, and turn to God in faith that he will work for us, then he will give us the help we need. He will glorify the all-sufficiency of his resources and wisdom and power and grace by working to meet our needs rather than demanding that we work to meet his.

This is the distinguishing glory of God among all the gods: they exalt themselves by demanding to be served; the true God exalts himself in serving those who trust him. Look how Isaiah taunts the Babylonian gods, Bel and Nebo, precisely on this point:

> Bel bows down; Nebo stoops;
>> their idols are on beasts and livestock;
> these things you carry are borne
>> as burdens on weary beasts.
> They stoop; they bow down together;
>> they cannot save the burden,
>> but themselves go into captivity.
> "Listen to me, O house of Jacob,
>> all the remnant of the house of Israel,
> who have been borne by me from before your birth,
>> carried from the womb;
> even to your old age I am he,
>> and to gray hairs I will carry you.
> I have made, and I will bear;
>> I will carry and will save." (Isa. 46:1–4)

What sets God apart as uniquely glorious is that other gods must be carried by men (vv. 1–2), but God carries his people from birth to old age. It is a stunning picture: the false gods ride on carts; the true God is the cart. This is what I meant above when I said that the unifying mark of God's glory is that the majestic heights of God are glorified especially through the way he stoops in lowliness to save the weak.

Isaiah drives home again the truth that God's utter uniqueness lies in his unparalleled willingness to be merciful to the undeserving:

> Let the wicked forsake his way,
>   and the unrighteous man his thoughts;
> let him return to the LORD, that he may have compassion on him,
>   and to our God, for he will abundantly pardon.
> For my thoughts are not your thoughts,
>   neither are your ways my ways, declares the LORD.
> For as the heavens are higher than the earth,
>   so are my ways higher than your ways
>   and my thoughts than your thoughts. (Isa. 55:7–9)

What is the reason God gives here for why sinful and repentant people may turn to him and find the hope of pardon? Note the word "for" at the beginning of verse 8: "*For* my thoughts are not your thoughts, neither are your ways my ways." In other words, God is not only utterly different from the gods; he is also different from men. And that difference lies in this: he will abundantly pardon. To support this, God does not say, "For my ways and thoughts are lower than yours." He says, "For as the heavens are *higher* than the earth, so are my ways *higher* than your ways and my thoughts than your thoughts." In other words, "I glorify the heights of my ways by condescending to pardon unworthy sinners."

Again Isaiah presses this vision of God:

> Thus says the One who is high and lifted up,
>   who inhabits eternity, whose name is Holy:
> "I dwell in the high and holy place,
>   and also with him who is of a contrite and lowly spirit,
> to revive the spirit of the lowly,
>   and to revive the heart of the contrite." (Isa. 57:15)

The unique glory of the God of the Bible is that he is the highest of all beings in transcendent holiness, and this height and this holiness are glorified not merely in their majesty, but in the paradoxical juxta-position of the intrinsic height of holiness and intentional lowliness of service. Isaiah states the principle clearly: "He exalts himself to show mercy to you" (Isa. 30:18).

So Isaiah portrays God as self-authenticating in his glorious unique-ness. There is no god, and there is no human, like this God. He is too high to be the product of fear and too lowly to be the product of pride. He is not the creation of man, and he is not in the pantheon of the gods. He is real, and he is true.

The Glory of God in History and Psalms

This vision of the glory of God, as majestic in mercy and meekness, is not unique to Isaiah. It pervades the biblical books of history and poetry as well as prophecy. It explodes in the New Testament with unparalleled clarity in the incarnation of the Son of God, Jesus Christ.

For example, when Asa, the king of Judah, refused to humble him-self and trust God to fight for him but instead relied on the king of Syria, God censures him with remarkable words:

> Because you relied on the king of Syria, and did not rely on the LORD your God, the army of the king of Syria has escaped you. Were not the Ethiopians and the Libyans a huge army with very many chariots and horsemen? Yet because you relied on the LORD, he gave them into your hand. *For the eyes of the LORD run to and fro throughout the whole earth, to give strong support to those whose heart is blameless toward him.* (2 Chron. 16:7–9)

Verse 9 gives an astonishing picture of God. He is not waiting for people to come serve him or help him or fight for him. On the contrary, his eyes are running to and fro looking for people whom he can serve in their battles. God exalts his strength by searching out weak people whose heart is blameless toward him, so that he can fight for them and work for them.

Similarly, in the Psalms, God takes his people to court, so to speak, in Psalm 50. His case against them is that they are treating him as though he needed their service and their sacrifices. They have forgotten the peculiar glory that he has among all the gods. He does not need them. They need him. And his peculiar glory is to serve those who trust him. He is the benefactor, not the beneficiary. That is his glory.

> Hear, O my people, and I will speak;
>> O Israel, I will testify against you.
>> I am God, your God. . . .
> I will not accept a bull from your house
>> or goats from your folds. . . .
> If I were hungry, I would not tell you,
>> for the world and its fullness are mine. . . .
> Offer to God a sacrifice of thanksgiving,
>> and perform your vows to the Most High,
> and call upon me in the day of trouble;
>> I will deliver you, and you shall glorify me. (Ps. 50:7–15)

Charles Spurgeon loved this text and exulted in the way it glorified God precisely in his serving us:

> God and the praying man take shares. . . . First here is your share: "Call upon me in the day of trouble." Secondly, here is God's share: "I will deliver thee." Again, you take a share—"for you shall be delivered." And then again it is the Lord's turn—"Thou shalt glorify me." Here is a compact, a covenant that God enters into with you who pray to him, and whom he helps. He says, "You shall have the deliverance, but I must have the glory." . . . Here is a delightful partnership: we obtain that which we so greatly need, and all that God getteth is the glory which is due unto his name.[8]

Indeed this "delightful partnership" is at the heart of what makes the Christian God glorious and what makes the Scriptures unique.

Jesus Christ, the Embodiment of the Peculiar Glory

As we come over into the New Testament, the peculiar glory of God's paradoxical juxtapositions comes to a supremely beautiful expression in Jesus Christ. When Paul stood before the philosophers on Mars Hill in Athens, he described the very God of Isaiah and 2 Chronicles and the Psalms, whose glory is that he does not need man but blesses man.

---

[8] Charles Spurgeon, *Twelve Sermons on Prayer* (Grand Rapids, MI: Baker, 1971), 105.

"He is not served by human hands, as though he needed anything, since he himself gives to all mankind life and breath and everything" (Acts 17:25). His glory is not in how many servants he can gather but in his willingness to assemble a humble people who will trust him to serve them.

When Jesus, the eternal Son of God, steps down into humanity, this is what he claims for himself: "The Son of Man came not to be served but to serve, and to give his life as a ransom for many" (Mark 10:45). His glory was not in the recruitment of servants to meet his needs, but in the extreme willingness to serve, even to the point of giving his life for those who would trust him.

Paul soars in amazement and wonder when he contemplates the fact that God does not need counsel, but gives it, and that he does not repay people, because he never needs to borrow anything.

Oh, the depth of the riches and wisdom and knowledge of God!
How unsearchable are his judgments and how inscrutable his ways!

"For who has known the mind of the Lord,
    or who has been his counselor?"
"Or who has given a gift to him
    that he might be repaid?"

For from him and through him and to him are all things. To him be glory forever. Amen. (Rom. 11:33–36)

The climax of the first eleven chapters of Romans is, "To him be glory forever." But why? These verses put the reason negatively and positively. Negatively, no one has ever given a gift to God so that God owes him. No one has ever met any need of God. He has none. He is above all benefaction from men. No one has ever given him counsel. We can't offer God any advice that he does not already know.

Positively, all things are from him and through him and to him. He is infinitely self-sufficient. He cannot be improved by anyone's gifts or counsel. Instead, he is the fountain of life. He gives to all men life and breath and everything. Specifically, he has come to earth in Jesus Christ to serve and to give his life as a ransom, that is, to "have mercy on all" (v. 32), so that the nations might "glorify God for his mercy"

(Rom. 15:9). This is why Paul reaches the climax of all God's merciful work with the words, "To him be glory forever" (Rom. 11:36). This is God's unique glory—to be glorious in the condescension of his transcendent greatness in mercy toward sinful man.

Jesus's entire life and ministry were the embodiment of this peculiar glory of God. At the end of his life, Jesus prayed to his Father, "I glorified you on earth, having accomplished the work that you gave me to do" (John 17:4). His entire ministry was aimed at this: make the Father look glorious. Earlier, he had cried out,

> "Now is my soul troubled. And what shall I say? 'Father, save me from this hour'? But for this purpose I have come to this hour. Father, glorify your name." Then a voice came from heaven: "I have glorified it, and I will glorify it again." (John 12:27–28)

This was his mission. But how would it happen? By self-emptying and servanthood and humiliation and death:

> Though he was in the form of God, [he] did not count equality with God a thing to be grasped, but emptied himself, by taking the form of a servant, being born in the likeness of men. And being found in human form, he humbled himself by becoming obedient to the point of death, even death on a cross. (Phil. 2:6–8)

Because of this majestic lowliness, in love for sinners, God exalted Jesus and gave him a name above all names (Phil. 2:9). But the aim of it all was that "every tongue confess that Jesus Christ is Lord, *to the glory of God the Father*" (v. 11). This is the peculiar glory of God and of his Scriptures: the glory of God is everywhere the aim, and the central means is the self-humbling of God himself in Jesus Christ. This is the "light of the gospel of the glory of Christ, who is the image of God" (2 Cor. 4:4).

The glory of the paradoxical juxtaposition of seeming opposites in Jesus Christ is at the heart of how God shows himself glorious in the Scriptures. Jesus said that all the Old Testament Scriptures were pointing to him. "And beginning with Moses and all the Prophets, he interpreted to them in all the Scriptures the things concerning himself" (Luke 24:27). The coming together of these paradoxes in Christ, with beautiful harmony, is the center of the glory that shines through Scripture.

The Lion and the Lamb United

Jonathan Edwards summed it up in a great sermon called "The Excellencies of Christ." He drew attention to Revelation 5:5–6, where Christ appears as "the Lion of the tribe of Judah" and as "a Lamb standing, as though it had been slain." This is the picture of the paradoxes of Lion and Lamb. He is both a lion-like Lamb and a lamb-like Lion. A lion is admirable for its ferocious strength and imperial appearance. A lamb is admirable for its meekness and servant-like provision of wool for our clothing. But even more admirable is the union of seeming opposites—a lion-like Lamb and a lamb-like Lion. What makes Christ glorious, as Edwards put it, is "an admirable conjunction of diverse excellencies."[9]

For example, echoing Edwards,[10] we admire Christ for his transcendence, but even more because the transcendence of his greatness is mixed with submission to God. We marvel at him because his uncompromising justice is tempered with mercy. His majesty is sweetened by meekness. In his equality *with* God he has a deep reverence *for* God. Though he is worthy of all good, he was patient to suffer evil. His sovereign dominion over the world was clothed with a spirit of obedience and submission. He baffled the proud scribes with his wisdom but was simple enough to be loved by children. He could still the storm with a word but would not strike the Samaritans with lightning or take himself down from the cross.

There is a template in the human heart created by God ready to receive with self-authenticating certainty such divine glory. We were made to know and enjoy this person, Jesus Christ, the lowly incarnation of the all-glorious God. We may sense it in our weariness or in our worldwide dreams. But we know. It is written in our hearts: this God-man is true.

Jesus said, "Come to me, all who labor and are heavy laden, and I will give you rest. Take my yoke upon you, and learn from me, for I am gentle and lowly in heart, and you will find rest for your souls. For my yoke is easy, and my burden is light" (Matt. 11:28–30). The lamb-like gentleness and humility of this Lion woos us in our weariness. And we

---

[9] Jonathan Edwards, "The Excellency of Christ," in *Sermons and Discourses: 1734–1738*, vol. 19, *The Works of Jonathan Edwards*, ed. M. X. Lesser (New Haven, CT: Yale University Press, 2001), 565.

[10] In this section, I am using some thoughts from John Piper, *Seeing and Savoring Jesus Christ* (Wheaton, IL: Crossway, 2004), 29–34.

love him for it. If he recruited only like the Marines, who want strength, we would despair of coming.

But this quality of meekness by itself, separated from Christ's majesty, would not be glorious. The gentleness and humility of the lamb-like Lion become brilliant alongside the limitless and everlasting authority of the lion-like Lamb. Only this fits our worldwide dreams. To be sure, we are weak and weary and heavy laden. But there burns in every heart, at least from time to time, a dream that our lives will count for something great. To this dream Jesus said, "All authority in heaven and on earth has been given to me. Go therefore and make disciples of all nations. . . . And behold, I am with you always, to the end of the age" (Matt. 28:18–20).

We know, from the built-in template of our own weakness together with our longing for transcendent greatness, that the glory of Jesus Christ—the Lion and the Lamb—is the glory we were made for. This is the heart of the glory that shines into our hearts through the Scriptures by the power of the Holy Spirit and convinces us that they are the very words of God.

Majesty Expressed through Meekness

We are still probing into the meaning of the answer of the Larger Catechism that "the Scriptures manifest themselves to be the word of God, by . . . the scope of the whole, which is to give all glory to God." I argued in this chapter that the Scriptures do, in fact, give all glory to God. Not only that, but from beginning to end they present God himself as giving all glory to God. He does all that he does with the aim of communicating his glory. What gives this portrait a distinct and compelling glory is that God magnifies his greatness by making himself the supreme treasure of our hearts, at great cost to himself (Rom. 8:32), and so serving us in the very act of exalting his glory.

The heart of God's glory, as he reveals it in the Scriptures, is the way his majesty is expressed through his meekness. I called this God's paradoxical juxtaposition of seemingly opposite traits. Jonathan Edwards called it "an admirable conjunction of diverse excellencies." This pattern of God's self-revelation in lion-like majesty and strength together with lamb-like meekness and service runs through the whole Bible and comes to its most beautiful climax in the person and work of Jesus Christ in dying and rising for sinners.

When Paul teaches in Romans 1:21 that all human beings, deep down, know God but fail to acknowledge him, the language he uses corresponds to this paradoxical glory. He says that we have all failed "to *honor* God and give him *thanks*." In other words, we have failed to see his soul-satisfying majesty, and we have failed to taste his need-meeting kindness. And we have failed to see their beautiful juxtaposition. We suppress the truth.

Nevertheless, there is in every human being a "knowledge" of this God. There is a built-in template that is shaped to receive as its perfect counterpart this peculiar communication of God's glory. When God opens our eyes (2 Cor. 4:6) and grants us the knowledge of the truth (2 Tim. 2:25), through the Scriptures (1 Pet. 1:23), we know that we have met ultimate reality. And in this way, God testifies that his word is true.

One of the ways this peculiar communication of the glory of God is woven into the Scriptures, confirming them to be the word of God, is the way the Old Testament Scriptures find fulfillment in the New Testament. It is not only the amazing wonder of God's foreknowledge and providence that captures us. It is, even more, the way the New Testament treats the fulfillment of Scripture as a display of the peculiar glory of God. That is what we turn to next.

Concerning this salvation, the prophets who prophesied about the grace that was to be yours searched and inquired carefully, inquiring what person or time the Spirit of Christ in them was indicating when he predicted the sufferings of Christ and the subsequent glories.

1 PETER 1:10–11

14

In the Fulfillment of Prophecy

In this chapter we continue to search the Scriptures for an understanding, and confirmation, of the claim that "the Scriptures manifest themselves to be the word of God, by . . . the scope of the whole, which is to give all glory to God." This is the answer of the Westminster Larger Catechism to the question, "How doth it appear that the Scriptures are the word of God?" I have argued that the catechism is right to say that the Scriptures have this unified aim—to give all glory to God.

More specifically, they uniformly reveal a God who aims at the praise of his glory in all that he does. In nature, history, and Scripture, God magnifies the supremacy of his glory. This is not the work of an egomaniac, because the human soul is created to find its deepest pleasures by seeing and savoring the God of glory as the soul's highest treasure. God's self-exaltation is an act of love for people whose joy is in God's greatness. We were created for this. The truth of God's glory is written on the human heart. Therefore, a glimpse of that glory through the Scriptures is self-authenticating. It is the means by which God attests to the truth of his word.

Innumerable Divine Glories Shine through the Scriptures

I am arguing that Jonathan Edwards is right, therefore, when he draws out of 2 Corinthians 4:4–6 the truth that "a saving belief of the gospel arises from the mind's being enlightened to behold the divine glory of the things it exhibits."[1] In other words, the simplest and least educated persons, as well as scholars, come to a well-grounded faith when "the light of the knowledge of the glory of God" (2 Cor. 4:6) touches that innate awareness of God that every human being has (Rom. 1:21). This happens through the Scriptures. In this way, God confirms not only the gospel, but the inspired Scriptures that bring it to us.

The Scriptures are confirmed in this way by the pervasive and innumerable ways God's glory shines through them. The Scriptures are like a diamond with countless facets that can send the rays of God's glory into the human heart in more ways than any of us have dreamed. Parts of Scripture that puzzle us may truly break forth with irresistible glory and truth among those of different cultures. Therefore, it is risky to attempt, as I did in the previous chapter, to dig into the Scriptures looking for the heart or the essence of the glory of God that makes it compelling to the human soul.

Nevertheless, it seems to me that the Scriptures encourage us to do this. The Scriptures do not just speak in broad, general terms about the glory of God. They point us to the specific glories of God's glory. They want us to see the *ways* God is glorious. They lead us to the *peculiar* glory of God that sets him off from all gods (Isa. 64:4) and from all human ways and thoughts (Isa. 55:8). That is what we began to see in the previous chapter. And that is what we continue to do here.

The aim of the next three chapters is to see how the Scripture puts the glory of God on display through the fulfillment of prophecy, the miracles of Jesus, and the fruit of love in the lives of his disciples. In other words, we continue digging into how "the Scriptures manifest themselves to be the word of God, by the scope of the whole, which is to give all glory to God." The Scriptures do not just say God acts for his glory. They show us how.

The Sheer Fact of Fulfilled Prophecy Is Glorious

We turn in this chapter to the astonishing way that the Scriptures of the New Testament reveal the fulfillment of Old Testament prophecies from hundreds of years earlier. I put the stress on *the way* the New Testament fulfills the Old Testament. That's what this chapter focuses on. There is

---

[1] Jonathan Edwards, *A Treatise Concerning Religious Affections*, vol. 2, *The Works of Jonathan Edwards*, ed. John Smith (New Haven, CT: Yale University Press, 1957), 299.

a remarkable attention to the peculiar glory of Christ in the very way the New Testament takes up the Old Testament prophecies of Christ.

But it should be said that the sheer fact of fulfilled prophecy is a revelation of the glory of God in Christ—not just *the way* it happens, but *that* it happens. This amazing fact has been used by God to awaken many people to the reality of his work in inspiring the Scriptures. I won't list the hundreds of examples from Scripture since these are so readily available.[2] But I will give a small taste before turning to the precise focus of this chapter.

One of the most astonishing portrayals in the Bible of the sufferings of God's messianic servant is found in Isaiah 53, written about seven hundred years before the time of Jesus. If we take just this chapter and trace its fulfillments and echoes in the New Testament, we will taste the wonder that God planned and predicted the path of Jesus centuries before he arrived. Luke recorded this truth in a sweeping statement about Jesus's final days:

> Truly in this city there were gathered together against your holy servant Jesus, whom you anointed, both Herod and Pontius Pilate, along with the Gentiles and the peoples of Israel, to do whatever your hand and your plan had predestined to take place. (Acts 4:27–28)

Below is a partial list of the fulfillments of Isaiah 53 in the New Testament.

Isaiah 53:1	John 12:37–38
Who has believed what he has heard from us? And to whom has the arm of the LORD been revealed?	Though he had done so many signs before them, they still did not believe in him, so that the word spoken by the prophet Isaiah might be fulfilled: "Lord, who has believed what he heard from us, and to whom has the arm of the Lord been revealed?"
	Romans 10:16
	But they have not all obeyed the gospel. For Isaiah says, "Lord, who has believed what he has heard from us?"

---

[2] E.g., I simply searched online "Lists of Old Testament prophecies fulfilled in the New Testament" and found ten significant lists. The most complete commentary on how the New Testament uses the Old Testament is *Commentary on the New Testament Use of the Old Testament*, ed. G. K. Beale and D. A. Carson (Grand Rapids, MI: Baker Academic, 2007).

Isaiah 53:4	Matthew 8:16–17
Surely he has borne our griefs and carried our sorrows; yet we esteemed him stricken, smitten by God, and afflicted.	That evening they brought to him many who were oppressed by demons, and he cast out the spirits with a word and healed all who were sick. This was to fulfill what was spoken by the prophet Isaiah: "He took our illnesses and bore our diseases."
Isaiah 53:4–5	1 Peter 2:24
Surely he has borne our griefs and carried our sorrows; yet we esteemed him stricken, smitten by God, and afflicted. But he was pierced for our transgressions; he was crushed for our iniquities; upon him was the chastisement that brought us peace, and with his wounds we are healed.	He himself bore our sins in his body on the tree, that we might die to sin and live to righteousness. By his wounds you have been healed.
Isaiah 53:6	1 Peter 2:24–25
All we like sheep have gone astray; we have turned—every one—to his own way; and the LORD has laid on him the iniquity of us all.	He himself bore our sins in his body on the tree, that we might die to sin and live to righteousness. By his wounds you have been healed. For you were straying like sheep, but have now returned to the Shepherd and Overseer of your souls.
Isaiah 53:7–8	Acts 8:32–33
He was oppressed, and he was afflicted, yet he opened not his mouth; like a lamb that is led to the slaughter, and like a sheep that before its shearers is silent, so he opened not his mouth. By oppression and judgment he was taken away; and as for his generation, who considered that he was cut off out of the land of the living, stricken for the transgression of my people?	Now the passage of the Scripture that he was reading was this: "Like a sheep he was led to the slaughter and like a lamb before its shearer is silent, so he opens not his mouth. In his humiliation justice was denied him. Who can describe his generation? For his life is taken away from the earth."
Isaiah 53:9	1 Peter 2:21–22
And they made his grave with the wicked and with a rich man in his death, although he had done no violence, and there was no deceit in his mouth.	For to this you have been called, because Christ also suffered for you, leaving you an example, so that you might follow in his steps. He committed no sin, neither was deceit found in his mouth.

Isaiah 53:12	Luke 22:37
Therefore I will divide him a portion with the many, and he shall divide the spoil with the strong, because he poured out his soul to death and was numbered with the transgressors; yet he bore the sin of many, and makes intercession for the transgressors.	For I tell you that this Scripture must be fulfilled in me: "And he was numbered with the transgressors." For what is written about me has its fulfillment.

One of the reasons for this widespread and detailed reference to the Old Testament in the New Testament is to magnify the glory that God is God, and that God is ruling the history that climaxed in Jesus.

> I am God, and there is no other;
> > I am God, and there is none like me,
> declaring the end from the beginning
> > and from ancient times things not yet done,
> saying, "My counsel shall stand,
> > and I will accomplish all my purpose." (Isa. 46:9–10)

God's deity—his Godness—is shown in declaring his purpose before it happens and then seeing to it that it happens by "accomplishing all my purpose." God does not just predict. He plans and accomplishes. The sheer fact of fulfilled prophecy is not owing to God's gift of clairvoyance but to God's sovereignty over the world. "The counsel of the LORD stands forever, the plans of his heart to all generations" (Ps. 33:11). His predictions are certain, not mainly because he foresees without error, but because he executes without fail. This is no small aspect of his glory in fulfilling Scripture.

The Fulfillment of Scripture Depicts the Peculiar Glory of God

But that is not the main focus of this chapter, wonderful as it is. Rather, I want to draw attention to how the fulfillment of prophecy is part of the display of God's peculiar glory. In the last chapter, I argued that at the heart of what makes the glory of God uniquely glorious is the way his majesty and his meekness combine. In other words, God's peculiar glory is never seen when his power is viewed in isolation from his readiness to dwell with "the contrite and lowly in spirit" (Isa. 57:15).

What is most compelling about the way Scripture presents the fulfillment of prophecy is not merely that it validates the divine origin of the prophecy and the divine agency of its fulfillment, but, even more, that this fulfillment serves God's peculiar glory of majesty in meekness—the peculiar glory of supreme strength in voluntary suffering for others.

The Foreknowledge of Jesus and His Divine Glory

According to the apostle John, Jesus's incarnate presence was a manifestation of the glory of God. "And the Word became flesh and dwelt among us, and we have seen his glory, glory as of the only Son from the Father, full of grace and truth" (John 1:14). Jesus expected his disciples to see this, and to be persuaded that he was a true incarnate presence of God. So when one of his disciples said, "Show us the Father," Jesus responded, "Have I been with you so long, and you still do not know me, Philip? Whoever has seen me has seen the Father" (John 14:9).

But Jesus did not just speak in generalities about his divine glory. He got specific. And one of the specifics is the way he connected himself with prophecy. For example, he cited the prophecy that he would be betrayed by one of his disciples, and then he added his own specific prophetic application to his immediate situation and drew out an implication for his divine glory:

> If you know these things, blessed are you if you do them. I am not speaking of all of you; I know whom I have chosen. But the Scripture will be fulfilled, "He who ate my bread has lifted his heel against me" [Ps. 41:9]. I am telling you this now, before it takes place, that when it does take place you may believe that I am he. (John 13:17–19)

"I am telling you this before it takes place that you may believe." In other words, fulfilled prophecy provides a good foundation for well-grounded belief. Belief in what? "That you may believe that I am he." What does that mean? In the original, there is no word for "he." It simply says, "That you may believe that I am." Jesus had already stunned the disciples and brought down the wrath of the Jewish leaders by saying, "Before Abraham was, I am" (John 8:58). In other words, Jesus was identifying himself with the name of God in Exodus 3:14: "God said to Moses, 'I AM WHO I AM.' . . . Say this to the people of Israel, 'I AM has sent me to you.'"

So in John 13:19, Jesus was not only saying that the fulfillment of Psalm 41:9 in life confirmed him as the Promised One, but, more amazingly, his own prophetic application of the prophecy to the situation right before him demonstrated him to be "I am"—the absolutely self-sufficient God of Israel.[3] Thus we behold his glory, glory as of the only Son from the Father. And here is the point: this illustration of fulfilled prophecy not only validated Jesus's divine glory, but it also revealed the peculiar nature of this glory because the prophecy tells that Jesus would be betrayed and suffer. Thus Jesus, even as he declares himself to be God, embraces his mission to die. This is his glory.

Pointing to the Peculiar Glory Is Typical of Prophetic Fulfillment

This is not exceptional in Scripture. It is the typical way the fulfillment of Scripture functions in the New Testament. The Scriptures don't just point to divine glory. They point to the peculiar glory that the Promised One will show his majesty in suffering. In other words, this essential feature of God's glory in Scripture is woven into the fabric of prophecy and fulfillment. The clearest statement of this is found in 1 Peter 1:10–11:

> Concerning this salvation, the prophets who prophesied about the grace that was to be yours searched and inquired carefully, inquiring what person or time the Spirit of Christ in them was indicating when *he predicted the sufferings of Christ and the subsequent glories.*

Here is a general statement about prophecy and fulfillment in Scripture. It is remarkable that Peter's way of summing up what the prophets were doing was to predict sufferings and glory (Lamb and Lion). In other words, the path to glory for God's incarnate representative on earth was the path through suffering. The path to majesty was through meekness. The path to exaltation was through humility. The path to power was through weakness.

---

[3] The testimony of prophecy itself was that it was the mark of divinity. Only God could name the future and then see to it that it came to pass. E.g., "I am God, and there is no other; I am God, and there is none like me, declaring the end from the beginning and from ancient times things not yet done, saying, 'My counsel shall stand, and I will accomplish all my purpose'" (Isa. 46:9–10; cf. Isa. 48:1–8).

Jesus had said the same thing on the road to Emmaus:

> "O foolish ones, and slow of heart to believe all that the prophets have spoken! Was it not necessary that *the Christ should suffer these things and enter into his glory?*" And beginning with Moses and all the Prophets, he interpreted to them in all the Scriptures the things concerning himself. (Luke 24:25–27; cf. v. 44)

Jesus summed up the Prophets and Moses by saying the Christ will enter his glory through suffering. And he was that Christ. This was his mission. He knew it, and he chose it, and this was his peculiar glory. Glory through voluntary suffering for the sake of others.

Similarly, Paul said to the Jews of Rome that this gospel of a crucified and reigning Christ was what the Old Testament foresaw:

> To this day I have had the help that comes from God, and so I stand here testifying both to small and great, saying nothing but what the prophets and Moses said would come to pass: that *the Christ must suffer and that, by being the first to rise from the dead, he would proclaim light both to our people and to the Gentiles.* (Acts 26:22–23)

The one who suffered and died was now exalted to proclaim light to all the nations.

The Golden Thread of Prophecy

In summary, then, Scripture is woven together by prophecy and fulfillment. This, in itself, is a great glory of Scripture. There is no other book like it with so many, and such clear, prophecies fulfilled in such a variety of ways.[4] It is in itself a witness to the divine origin of Scripture. But my point here is that there is a peculiar glory in the way the Scriptures reveal the fulfillment of prophecy.

---

[4] "As for material use of the OT in the NT, there is great diversity in that as well. Sometimes the citations serve as proof and confirmation of a given truth (e.g., Matt. 4:4, 7, 10; 9:13; 19:5; 22:32; John 10:34; Acts 15:16; 23:5; Rom. 1:17; 3:10f.; 4:3, 7; 9:7, 12, 13, 15, 17; 10:5; Gal. 3:10; 4:30; 1 Cor. 9:9; 10:26; 2 Cor. 6:17). Very often the OT is cited to prove that it *had to* be fulfilled and was fulfilled in the NT, either in a literal sense (Matt. 1:23; 3:3; 4:15, 16; 8:17; 12:18; 13:14, 15; 21:42; 27:46; Mark 15:28; Luke 4:17f.; John 12:38; Acts 2:17; 3:22; 7:37; 8:32; etc.) or typologically (Matt. 11:14; 12:39f.; 17:11; Luke 1:17; John 3:14; 19:36; 1 Cor. 5:7; 10:4; 2 Cor. 4:13; 8:15; 13:1; Heb. 2:6–8; 7:1–10; etc.). Citations from the OT repeatedly serve simply to clarify, inform, admonish, console, etc. (e.g., Luke 2:23; John 7:38; Acts 7:3, 42; Rom. 8:36; 1 Cor. 2:16; 10:7; 2 Cor. 4:13; 8:15; 13:1; Heb. 12:5; 13:15; 1 Peter 1:16, 24, 25; 2:9)." Herman Bavinck, *Reformed Dogmatics*, vol. 1, *Prolegomena* (Grand Rapids, MI: Baker Academic, 2003), 396.

The peculiar glory is that the Promised One displays the fullness and the uniqueness of his glory by moving to majesty through meekness and to splendor through suffering. He attains the height of his glory through humble service. This is the golden thread of prophecy. Crowning this glory of prophecy is the truth that it was the spirit of Christ himself prophesying the suffering and the glory of Christ. "The Spirit of Christ in them predicted the sufferings of Christ and the subsequent glories" (1 Pet. 1:11).

So when Jesus says that *such* prophecy is a good ground for our faith (John 13:19), he has in mind not only the sheer transcendent glory required to predict the future and carry it through but also the peculiar glory that is woven through the whole fabric of biblical prophecy: the "glory of the gospel of Jesus Christ" (2 Cor. 4:4) manifest in the majesty of his meekness, the strength of his weakness, and the supreme power of his voluntary suffering. This is the glory that called the Scriptures into being. And when we see it shining through these inspired writings, God confirms to our heart that these are the very words of God.

In the next chapter, we turn to the miracles of Jesus. Jesus and the apostles believed his miracles were good grounds for faith in the truth of their message and the integrity of their persons. But clearly the raw display of power in a miracle was not convincing to many. Judas saw them. The Pharisees saw them. But they did not see anything that compelled them to believe. There must have been a peculiar glory in these works that Jesus expected people to see and which would be a good ground of their belief in his person and his word. That is what we turn to now.

I know that you do not have the love of God within you. I have come in my Father's name, and you do not receive me. If another comes in his own name, you will receive him. How can you believe, when you receive glory from one another and do not seek the glory that comes from the only God?

JOHN 5:42–44

15

In the Miracles of Jesus

Continuing the point of the previous chapter, we shift our focus from the fulfillment of prophecy to the miracles of Jesus. We are arguing that the Scriptures put the glory of God on display through the fulfillment of prophecy, the miracles of Jesus, and the fruit of love in the lives of his disciples. We are pressing into the biblical warrant for the claim of the Westminster Catechism that "the Scriptures manifest themselves to be the word of God, by . . . the scope of the whole, which is to give all glory to God." The Scriptures do not just say God acts for his glory. They show us how. They draw our attention to a peculiar glory of God.

Similar to the way that the fulfillment of prophecy reveals the peculiar glory of God in Christ, so also Jesus's miracles do the same. The miracles did not provide a foundation for well-grounded faith merely because they were signs of power. They gave rise to saving faith in those who saw in the miracles the God-exalting, self-denying power of one who would save sinners not by nature-subduing power but by soul-subduing suffering. "I, when I am lifted up from the earth, will draw all people to myself" (John 12:32). The seeming weakness of the cross, endured by the most majestic and innocent person, is the peculiar glory that draws us to a well-grounded faith. Jesus's miracles were the foundation of faith because they had a peculiar glory about them. Where do we see that in Scripture?

The Links between Miracles, Glory, and Faith

When John wrote, "We have seen his glory, glory as of the only Son from the Father, full of grace and truth" (John 1:14), part of that glory was the glory of his miracles, which John regularly calls "signs." We know this because after Jesus's first miracle, John said, "This, the first of his signs, Jesus did at Cana in Galilee, *and manifested his glory*" (John 2:11). So Jesus knew what he was doing with his miracles. He was giving signs. And the signs were pointing to his glory.

This was intended to be the foundation for a well-grounded faith. Repeatedly Jesus spoke of his works as a good reason to believe in him. "The works that the Father has given me to accomplish, *the very works that I am doing, bear witness about me that the Father has sent me*" (John 5:36). "*The works that I do in my Father's name bear witness about me*" (John 10:25). "Even though you do not believe me, *believe the works,* that you may know and understand that the Father is in me and I am in the Father" (John 10:38). "Believe me that I am in the Father and the Father is in me, or else *believe on account of the works themselves*" (John 14:11).

Faith without the Sight of Glory

But Jesus gives us a warning that miracles can win him a following without winning saving faith. There is a way to "believe" in Jesus's miracles without believing in Jesus as he really is. John's Gospel bears clear witness to this danger and points us to the peculiar glory of the miracles that many people did not see.

For example, on one occasion, John reports that "as he was saying these things, many believed in him. So Jesus said to the Jews *who had believed him,* 'If you abide in my word, you are truly my disciples, and you will know the truth, and the truth will set you free'" (John 8:30–32). Keep that in mind: he is talking to those who in some sense had "believed" him. Surprisingly, they respond critically, "We are offspring of Abraham and have never been enslaved to anyone. How is it that you say, 'You will become free'?" Then Jesus stuns us (remember he is talking to those "who had believed") by saying, "You seek to kill me because my word finds no place in you" (John 8:37).

Jesus taught so clearly, "Whoever believes in the Son has eternal life"

(John 3:36). But now he is saying that they "believe," even though his word "finds no place" in them and even though they want to kill him. What kind of belief is that? Before we answer, notice that this is not the only situation where Jesus commented on a kind of "belief" that was not saving belief.

When Jesus went to the Passover in Jerusalem, John comments, "Many believed in his name when they saw the signs that he was doing" (John 2:23). But then he adds, "But Jesus on his part did not entrust himself to them, because he knew all people and needed no one to bear witness about man, for he himself knew what was in man" (John 2:24–25). Evidently this "belief" was not a kind Jesus could trust. Something was wrong with it. They had seen signs and believed he was doing them, but that was not what Jesus was looking for.

Similarly, after the feeding of the five thousand, the crowds followed him with great enthusiasm: "They were about to come and take him by force to make him king" (John 6:15). This sounds like great faith and allegiance. But Jesus says to them, "You are seeking me, not because you saw signs, but because you ate your fill of the loaves" (John 6:26). I take that to mean that they saw the miracle of the feeding of the five thousand, but instead of seeing it as a sign of a peculiar glory, they saw it as proof that Jesus had the power to meet their physical needs and be a king who could make their lives safe and prosperous. Jesus was not interested in that kind of "belief." What was wrong with it? What were they missing?

Even His Brothers Saw the Miracles but Did Not Believe

A key to the answer is found in the "belief" of Jesus's brothers, which John calls "unbelief":

> Now the Jews' Feast of Booths was at hand. So his brothers said to him, "Leave here and go to Judea, *that your disciples also may see the works you are doing*. For no one works in secret if he seeks to be known openly. If you do these things, show yourself to the world." For *not even his brothers believed in him*. (John 7:2–5)

That is a jolting statement: "Not even his brothers believed in him." And what is more jolting is that John gives this statement as the ground ("for") for what they had just said. And what had they said—"You are doing great works—great miracles. Go up to Jerusalem and show yourself to the world"—that's what John called "unbelief."

Up to this point in John's Gospel, Jesus had turned water into wine (2:1–11), healed an official's son (4:46–54), healed a man paralyzed for thirty-five years (5:1–12), fed five thousand with five loaves and two fish (John 6:1–14), and walked on water (6:19–21). Evidently, Jesus's brothers were following all this and were very excited about the possibilities of a great movement of people behind Jesus. So they say, in effect, "Stop being so low-key. No one works in secret if he seeks to be known openly. Show yourself to the world." And John says that the reason they said this is, "For *not* even his brothers believed in him."

So his brothers see the miracles, believe that Jesus is doing them, are excited about the impact they will have, and do not "believe." What are they missing? The clue lies in the fact that they tell Jesus to go to Jerusalem publicly, but Jesus says no and then goes privately: "After his brothers had gone up to the feast, then he also went up, not publicly but in private" (John 7:10). They want him to go and work wonders and be exalted by the crowds. But Jesus goes up without a splash and starts *teaching*. Indeed, the content of his teaching, if anything, is going to ruin his chances of being exalted by the crowds. He told his brothers before they left for the feast, "The world cannot hate you, but it hates me because I testify about it that its works are evil" (John 7:7).

The Peculiar Glory Can Be Seen Only by the Right Heart

What he says in Jerusalem, after refusing to seek a great crowd, shows us what was wrong with his brothers' faith. He says to the Jews,

> My teaching is not mine, but his who sent me. If anyone's will is to do God's will, he will know whether the teaching is from God or whether I am speaking on my own authority. The one who speaks on his own authority seeks his own glory; but the one who seeks the glory of him who sent him is true, and in him there is no falsehood. (John 7:16–18)

Here's the key. What is the mark of the man who is true and in whom is no falsehood? He does not seek his own glory but the glory of the one who sent him. The mark of authenticity in Jesus's miracles is not their raw power but that their power was in the service of God-exalting humility, not self-exalting crowd pleasing. This was the peculiar glory of his miracles. This is what the signs pointed to. This Messiah was not what the brothers of Jesus (or anyone else) expected.

To be sure, Jesus was to be "called the Son of the Most High." To be sure, he would "sit on the throne of his father David, and of his kingdom there will be no end" (Luke 1:32–33). But the pathway to that great glory was not what anyone expected. It would be through self-denying suffering, not self-exalting popularity. His brothers did not see this. And their enthusiasm for his miracles was, in fact, unbelief (John 7:5). It was not based on a sight of the peculiar glory.

Jesus does not trace this unbelief back to ignorance about Old Testament prophecies about the suffering Messiah. He traces it back to a human heart that does not have a will in tune with God's will. He says in John 7:17, "If anyone's will is to do God's will, he will know whether the teaching is from God or whether I am speaking on my own authority." The deepest problem is not ignorance but a will that does not will to do God's will. In the context, God's will is the surrender of self-exaltation and the embrace of God-exaltation. "The one who speaks on his own authority seeks his own glory; but the one who seeks the glory of him who sent him is true" (John 7:18).

So where the human will enjoys and pursues self-exaltation rather than God-exaltation, the true Jesus will not be attractive or recognized for who he really is. The glory will be invisible. And his miracles will, therefore, be misunderstood. The human heart must be brought into harmony with the will of God in order for God's design for Jesus's miracles to be seen. Their peculiar glory was not power in the service of self-exaltation but power in the service of God-exaltation and self-denying service of human liberation. Jesus would use this power to relieve the suffering of others, but not his own. Anyone who did not share this disposition would not see the glory. And therefore, their excitement about his miracles was not saving belief.

You Can't Believe If You Are in Love with Human Praise

Jesus makes this even more clear in John 5:41–44, where he says,

> I do not receive glory from people. But I know that you do not have the love of God within you. I have come in my Father's name, and

you do not receive me. If another comes in his own name, you will receive him. How can you believe, when you receive glory from one another and do not seek the glory that comes from the only God?

That last rhetorical question has a devastating answer. The answer to the question, "How can you believe?" is, "You can't." Restate the question as a statement, since Jesus really is making a strong statement with it: "You who receive glory from one another, and do not seek the glory that comes from God, *cannot* believe." Why not? Because of what Jesus says in verse 43: "I have come in my Father's name, and you do not receive me. If another comes in his own name, you will receive him." Why would they have received one who comes in his *own* name? Because that mind-set would fit with their own. One who comes in his own name, seeking his own glory, would be one like them. His ways would be their ways. He would endorse their self-centeredness. Even if he became their competition, he would not become their condemnation. They might feel envy, but they would not feel guilt.

This is why they "cannot believe." They love the glory of man more than the glory of God. "I know that you do not have the love of God within you" (v. 42). They love themselves. They love the praise of man. So when Jesus says, "I do not receive glory from people" (v. 41), he means this: "The kind of human exaltation that people give who have no love for God is of no interest to me and does not fit with who I am." Therefore, people who want that kind of "glory from people" will not know Jesus. They will fundamentally miss what he is about. And therefore, they will not see what his signs—his miracles—are pointing to. They cannot recognize the peculiar glory of Jesus in his miracles, because they do not will his will (John 7:17). They do not share his love for the glory of God (7:18; 5:44). And they do not intend to join him in the self-sacrifice that puts his power in the service of love, not pride.

Transfiguration: The Coming, the Glory, and the Scriptures

There was one moment in the life of Jesus when the majesty of Jesus stood forth in an absolutely unique way. It was notable precisely because it was exceptional. On the Mount of Transfiguration, Jesus's divine glory shone in a more immediate and spectacular way. For our purposes here, what is most significant about this exceptional revelation of glory is the impact it made on the apostle Peter and what he made of it. Peter saw in this revelation a confirmation of the written word of God in the Old Testament, especially as it relates to the second coming of Christ in glory at the end of the age.[1]

In the Gospels of Matthew, Mark, and Luke the story of the transfiguration is immediately preceded by a promise of Jesus that appears to be concerning his future, second coming:

- "Truly, I say to you, there are some standing here who will not taste death until they see the Son of Man coming in his kingdom." (Matt. 16:28)

- "And he said to them, 'Truly, I say to you, there are some standing here who will not taste death until they see the kingdom of God after it has come with power.'" (Mark 9:1)

- "But I tell you truly, there are some standing here who will not taste death until they see the kingdom of God." (Luke 9:27)

My understanding of what Jesus was doing (followed by Matthew, Mark, and Luke) was pointing to his second coming by predicting a preview of it that would happen shortly on the Mount of Transfiguration. So when Jesus said that some will see the kingdom of God come with power (or will see the Son of Man coming in his kingdom) before they die, he meant that Peter, James, and John (as each of these Gospels records) would see an extraordinary preview of Christ's future glory, which he will have when he comes in his final kingdom. In effect, Peter, James, and John saw the power and glory of the Son of Man coming in his kingdom when Jesus was transfigured before them.

As Mark records the event,

After six days Jesus took with him Peter and James and John, and led them up a high mountain by themselves. And he was transfigured before them, and his clothes became radiant, intensely white, as no one on earth could bleach them. And there appeared to them

---

[1] This section on the Transfiguration was inspired by an email exchange with Alastair Roberts, who has written insightfully on the wider implications of the Transfiguration. His as yet unpublished essay is entitled "Transfigured Hermeneutics." He is not responsible for any inadequacies or inaccuracies of this section.

> Elijah with Moses, and they were talking with Jesus. And Peter said to Jesus, "Rabbi, it is good that we are here. Let us make three tents, one for you and one for Moses and one for Elijah." For he did not know what to say, for they were terrified. And a cloud overshadowed them, and a voice came out of the cloud, "This is my beloved Son; listen to him." And suddenly, looking around, they no longer saw anyone with them but Jesus only. (Mark 9:2–8)

Matthew and Luke record aspects of the encounter that Mark omits. Matthew says that Jesus's face "shone like the sun" (17:2), and Luke adds that Moses and Elijah "appeared in glory and spoke of his departure [lit., 'his exodus'], which he was about to accomplish at Jerusalem" (Luke 9:31).

Putting some pieces together, we can see that the transfiguration is looking in two directions. It is looking forward to the second coming of Jesus in his kingdom and glory. And it is looking back to Moses and Elijah, who represent the Law and the Prophets that prophesied that glorious event. In the middle of that historical sweep stands Jesus whom God declares to be his beloved Son, and who is about to accomplish "his exodus" of deliverance in Jerusalem. God says he should be "listened to" at all costs. "This is my beloved Son; listen to him." So even as we are seeing a glorious preview of the second coming, we are reminded of what he will have to endure in Jerusalem to deliver his people out of the bondage of sin.

Now, what will the apostles make of this amazing event? Remarkably we have Peter's actual testimony of what the event meant to him— or at least part of what it meant. In 2 Peter 1:16–19 we read this account of the transfiguration and its significance:

> We did not follow cleverly devised myths when we made known to you the power and coming of our Lord Jesus Christ, but we were eyewitnesses of his majesty. For when he received honor and glory from God the Father, and the voice was borne to him by the Majestic Glory, "This is my beloved Son, with whom I am well pleased," we ourselves heard this very voice borne from heaven, for we were with him on the holy mountain. And we have the prophetic word more fully confirmed, to which you will do well to pay attention as to a lamp shining in a dark place, until the day dawns and the morning star rises in your hearts.

Similarly to Matthew, Mark, and Luke, Peter connects the transfiguration to the second coming of Jesus. According to Matthew, Jesus said that on the Mount of Transfiguration, Peter and James and John would "see the Son of Man coming in his kingdom" (Matt. 16:28). Peter says that in his teaching he had "made known to you the power and coming of our Lord Jesus Christ" (2 Pet. 1:16). He argues that the reason this should not be regarded as "myth" is that he was an "eyewitness" of the "majesty." In other words, he says, I saw the preview of the second coming. I saw the curtain of the future lifted and the majesty of Jesus in his future glory.

Then he goes further and adds hearing to seeing. He was not just an eyewitness, but also an ear-witness. "When . . . the voice was borne to him by the Majestic Glory, 'This is my beloved Son, with whom I am well pleased,' we ourselves heard this very voice borne from heaven, for we were with him on the holy mountain" (2 Pet. 1:17–18). So with his ears and his eyes, Peter experienced a preenactment of the majesty of Jesus at his second coming.

Then Peter makes the connection that is so relevant for our purposes here. He connects this event with the Old Testament Scripture that predicts the second coming: "And we have the prophetic word more fully confirmed, to which you will do well to pay attention as to a lamp shining in a dark place, until the day dawns and the morning star rises in your hearts."

In other words, as we have seen before, Jesus confirms the authority of the Old Testament Scriptures. This time he does so not by saying, "Do not think that I have come to abolish the Law or the Prophets; I have not come to abolish them but to fulfill them" (Matt. 5:17); rather, he confirms the Scriptures by revealing the very glory that he will have when he comes at the last day to fulfill all that had been written about him. He confirms the Scriptures by a stunning pre-fulfillment of their most glorious hope.

The point Peter is making is not that the prophetic writings lacked solidity or sureness, and Jesus provided it. The point is that the Scriptures were already "firm" (βέβαιος). Now they are "more firm" (βεβαιότερον). Moses and Elijah, representing the Law and the Prophets, are vindicated by their presence with Jesus "in glory" (Luke 9:31). Now, in the shadow of Jesus's superior glory, they do not lose their authority, but rather gain confirmation from the Son of God. Peter says that we are to look to the truth and the glory they reveal as to "a lamp shining in a dark place, until the day dawns and the morning star rises in your hearts."

Christ has not come to abolish the Law and the Prophets (Moses and Elijah), but to fulfill them. On the Mount of Transfiguration, he pre-fulfills their promises of ultimate hope. In this way, these Scriptures come to burn with all the more brightness as a lamp for our dark world.

For one brief moment, the transfiguration broke the pattern of the incarnation. It pulled back the curtain on the future when the glory of Christ would not be clothed in fragile lowliness any longer. And that too is part of the peculiar glory of Jesus Christ—the sheer brevity yet wonder of it. And all of it serving to make the Scriptures—the prophetic writings, as Peter calls them—more sure. The transfiguration itself becomes a kind of dramatization of the point of this book: it is the peculiar glory of Jesus that awakens and wins our confidence in the truth of Scripture.

In summary, then, the miracles of Jesus are meant to provide a good foundation for well-grounded confidence that he is who he says he is and that his teachings are true (John 5:36; 10:25, 36; 14:11). But the miracles, as mere demonstrations of supernatural power, do not have this effect. Even demons know that Jesus does such miracles (Mark 1:24). So do Jesus's brothers. And their excitement about his miracles, and their desire to see him do more of them for the sake of more notoriety, is called "unbelief."

To see the miracles of Jesus as the foundation for true and saving faith, one must see the peculiar glory they display. "This, the first of his signs, Jesus did at Cana in Galilee, *and manifested his glory*" (John 2:11). This glory can only be seen by those whose hearts are brought into conformity with the glory. The peculiar glory of Jesus's miracles is that their supernatural power is in the service of humble God-exaltation, not crowd-pleasing self-exaltation. They are in the service of relieving suffering, not escaping suffering. They will take Jesus to the cross, not keep him from it (Matt. 16:21–23). Hearts that do not share this love for the glory of God and the good of others in the humility of self-denial will not see the glory of Jesus in his miracles.

But where God does his merciful, blindness-removing work (2 Cor. 4:6; Matt. 11:25; John 9:39), Jesus is seen for who he really is, and the peculiar glory of his miracles becomes a good foundation for well-grounded faith. "Blessed are you, Simon Bar-Jonah! For flesh and blood has not revealed this to you, but my Father who is in heaven" (Matt. 16:17). The human heart must be set free from its blinding love affair with the praise of men (John 5:44), and must will the will of God. That is, the heart must be conformed to the peculiar way God glorifies himself in history and in Scripture: through majesty in meekness and strength in suffering—the wealth of his glory in the depth of his giving.

The Peculiar Glory of the Miracles and the Scriptures

John makes the connection between the miracles of Jesus and the *Scriptures*. His own profound apostolic record—the Gospel of John—is the unfolding of seven signs (miracles). He states the aim of this written unfolding of these seven signs: "These are *written* so that you may believe that Jesus is the Christ, the Son of God, and that by believing you may have life in his name" (John 20:31). In other words, John intends for his *writing* to put the glory-revealing signs on display for future generations—for us. Just as the miracles of Jesus displayed the peculiar glory of Christ in his earthly life, so they do the same for us as we read. John's Gospel preserves and portrays them for us. This was clearly his intention, as he shows in his first epistle:

> The life was made manifest, and we have seen it, and testify to it and proclaim to you the eternal life, which was with the Father and was made manifest to us—that which we have seen and heard we proclaim also to you, so that you too may have fellowship with us; and indeed our fellowship is with the Father and with his Son Jesus Christ. (1 John 1:2–3)

This is how Jesus intended the Spirit-guided Scriptures of his apostles to work. They would be the way later generations would see what the first generation saw: the glory of Christ. That's what Jesus said:

> When the Spirit of truth comes, he will guide you into all the truth, for he will not speak on his own authority, but whatever he hears

he will speak, and he will declare to you the things that are to come. *He will glorify me*, for he will take what is mine and declare it to you. (John 16:12–14)

The Holy Spirit of God will guide the apostles into all the truth, the aim of which is to glorify Jesus. That is, the writings of the apostles are designed to make the peculiar glory of Jesus's life, including his miracles, visible to generations to come as they read the inspired Scriptures.

Peculiar Glory on Display

This is how "the Scriptures manifest themselves to be the word of God" (Larger Catechism). Pervasively and profoundly, they put the peculiar glory of God on display. When God mercifully clears away the corroding effects of sin on the template of God's glory in our hearts, we see "the light of the knowledge of the glory of God in the face of Jesus Christ" (2 Cor. 4:6). It fits. This is what we were made for. We know it.

This light is its own confirmation, just as natural light is its own confirmation. We know we are seeing reality. In the end, we do not deduce by logical inference that the eyes of our heads are seeing objects in the world. Sight is its own argument. Similarly, in the end, we do not deduce by logical inference that the eyes of our hearts are seeing the peculiar glory of God in his word. Sight is its own argument. This is how the peculiar glory of Jesus's miracles confirms to us that the Scriptures are the word of God.

In the next chapter, we recognize an age-old reason that many have come to believe the Bible is true, namely, the effect it has had on people's lives. The astonishing truth is that the Bible addresses this and relates it directly to the peculiar glory of God we have been seeing. Therefore, the effect of the word in changing lives is part of the overall intention of God to reveal his self-authenticating glory in and by the word.

And we all, with unveiled face, beholding the glory of the Lord, are being transformed into the same image from one degree of glory to another. For this comes from the Lord who is the Spirit.

2 CORINTHIANS 3:18

16

In the People the Word Creates

When we consider that the Scriptures manifest themselves to be the word of God by the way they give all glory to God, we are drawn into a dazzling display of light shining from the innumerable facets of the diamond we call Scripture. New cultures and new generations and new individuals see an ever-expanding vista of the glory of God that is really there in the biblical revelation of God and his ways. Our exploration is not exhaustive, therefore, but illustrative.

God's Peculiar Glory

In this book, I am trying to draw out of Scripture some of the connections between the particularities of God's self-glorification and the ways these confirm the Scriptures as the word of God. I have argued that the Scriptures not only show *that* their pervasive aim is to give all glory to God (as the catechism says[1]), but also to show the astonishing *ways* they do so.

What has emerged is an essence or a center or a dominant peculiarity in the way God glorifies himself in Scripture. We have seen this in the way he glorifies himself in working for those who wait for him (chapter 13), through fulfilled prophecy (chapter 14), and through the miracles of Jesus (chapter 15). That dominant particularity is the

---

[1] Westminster Larger Catechism, Question #4: "How doth it appear that the Scriptures are the word of God?" Answer [in part]: "The Scriptures manifest themselves to be the word of God, by . . . the scope of the whole, which is to give all glory to God."

revelation of God's majesty through meekness. It is the revelation of the heights of his holiness through his humble helpfulness. And it is the grandeur of his grace through his voluntary sufferings in the rescue of sinners. This is God's *peculiar* glory. It is at the heart of the gospel of Jesus Christ. Along with countless manifestations in Scripture, this is the central brightness of "the light of the gospel of the glory of Christ, who is the image of God" (2 Cor. 4:4). This is what bursts upon the heart and mind of the person in whom God shines with "the light of the knowledge of the glory of God in the face of Jesus Christ" (2 Cor. 4:6). Now we push our exploration another step further. What we will see now is that the Scriptures manifest themselves to be the word of God by their display of this peculiar glory of God in the transformation of self-ish people into God-centered, Christ-exalting servants who live for the temporal and eternal good of others. More specifically, the Scriptures show themselves to be God's word both *by the new life they exhibit and by the new life they create.*

Beholding and Becoming the Glory of God

As we have noted, in 2 Corinthians 4:4–6 the apostle Paul connects the power of God's word, the glory of God, and the transformation of sinners. Verse 4 says that the reason people don't believe the gospel to be true is that they are blind to the light of this glory. But when God overcomes the blindness (v. 6), they see and believe. The seeing is the well-grounded foundation of faith. It is real. And the least educated and most educated hearers of God's word arrive at well-grounded certainty by the same final step: sight.

Five verses earlier, Paul had made the connection between this sight and the transformation of our lives. In 2 Corinthians 3:18 he shows how the glory of what we *behold* in the word creates a glory in the way we *behave* in the world. He wrote, "We all, with unveiled face, *behold-ing the glory of the Lord, are being transformed into the same image from one degree of glory to another.* For this comes from the Lord who is the Spirit" (2 Cor. 3:18). Beholding is becoming. We are transformed by seeing. And the nature of the transformation is shaped by the nature of what is seen. We see "the glory of the Lord." And we are changed "from one degree of glory to another."

This means that the word of God, with the gospel at its center, exhibits the glory of God in Christ and creates an exhibition of the glory of God in those who see and believe. The authentication of the Scriptures, therefore, arises both from the self-authenticating glory of God that they *display* and the living demonstration of that glory that they *create*.

The Lord of Glory Appears in the Word

Paul makes clear in the flow of his thought that this "beholding the glory of the Lord" happens through the "*gospel* of the glory of Christ" (2 Cor. 4:4), or the "*knowledge* of the glory of God in the face of Jesus Christ" (v. 6). In other words, for those who were not there in the first century to see Christ face-to-face, the sight of his glory is mediated by *words*. The "gospel" is a narration of once-for-all events. It is news. It is a true story. It is the word of God (cf. 1 Pet. 1:23, 25). But the event of God's self-glorification through the word of God is not limited to only one part of God's word called the "gospel."

The principle is that when God speaks, God himself stands forth for those who have eyes to see. "The LORD *appeared* again at Shiloh, for the LORD revealed *himself* to Samuel at Shiloh *by the word of the LORD*" (1 Sam. 3:21). The Lord himself "appeared." The Lord "revealed himself." These are astonishing statements. And notice *how* this self-revelation happens: "by the word of the Lord." We see *the Lord* by the *word* of the Lord. This is how Paul understands "beholding the glory of the Lord" in 2 Corinthians 3:18. We see this from the way Paul describes this self-revelation ("glory of the *Lord*") in terms of "the light of the *gospel* of the glory of Christ" in 2 Corinthians 4:4–6.

The apostles, and others in that day, saw the glory of the Lord face-to-face. They say, "We have seen his glory, glory as of the only Son from the Father, full of grace and truth" (John 1:14). Then Jesus promised to give them the Holy Spirit so that they could glorify the Lord as they depict him in their writings. The Lord said, "He [the Holy Spirit] will *glorify* me" (John 16:14). Thus, when we read the apostolic writings, we can see the "light of the knowledge of the glory of God in the face of Jesus Christ." The writings are of such a nature that it is, in one sense, as good as being there and seeing Jesus face-to-face. In fact, we probably have a significant advantage over those who were there, because we have the whole inspired apostolic interpretation of the events in the New Testament, whereas they were seeing things much more incrementally.

We should never think that Paul thought of his inspired portrayal of Christ (1 Cor. 2:13) as limited to a fraction of his message called "the gospel." In one sense, Paul saw all that he did as unfolding and clarifying aspects and implications of the gospel (1 Cor. 2:1–2). And it is clear from the way he spoke of his own authority that he saw all of his official teaching as God-given and having final authority (1 Cor. 14:37–38). When he was leaving the Ephesian elders, he said their blood was not on his hands—that is, if they failed to see and believe the truth of Christ, he was not responsible—because "I did not shrink from declaring to you *the whole counsel of God*" (Acts 20:27). It was not some part of his message that they were responsible to believe but the *wholeness* of it.

Therefore, when I say that "beholding the glory of the Lord" happens through "the word of the LORD" (1 Sam. 3:21), I am referring to all of God's inspired word. That is where the miracle of 2 Corinthians 3:18 happens: "Beholding the glory of the Lord, [we] are being transformed into the same image from one degree of glory to another."

Are We Made New by the Word or the Spirit?

The next step in pondering how the Scriptures are shown to be the word of God by the way they display and create the glory of God in people's lives is to clarify something that may have been misleading in the previous chapter on the miracles of Jesus. I argued that unless the human heart is brought into tune with God's will, it will never recognize the truth and beauty of God's peculiar glory in the miracles of Jesus. Jesus said as much: "If anyone's will is to do God's will, he will know whether the teaching is from God or whether I am speaking on my own authority" (John 7:17). If the human heart is in love with the praise of man, it will not be able to see and believe in a Christ who lives and teaches a radically different way of life. "How can you believe, when you receive glory from one another and do not seek the glory that comes from the only God?" (John 5:44).

The reason this may be misleading is that it sounds like something *other* than the word of God imparts the meaning and truth of the word. But if that were true, then the whole point that I am trying to make now would be contradictory. I am trying to show that it is precisely the glory of God *seen in the word* that brings about the change in us which is needed in order to see the truth and beauty of the word. Beholding the glory of the Lord, *in the word*, we are transformed. So the instrument of change in the human heart is the word of God. This is not in contradiction with the statement that our hearts must be changed in order to see the truth and beauty of the word.

The word itself is the instrument by which the Holy Spirit makes it possible for us to see the truth and beauty of the word. We see this in the way Peter describes the new birth, which is the most fundamental transformation that must happen in order for us to see the glory of Christ and believe. He writes, "You have been born again, not of perishable seed but of imperishable, *through the living and abiding word of God. . . .* And this word is the good news that was preached to you" (1 Pet. 1:23, 25). So the new birth does not happen apart from the word of God. God is the miracle worker in the new birth. "*He* has caused us to be born again" (1 Pet. 1:3). But the word of God is the *instrument* of the change.

Similarly James says, "Of his own will he brought us forth *by the word of truth*, that we should be a kind of firstfruits of his creatures" (James 1:18). We are new creatures—born again—"by the word of truth." The word is not passive in our transformation. Paul says, "We also thank God constantly for this, that when you received the word of God, which you heard from us, you accepted it not as the word of men but as what it really is, the word of God, *which is at work in you believers*" (1 Thess. 2:13). The word of the cross may be folly to those who are perishing, "but to us who are being saved it is *the power of God*" (1 Cor. 1:18). Thus John can teach that faith is owing to the new birth (1 John 5:1), and Paul can say, "Faith comes from hearing, and hearing through *the word of Christ*" (Rom. 10:17).

The word is the instrument in the hands of the Holy Spirit in the miracle of new birth, which brings about faith. But the effectiveness of the word in this miracle depends on the Holy Spirit's giving us life

(John 3:3, 7–8). It depends on God saying to the dark heart, "Let there be light." It depends on the Father's doing what flesh and blood cannot do (Matt. 16:17). That is, the effectiveness of the word depends on our being freed from the pride that values man above God (John 7:17; 5:44). And it is the word itself that brings this about.

We Are Made New by the Word in the Hand of the Spirit

I admit it may sound confusing to say that the word does the work. So how does this all fit together? How does the truth and beauty of the word itself do the transforming, yet a transformation must happen in order for us to see the truth and beauty of the word?

The clue lies in realizing that when God the Holy Spirit acts in our hearts so that we see the truth and beauty of Christ in his word, he does not add any knowledge that is not in the word. No truth and no beauty are added to what comes through the word. It is the Scriptures themselves that present Christ as compellingly glorious. Our conscious experience of this miracle is that the word breaks through. The word convinces. The word does the work of changing our mind. That is what we experience. And this conscious experience is true.

But the reason why the word did this work on a particular day—which it had not done, say, for the previous twenty years—is something other than the word. The word has always been what it is. It has always revealed the truth and beauty of Christ. The change happened in us, not in the word. It is as though the sun of truth has broken through the clouds after a long storm of darkness. Something blew the clouds away. But in our experience, it is the word that breaks through. The breaking through of the word and the blowing away of the clouds are as simple as opening the eye and seeing. The brightness of the word wakes us and convinces us. The Holy Spirit blows the blinding clouds away. But our experience is that the sword of the Spirit, the word of God (Eph. 6:17), cuts through them with irresistible light. The Spirit does not make the sun bright. The Spirit enables us to see the sun for what it really is. But it is the seeing that produces the conscious change. The Holy Spirit does not contribute any new light to "the light of the knowledge of the glory of God" (2 Cor. 4:6).

So was it wrong to say, as I did, that the human heart must be freed from its love affair with the praise of men in order to see and savor the glory of God in the miracles of Jesus and in the word of God? No.

Picture it like this. The work of the Holy Spirit and the work of the word of God in giving light to the soul are simultaneous in their effect. The reason is that the word is like an instrument or tool in the hands of the Holy Spirit. The soul has a template for the light of the glory of God in the word. That template possesses indented shapes, so to speak, which are a perfect fit for the glory of God. This template is a lifelong witness in our souls that we were made for God and that his glory is real. Sin has corroded this template and filled the indentations with corrosive deceptions of false glories. The glory of God becomes real to us when the Holy Spirit takes the tool of the word and by it removes the corrosive deceptions and fills the indentations of the template with truth. "You are clean because of the word that I have spoken to you" (John 15:3). "Sanctify them in the truth; your word is truth" (John 17:17).

Thus it is true to say that the human heart must be changed "before" it can see the glory of God in the word, because those corrosive blockages must be removed. But the word "before" has a causal meaning, not a temporal one—as if I were to say, "You must open your eyes *before* you can see the light." In fact, the opening of the eye and the seeing of light are simultaneous. The opening of the eye is a kind of cause without which light will not shine through, yet the removal of the obstacle and the seeing of light are simultaneous. So the corrosives of deception in the heart must be removed "before" the light of the glory of God can be seen. Yet the glory of God in the word is the instrument that removes the blinding corrosives.

So, for example, the corrosive deception that the praise of man is preferable to the glory of God must be removed "before" we can see the supremely beautiful glory of God as our greatest treasure. But how do we experience this? We experience it when the glory of God in the word utterly obliterates that dark corrosive with its superior brightness. The removal of the deception and the seeing of the superior glory are simultaneous. The deception goes and the truth arrives in the same instant. But the removal of deception was causally "prior" because this truth and this deception could not coexist. Yet, in the hands of the Holy Spirit, it was the truth that destroyed the deception.

The Word Is Confirmed by the Glory It Creates

What we have seen so far in this chapter is that the reality of the glory of God, shining through the word of God, adds this to its self-authenticating powers: it creates in human hearts images of its own divine glory (2 Cor. 3:18). The peculiar glory of God in Scripture is reflected in his people: they are transformed from self-centered, self-exalting people to God-centered, Christ-exalting servants, who live for the good of others. In this, they are like Christ, the perfect embodiment of the peculiar glory of love through lowliness. This change extends the self-authenticating evidence of the glory of God through the word into the character and the good works of God's people. Thus the people who are most transformed *by* the word become evidences for the reality of the God *of* the word.

The Salt and Light of the World

For example, Jesus said to his disciples,

> You are the light of the world. A city set on a hill cannot be hidden. Nor do people light a lamp and put it under a basket, but on a stand, and it gives light to all in the house. In the same way, let your light shine before others, so that they may see your good works and give glory to your Father who is in heaven. (Matt. 5:14–16)

First, Jesus had appeared in the world as the light of the world. "I am the light of the world. Whoever follows me will not walk in darkness, but will have the light of life" (John 8:12). Now the disciples have beheld the glory of the Lord and have been changed from one degree of glory to another into his image (2 Cor. 3:18). So he calls them the light of the world. They are extending the glory they have seen into the world by the transformation of their lives.

Specifically, Jesus says, "They will see your *good works* and give glory to your Father who is in heaven" (Matt. 5:16). In some way, through the works of the followers of Jesus, the glory of God is visible. But this is not automatic. Not everyone who sees the disciples' transformed lives gives glory to God. This should remind us of the miracles of Jesus, which we focused on in chapter 15. Not everyone who saw the miracles saw the glory of God. And not everyone who sees the good deeds of Jesus's disciples sees the glory of God. As with Jesus's miracles, so with the disciples' good deeds, there is something peculiar about the glory of these works. What is it?

Jesus had just said about his disciples:

> Blessed are those who are persecuted for righteousness' sake, for theirs is the kingdom of heaven. Blessed are you when others revile you and persecute you and utter all kinds of evil against you falsely on my account. Rejoice and be glad, for your reward is great in heaven, for so they persecuted the prophets who were before you. (Matt. 5:10–12)

So it is clear that not all who see the disciples' "righteousness" (v. 10) are moved to give glory to God. Some people persecute and revile them (v. 11). But amazingly, Jesus says that his people—those who have been "called out of darkness into his marvelous light" (1 Pet. 2:9)—must not grumble, but rather rejoice. This kind of response to suffering is so utterly extraordinary that Jesus immediately says, "You are the salt of the earth. . . . You are the light of the world" (Matt. 5:13–14). The stunning taste and brightness of the disciples' *joy in suffering for righteousness' sake* is the salt and light of the world.[2] This is the peculiar glory Jesus brought into the world. This is the light of the glory of Christ that we see in the gospel (2 Cor. 4:4). And this is the peculiar glory his followers reflect when they "behold the glory of the Lord" (2 Cor. 3:18).

So when Jesus says in Matthew 5:16, "Let your light shine before others, so that they may see your good works and give glory to your Father who is in heaven," the light he has in mind is the peculiar brightness described in verses 10–12. The light that moves people to give glory to God is not mere good deeds but *deeds of love done with Christ-dependent joy in spite of mistreatment*. When people have their eyes opened by the Spirit of God, they see the God-given beauty in such deeds and give glory to God. Others see just another moral performance and chalk it up to natural causes.

---

[2] Another evidence for this interpretation is Paul's line of thought in Phil. 2:14–15: "Do all things *without grumbling or disputing*, that you may be blameless and innocent, children of God without blemish in the midst of a crooked and twisted generation, among whom *you shine as lights in the world*." Notice that the specific behavior that shines as "light" in the world is "not grumbling," which is another way of saying: when things go badly, do the opposite of grumbling, namely, rejoice, which is what Matt. 5:12 says.

This extraordinary saltiness and brightness in the glory of the disciples' lives is the reflected radiance of the glory of Christ, mediated through the words of God. This is true not only for us who know the glory of Christ through the inspired narratives of his followers, but also for those who followed him in his earthly days. They too were dependent on the words of the Lord for their transformation. They knew him not only because of what he did but also because of what he said.

Christ Gave Them the Words of God and the Glory of God

We see this in Jesus's prayer in John 17: "I have given them your word, and the world has hated them because they are not of the world, just as I am not of the world" (v. 14). It was the word of God through Jesus that transformed the disciples so that they were out of step with the world. This is perhaps what Jesus has in mind when he says, "The *glory* that you [Father] have given me I have given to them" (v. 22). The glory that rested on Jesus was reflected in the disciples. And parallel to this were the words: "I have given them the *words* that you gave me" (v. 8). So Jesus gave the *words* of God to his disciples and the *glory* of God to his disciples, and thus they were radically out of step with the world. And some hated them. And some believed.

And their Christ-dependent joy in spite of mistreatment has the same origin, namely, in Christ's words. In the prayer of John 17, Jesus says, "These things I *speak* in the world, that they may have my joy fulfilled in themselves" (v. 13). Again in John 15:11, he says the same thing: "These things I have *spoken* to you, that my joy may be in you, and that your joy may be full." Notice, the joy of the disciples is not just a joy in response to Jesus. It is the very joy *of* Jesus in them. Yet Jesus says it is owing to "these things I have spoken." Which means, therefore, that the joy that Jesus experiences becomes the joy that the disciples experience, mediated to them through his words.

Joy That Sustains Love in Suffering

This Christ-dependent, Christ-displaying joy is a joy in spite of mistreatment. And for both Jesus and the disciples, it flows from the hope of the glory of God. "For the *joy* that was set before him [he] *endured the cross*, despising the shame, and is seated at the right hand of the throne of God" (Heb. 12:2). Parallel to this is: "Blessed are you when others . . . persecute you. . . . Rejoice and be glad, for your reward is great in heaven" (Matt. 5:11–12). Christ loved the world as he endured sufferings in the hope of great reward. And this is the same joy that sustains his followers in their *deeds of love done with Christ-dependent joy in spite of mistreatment*, as they look to a great reward.

Jesus prays, "Father, glorify me in your own presence with the glory that I had with you before the world existed" (John 17:5). And then he prays for his disciples to share the same: "Father, I desire that they also, whom you have given me, may be with me where I am, to see my glory that you have given me because you loved me before the foundation of the world" (v. 24). This is the great reward both Jesus and we look to in our suffering. It is the key to our joy in sorrow and therefore the key to enduring in love in spite of suffering. This peculiar beauty of this final glory came into the world in Jesus and is reflected in his disciples. This happened then and happens now through the word of God. The word exhibits and creates the glory of Christ in the lives of Christ's followers, and this too is how the Scriptures manifest themselves to be the word of God.

To Convince and Convert, Comfort and Build Up

The Scriptures "manifest themselves to be the word of God, by . . . the scope of the whole, which is to give all glory to God." The words that God inspired carry a divine and human intention that is interpenetrated with the light of the glory of God. The shining of this light, by the Scriptures, into the human heart confirms that these Scriptures are the word of God. This is true both generally and specifically. The general thrust of Scripture is that God get . . . all the glory. Together with their claim to be God's word, this thrust of the Scriptures is a confirmation to the glory-shaped template of the human heart that the Scriptures are the word of God.

But along with the general thrust of the Scriptures to give all the glory to God, there are the specific ways that Scripture embodies the peculiar glory of God. We have seen this in the way God works for those who wait for him (chapter 13), in the fulfillment of prophecy (chapter 14), in the miracles of Jesus (chapter 15), and now in the way

the Scriptures exhibit and create human lives that embody this peculiar glory. That peculiar glory is majesty in meekness, strength through
weakness, and *deeds of love done with Christ-dependent joy in spite
of mistreatment.*

We saw that this astonishing change in the self-exalting human soul
is the light of the world (Matt. 5:14). When Christians live lives of love
in this peculiar spirit, those who see, with the Spirit-given sight, give
glory to the Father who is in heaven (Matt. 5:16). It is not the good
deeds alone that convince, just as it is not the miracles of Jesus alone
that convinced. It is the peculiar glory of God embedded in the deeds—
and in the miracles—that must be seen. When it is seen, the reality of
God is confirmed.

This new heart of *love*—expressed with *Christ-dependent joy in
spite of mistreatment*—is the creation of the Spirit *through the word
of God.* Love and joy are the fruit of the Spirit (Gal. 5:22). And love
and joy are the work of the word (1 Tim. 1:5; Gal. 3:5; John 15:11).
The word reveals the Lord Jesus (1 Sam. 3:21), who is the embodiment
of this peculiar glory (2 Cor. 4:4). And as we behold this glory in the
word, we are changed into that image from glory to glory (2 Cor. 3:18).

One way to understand this chapter would be to see it as the unfolding of another answer of the Larger Catechism. In answer to the question about how the Scriptures show themselves to be the word of God,
it also answers, "The Scriptures manifest themselves to be the Word of
God . . . *by their light and power to convince and convert sinners, to
comfort and build up believers unto salvation.*" Instead of unpacking
these words in detail, I have gone beneath them to the connection they
have with that other answer: "The Scriptures manifest themselves to be
the word of God, by . . . the scope of the whole, which is to give all glory
to God." My discovery is that the *way* the Scriptures "convince and
convert and comfort and build up" is by the revelation of the peculiar
glory of God in Christ.

If we wanted to make a book out of this one chapter, we could press
into other Scriptures that exhibit the peculiar glory of Christ in the lives
of believers. For example, we would turn to Philippians 2:5–11 ("Let
this mind be in you which was also in Christ Jesus," v. 5, NKJV); and
1 Peter 2:19–24 ("To this you have been called, because Christ also

suffered for you," v. 21); and Ephesians 4:32–5:2 ("Walk in love, as Christ loved us and gave himself up for us," v. 2). Careful study would show that Christ's self-emptying (Phil. 2:7), suffering (1 Pet. 2:23), and patient forgiving (Eph. 4:32) are replicated in the lives of his disciples *through the word of God.*

This word is what Jesus bequeathed to his church through the apostolic Scriptures, the New Testament. This is where we see the glory of God exhibited in the lives of Jesus's disciples and their teaching about the Christian life. But even more compelling is the power of these Scriptures to impart Christ's peculiar glory to us as we behold the glory of the Lord, and "are being transformed into the same image from one degree of glory to another" (2 Cor. 3:18). It is the Scriptures that impart this glory. The words that God inspired have a divine and human meaning that is interpenetrated with the light of the glory of God. The shining of this light, through the Scriptures, into the human heart confirms that they are the word of God.

In the next chapter we acknowledge that the pathway we have taken, in quest of a well-grounded conviction that the Scriptures are true, is not the same as arguments from history. In fact, the approach we have taken raises questions about the legitimacy of such historical proofs and even of human reasoning in the task of Bible study. So the question that needs to be asked now is this: How does the sight of divine glory in Scripture relate to the ordinary use of human reason and historical data in the way we understand and corroborate the Bible?

When you read this, you can perceive my insight into the mystery of Christ.

17

The Place of

Historical Reasoning

The question we ask in this chapter is, How do human reasoning and historical scholarship (or any mental effort in Bible study) relate to the spiritual sight of the glory of God in the Scriptures? Another way to ask it would be, How does knowledge gained by "beholding the glory of the Lord" in the word (2 Cor. 3:18) relate to knowledge gained by logical inference from historical data (such as biblical texts)? Or another way to ask it would be, How does the knowledge of honey gained by tasting relate to the knowledge of honey gained by observation (golden-brown, highly viscous, coming from beehives)? Or how does the knowledge of daylight gained by sight relate to the knowledge of daylight gained by inferences from other senses (warmth on the skin, the clock strikes noon, other people say the sun is shining)?

The reason this question matters is that someone might infer from what I have said so far that the observation of the world with our physical senses and the use of reason to draw valid inferences are of little importance, since God reveals the truth of his word directly to our hearts by a sight of his glory. This would be a fatal mistake. *Fatal* is the right word—not a minor mistake, but fatal. The reason it would be fatal, as we are going to see, is that the glory of God is mediated to our souls *through* biblical texts, which exist for us today and are understood by us today only with the help of observation, reasoning, and historical data (such as texts).

Persuasion by Reason and Persuasion by the Spirit

We took seriously John Calvin's teaching on the testimony of the Holy Spirit: "Then only, therefore, does Scripture suffice to give a saving knowledge of God when its certainty is founded on the inward persuasion of the Holy Spirit."[1] The Holy Spirit is decisive in opening our eyes to see God's glory in the Scriptures. Nevertheless, Calvin acknowledges that there are other arguments and reasons for the truth of Scripture:

> There are other reasons, neither few nor feeble, by which the dignity and majesty of the Scriptures may be not only proved to the pious, but also completely vindicated against the cavils of slanderers. These, however, cannot of themselves produce a firm faith in Scripture until our heavenly Father manifest his presence in it, and thereby secure implicit reverence for it.[2]

So there is spiritual usefulness in tracing out "reasons" for the truth of Scripture other than the immediate sight of their glory. Yet even here the question is not posed the way I am posing it. Calvin is not asking (as I am), How did the average person even come to have a Bible? And how did a person learn to read (French, or Greek, or English) in the first place, or to construe language orally? And what mental processes does a person go through in order to find the true meaning of a text instead of a false one?

But these questions are crucial if we are to know the proper relationship between knowledge by spiritual sight and knowledge by empirical observation and rational inference. Jonathan Edwards is aware of the issue and comes closer to asking the question that concerns me:

> A Christian is a knowing, understanding person, not only with spiritual saving knowledge, but in doctrinal knowledge of religion, for saving knowledge depends upon it. 'Tis not possible that any should know the excellency of Jesus Christ, that he is a mediator,

---

[1] John Calvin, *Institutes of the Christian Religion*, trans. F. L. Battles, ed. J. T. McNeill (Philadelphia: Westminster Press, 1960), 1.8.13.
[2] Ibid.

except he knows who Christ is, that he is mediator, and how he is mediator, and that he is God. And many other things are necessary to be known of Christ in order to see his excellency. There must be a knowledge what the things of the gospel are, before we can be sensible of the truth and reality and excellency of the things of the gospel.[3]

That last sentence is the crucial observation: "There must be a knowledge what the things of the gospel are, before we can be sensible of the truth and reality and excellency of the things of the gospel." Or, as he says earlier, "saving knowledge depends [on] doctrinal knowledge." That is, we must know what the Bible teaches before we can see the glory of God in that teaching.

The Mental Work of Preserving and Interpreting Texts

This means that the Bible must be preserved from generation to generation so that its truth can be known in our own day. And that preservation involves the mental work of reading and transmitting the text. Then there must also be faithful translations so that those who don't know Greek and Hebrew may have access to the true meaning of Scripture. And such translations depend on a rigorous mental effort to know at least two languages—the original one and the one into which we are translating. And then there are mental skills involved in reading, some of which we learned as children, but others of which we have learned later in order to read with greater care.

All the processes of preserving the original text, transmitting it, translating it, and learning to construe its true meaning involve the natural uses of our senses in observation and mental capacities of reason and inference. These processes are essential for any of us to have access to the meaning of biblical texts where God's glory is seen. Therefore, as Edwards says, spiritual, saving knowledge—the sight of "the light of the gospel of the glory of Christ" (2 Cor. 4:4)—is dependent on the natural knowledge of what the Scripture teaches.

---

[3] Jonathan Edwards, "A Spiritual Understanding of Divine Things Denied to the Unregenerate," in *Sermons and Discourses, 1723–1729*, vol. 14, *The Works of Jonathan Edwards*, ed. Harry S. Stout and Kenneth P. Minkema (New Haven, CT: Yale University Press, 1997), 92.

Faith Comes by Hearing, Sight by Reading

Faith comes by hearing, sight by reading—this is, in fact, what the Scriptures tell us. There can be no saving faith where there is no knowledge of the gospel.

> "Everyone who calls on the name of the Lord will be saved." How then will they call on him in whom they have not believed? And how are they to believe in him of whom they have never heard? And how are they to hear without someone preaching? And how are they to preach unless they are sent? As it is written, "How beautiful are the feet of those who preach the good news!" But they have not all obeyed the gospel. For Isaiah says, "Lord, who has believed what he has heard from us?" So faith comes from hearing, and hearing through the word of Christ. (Rom. 10:13–17)

Paul is addressing the very thing that concerns us here: How do knowledge by hearing the word and knowledge by seeing glory in the word relate to each other? His answer is that there can be no knowledge by seeing the glory of God in the word if we don't hear the word.

Paul makes a similar point when he says to the Ephesians that the means by which they can know his insight into the mystery of Christ is by *reading* what he has written.

> I, Paul, a prisoner for Christ Jesus on behalf of you Gentiles—assuming that you have heard of the stewardship of God's grace that was given to me for you, how the mystery was made known to me by revelation, as I have written briefly. *When you read this, you can perceive my insight into the mystery of Christ.* (Eph. 3:1–4)

It is through reading what is accessible to the ordinary human eye and mind—the text of Scripture—that spiritual sight may happen. Reading with a view to right understanding is a rigorous mental effort. We worked hard at it in the first six years of our schooling. It was a human affair, not necessarily a spiritual one. Since our childhood, we have, perhaps, learned even more demanding skills of reading carefully. All of this involved our powers of observation and our rational ability. This, Paul says, is the way you can "perceive my insight into the mystery of Christ." There is no access to the mystery of Christ (where the "riches of his glory" are found, Col. 1:27) without reading (or hearing) the inspired writings. Paul does not believe in a spiritual revelation of the glories of the mystery of Christ apart from a right understanding of inspired Scripture.

The Only Pathway to Seeing Glory Is Human Thinking

One had to see the human Jesus in order to see that he was more than human. One had to see the human enactment of the miracles of Jesus in order to see the peculiar divine glory of the miracles. And one has to see the behavior of a follower of Jesus in order to discern the glory of Christ's image. In the same way, one must see and interpret the human language of the Scriptures in order to see the light of the gospel of the glory of Christ in them. Which means that the only pathway to the self-authenticating light of the glory of God in Scripture is the path of human observation and human reasoning.

Notice, it is not just that we must *have* the Scriptures and that we must *read* (or hear) them, but also that we must read them in some measure according to their original and true meaning. God's glory interpenetrates the true meaning of the Scriptures. It is the true meaning of texts that emits the divine glory. It is not magically attached to letters and words. It is embodied in the meaning that the words carry. Thus a false interpretation of some teaching or action of Jesus will not truly reveal his glory. The apostle Peter says that there are things in the Scriptures that "the ignorant and unstable twist to their own destruction" (2 Pet. 3:16). Twisted Scriptures do not convey the glory of God. They lead to destruction.

The implications of this are enormous. Parents will labor to teach their children to read, for this is the normal pathway to the mystery of Christ (Eph. 3:4). Schools will be established where the skills of reading in the most careful way will be taught. And we will all make a priority out of reading the Bible with great zeal and accuracy. As Edwards says, "If you would with success seek divine and spiritual knowledge, get that knowledge of divine things that is within your power, even a doctrinal knowledge of the principles of the Christian religion."[4] If you want to

---

[4] Ibid.

see the glory of a painting, keep looking at the painting. Study it. If you want to see the glory of the sunrise, get up before dawn and face east.

The glory of God is not contained in the Scriptures the way a jewel is contained in a box. It is contained in the Scriptures the way light is contained in fire, the way sweetness is contained in honey, the way redness and fragrance are contained in the rose. When the spiritual nerve endings and spiritual taste buds and spiritual retina are made alive by the Spirit, these glories are tasted and seen. But not without a natural contact with the fire and the honey and the rose.

How Do We Depend on Scholarship and Other Human Agency?

Does this mean that we are back to depending on the scholars for our faith? The answer is mixed. We are not dependent on historians and apologists and scholars to prove to us that the Scriptures are true and that God is real. But we are dependent on human agents to give us access to the Bible. And we are dependent on human agency—our own and others'—to give us the ability to construe the meaning of the Bible through reading or hearing what it says. There is no access to the peculiar glory of God in his word without human agency. And there is no access to the true meaning of biblical texts without human agency. Seeing the truth and beauty of God in Scripture will always require more than human agency. But never less.

Reading well is a mediator of glory. When Paul observed that a veil lay over the hearts of the Jewish people (2 Cor. 3:15) when the Scriptures were read in the synagogue every week (Acts 13:27; 15:21), the solution was not to stop reading the Scriptures. The solution was to turn to the Lord Jesus. "When one turns to the Lord, the veil is removed" (2 Cor. 3:16). The veil is lifted to see what is there. If we turn away from reading, there is little reason to think the Lord will lift the veil. What would we see?

The Path of Apologetics Is the Path to Light

What does all this imply for the work of apologetics—the effort to give rational and historical arguments for the truth of the Christian faith? One way to describe the implication is to say that the actual *path* to rational persuasion from historical facts and valid inferences is the *same* as the path to spiritual sight. In other words, even though the closure with certainty at the end of the path is different, the path is the same. We prayerfully *observe* the facts before us, and we *think* about them in order to construe the meaning that the inspired author (and God) intended us to see. That is what we must do, whether we are seeking rational persuasion or spiritual illumination. This is because both kinds of knowledge are rooted in real human history and real human sentences.

One way to illustrate this shared pathway toward different aims— valid inference versus spiritual sight—would be to follow the apostle Paul's argumentation from his own life as a means to both ends. In the previous chapter, I argued that one way the Scriptures show themselves to be the word of God is by the way they create images of the glory of God in the lives of those who are transformed by the Scriptures. People behold the glory of Christ in the word of God, and they are changed "from one degree of glory to another" (2 Cor. 3:18). Paul is one of those people. And he believes that the impact of the word of God on his life is a good argument for the truth of the gospel. Let's follow his argument to see how it represents the single path toward well-grounded faith.

The Life of Paul as a Compelling Creation of the Word of God

Virtually all scholars agree that Paul wrote the epistle to the Galatians. Even scholars who do not believe in the truth of Christianity, or that Paul was an inspired spokesman of Christ, are convinced that he really wrote this letter. It is one of his most personal and passionate. In his letter, Paul deals with adversaries who think he is not a reliable apostle. So one of the first things he does is defend his apostleship. Here is the argument as he gives it:

> Am I now seeking the approval of man, or of God? Or am I trying to please man? If I were still trying to please man, I would not be a servant of Christ. For I would have you know, brothers, that the gospel that was preached by me is not man's gospel. For I did not receive it from any man, nor was I taught it, but I received it through a revelation of Jesus Christ. For you have heard of my former life in Judaism, how I persecuted the church of God violently and tried to destroy it. And I was advancing in Judaism beyond many of my own age among my people, so extremely zealous was I for the traditions

of my fathers. But when he who had set me apart before I was born, and who called me by his grace, was pleased to reveal his Son to me, in order that I might preach him among the Gentiles, I did not immediately consult with anyone; nor did I go up to Jerusalem to those who were apostles before me, but I went away into Arabia, and returned again to Damascus. Then after three years I went up to Jerusalem to visit Cephas and remained with him fifteen days. But I saw none of the other apostles except James the Lord's brother. (In what I am writing to you, before God, I do not lie!) Then I went into the regions of Syria and Cilicia. And I was still unknown in person to the churches of Judea that are in Christ. They only were hearing it said, "He who used to persecute us is now preaching the faith he once tried to destroy." And they glorified God because of me. (Gal. 1:10–24)

The argument goes like this:

Premise 1: You know how totally devoted I was to traditional Judaism (v. 14) and how violently I opposed Christianity (v. 13).

Premise 2: The very ones I once tried to destroy are now glorifying God because of what they see in me (v. 24).

Premise 3: I did not consult with the other apostles for the content or the authority of my new calling (vv. 16–23).

Conclusion: "I did not receive it from any man, nor was I taught it, but I received it through a revelation of Jesus Christ" (v. 12).

The crucial clue in the text that Paul is arguing this way is the word "For" at the beginning of verse 13:

I did not receive [my gospel] from any man, nor was I taught it, but I received it through a revelation of Jesus Christ. *For* you have heard of my former life in Judaism, how I persecuted the church of God violently and tried to destroy it.

From verse 13 through verse 24, Paul is building his case that his message and authority come directly from the risen Christ. He has more to say about the way the other apostles approved his apostolic authority

(Gal. 2:7–9), but for our purposes, we have seen in Galatians 1:10–24 the crucial way Paul argues for the truth of his apostleship.

His argument is for the validity of an inference based on human observation and thinking. Given how deep was his devotion to Judaism, and how radical was his opposition to Christianity, and how he has now done a 180-degree turn and is risking his life to spread the very faith he once opposed, we are justified in inferring the truth of his claim to have encountered the risen Christ and received his message from him. It is a valid inference.

Pursuing Paul's Way of Arguing Further

In this way, it seems to me, Paul gives warrant to the task of apologetics.[5] In fact, I think Paul would endorse pressing the argument further, since the evidence is there in his writings to sustain it. For example, the apologist might raise the question: But how do we know whether the change in Paul's behavior might be owing to (1) a serious psychosis, a kind of delusional mental illness that religious egomaniacs sometimes experience; or (2) a hoax put over on the churches and the world by a phenomenally clever con man; or (3) an honest mistake of some kind that Paul stumbled into?

Then the apologist, with Paul's help, would take these possible explanations of his transformation one at a time and test them to see if they are probable inferences from what we know.

The apologist would observe, first, that Paul's writings simply do not fit the way psychotics talk. This is not an unsupportable claim by a Christian advocate. This observation is readily available to anyone who can read English. In any bookstore or library or on the Internet, you can obtain a Bible with all of Paul's letters. You can read them for yourself in about seven hours, even if you are a slow reader.

What you find is that his writings (such as the book of Romans) are reasoned in an extended and coherent way. Alongside that reasonableness, his letters also bear the marks of warm, personal relationships.

---

[5] The word *apologetics* comes from the Greek *apologia*, which is used, e.g., in 1 Pet. 3:15 in a way that points to the meaning of apologetics: "In your hearts honor Christ the Lord as holy, always being prepared to make a defense (*apologian*) to anyone who asks you for a reason for the hope that is in you; yet do it with gentleness and respect." Thus, apologetics, for Christians, has come to refer to the effort to defend the faith and give solid reasons for why a person should be a Christian and believe the Christian Scriptures are true.

They show profound concern for others, even at great cost to himself. They show a wide and healthy range of human emotion rather than the pathological lopsidedness of the mentally ill. In other words, it is not possible to make a compelling case that Paul was mentally ill or psychotic or delusional. That explanation of his transformation is pure speculation without any basis in historical fact.

Then, second, the apologist would observe that year after year Paul embraced a life of suffering to spread the gospel for the salvation of others. This simply rules out the thought that he is using his apostleship as a cover for a con game. People often embrace suffering for what is false but not for what is known to be false. When we know what we are teaching is false, we are motivated to line our own pockets with money, not get whipped and beaten and imprisoned and killed. Paul repeatedly proved by his life that he was not being driven by money—making tents to earn a living, not taking offerings for himself, having others handle the money he collected for the poor, living simply. His sufferings for the sake of the churches were part of the open record (2 Cor. 6:3–10; 11:23–28). This suggestion, that his transformation is owing to his desire to deceive the churches, has no evidence to support it.

Third, the apologist would observe that Paul certainly was not a perfect man and could make honest mistakes. But to say that this explains his decades-long ministry is not compelling. The problem with such a suggestion is that the ostensible mistake at his conversion goes on for decades. Year after year, Paul would be making the most outrageous claims about his own revelatory experiences and the truth of Christ and the Holy Spirit and the nature of reality. This would not be an honest mistake. This would be a lifetime of sustained delusion or fabrication. Unless Paul is telling the truth.

And thus the apologist would point out that the evidence is strong that when Paul explains the divine origin of his apostleship, he is speaking as a reasonable and honest man who knows what he is saying and why. His explanation is that Christ appeared to him and that he is the ongoing recipient of divine revelation (1 Cor. 2:13). With this apostolic authority, Paul claims that all of the Old Testament is inspired by God (1 Tim. 3:16–17); presents a full portrait of the deity of Christ (Col.

1:19; 2:9; Phil. 2:5–11) and his saving work; and claims that his own teachings have the authority of God (1 Cor. 14:37–38; 1 Cor. 2:13).

My point here is that this kind of apologetic argument is in line with what Paul had begun in Galatians 1:10–24. It takes facts seriously. It reasons. It infers. And in Paul's mind, this kind of reasoning, on the basis of observation and inference, is valid. Such observation and reasoning is the same pathway we take whether we hope to find rational validation or spiritual illumination. We pray for God's help in both cases, and we are dependent, in both cases, on the Spirit both for the right use of reason and for the gift of spiritual sight.

The Path of Apologetics May, or May Not, Yield a Sight of Glory

But if we take this pathway and arrive only at a valid inference that Paul is a true spokesman of the risen Christ, what do we have? We have a conclusion that heightens our accountability to believe in Christ. We have a pattern of argumentation that may overcome numerous objections that unbelievers raise to the truth of Scripture. And we have a valid narrative of God's work in Paul's transformation.

But we do not yet have saving faith or a glimpse of the "light of the knowledge of the glory of God in the face of Jesus Christ" (2 Cor. 4:6). We do not have more than what the Devil has. He knows that Paul was genuinely converted by the risen Christ. He knows this with greater certainty than any historian who has ever lived.

But we have not wasted our time. For it is precisely through this "valid narrative of God's work in Paul's transformation" that the peculiar glory of God can break forth. In the previous chapter, we saw that not all the good deeds of believers cause people to give glory to God. But sometimes people see *through* the transformed lives of believers, behold the glory of God, and give glory to our Father in heaven (Matt. 5:16).

It is similar with Paul's divinely transformed life. The capstone of his argument in Galatians was this: "And they glorified God because of me" (Gal. 1:24). Not all did. He was hated and persecuted all his life. But some did. Some looked at the new man, Paul, or heard the story he told, or read something he wrote, and they saw the peculiar glory of God. Paul had beheld the glory of God in the risen Christ and was transformed by it. They saw this glory in Paul himself and embraced him as a true spokesman of the risen Christ. "They glorified God" because of him.

In other words, the path to this divine illumination and the path to the valid inference of Paul's truthfulness are the same path. The final closure of certainty is not the same. In one case, the heart sees *through* the narrative of Paul's transformation to the glory of Christ reflected in his change. In the other case, the mind infers that Paul is a true spokesman for the risen Christ and may or may not see the peculiar and compelling beauty of the work of God in Paul's life. The reader may conclude by inference that this is honey and yet not taste it, that this is a rose but not see red or smell the fragrance, that this is fire but not see the light.

Human Agency Necessary

What we have seen in this chapter is that the relationship between reason and faith is not hostile. The relationship between spiritual sight and empirical observation is not antagonistic. The relationship between divine illumination and human agency in the process of knowing are not at odds. Or, to put it positively, the divine and saving sight of the glory of God is always mediated by the (humanly preserved and humanly construed) word of God. "Faith comes from hearing, and hearing through the *word* of Christ" (Rom. 10:17). "When you *read* this, you can perceive my insight into the mystery of Christ" (Eph. 3:4).

Since the saving sight of the glory of God (2 Cor. 4:6) always comes through the word, it is necessarily dependent on human agency—the agency of others who *preserve* the word's presence in our hands, and the agency of ourselves who *construe* the word's meaning in our minds. If the word is not preserved for us, we have no access to the meaning where the glory shines. And if the word is not construed correctly, likewise, we have no access to the meaning where the glory shines.

So while we are not dependent on human observation and reasoning to provide certainty of the word's truth, we are dependent on human effort to bring the book to our hands and its meaning to our minds. God has ordained that it be this way. Faith comes by hearing. No sending, no preaching. No preaching, no hearing. No hearing, no believing.

No believing, no calling on the Lord. No calling, no salvation (Rom. 10:13–15). Hence the necessity of missions, and the necessity of scholarship, and the necessity of reading, and the necessity of the word.

The link between the previous chapter (about the kind of people that the word of God creates) and this one has been the conversion of the apostle Paul, whose newness as a Christian was both a reflection of the glory of Christ and the ground for a valid inference that he was a true apostle. Paul saw his own life both ways. He argued in Galatians that one could reasonably infer his apostleship from his life change. And he argued that one could also see the glory of God through that same life change (Gal. 1:24). The pathway to knowledge by observation and inference is the same—the pathway on which we receive divine light. But inferences by themselves do not save. Only the divine "light of the gospel of the glory of Christ" transforms the soul. Only divine light yields certainty that secures the soul for a life of love through the worst sufferings. Only the sight of God's glory in his inspired word gives certainty to the simplest and the most educated person.

Conclusion

My conclusion is that "the Bible, consisting of the sixty-six books of the Old and New Testaments, is the infallible Word of God, verbally inspired by God, and without error in the original manuscripts,"[1] and that this can be known with a well-grounded confidence because the peculiar glory of God shines in and through these Scriptures.

This also implies that the Scriptures are the supreme and final authority in testing all claims about what is true and right and beautiful. In matters not explicitly addressed by the Bible, it implies that what is true and right and beautiful is to be assessed by criteria consistent with the teachings of Scripture. All of this implies that the Bible has final authority over every area of our lives and that we should, therefore, try to bring all our thinking and feeling and acting into line with what the Bible teaches.

I do not write those words lightly. They make a staggering claim. Breathtaking. If they are not true, they are outrageous. The Bible is not the private charter of a faith community among other faith communities. It is a total claim on the whole world. God, the creator, owner, and governor of the world, has spoken. His words are valid and binding on all people everywhere. That is what it means to be God. And to our astonishment, his way of speaking with unique, infallible authority in the twenty-first century is through a book. One book. Not many. That is the breathtaking declaration of the Christian Scriptures.

---

[1] Taken from the Bethlehem Baptist Church Elder Affirmation of Faith, http://www.hopeingod.org /document/elder-affirmation-faith

An Understandable Obstacle

For some of you, this claim presents an enormous obstacle. You may belong to another religion with its own sacred scriptures. You may have no religion. Or you may have your hands in many spiritual pots, attempting to find the most inspiring and helpful parts from all of them. In all these cases, the totality of the claim that the Christian Scriptures lay on you may feel out of the question.

You may feel that the only things such a total claim can breed are intolerance, and then hate, and then violence. You may point to religiously motivated terror in our day or to historical violence in the name of Christianity. An answer to that concern is worthy of an entire book. But short of that, I would briefly ask you to consider another angle.

Does reason and history show that totalitarian abuses of ethnic and religious minorities are avoided by the avoidance of religious absolutes? The great horrors of the twentieth century were not perpetrated by lovers of God—six million Jews murdered in Germany, and sixty million people killed or starved under the Soviet regime, and forty million destroyed under the Chinese Cultural Revolution of Mao Zedong, and over a million purged in the Communist Killing Fields of Cambodia. These atrocities were pursued by those who considered biblical religion (and all other religions that give allegiance to God over the state) to be a threat. In other words, the solution to the historic problem of religious violence is not irreligion. We have tasted the horrors of those who exalt themselves above the absolutes of religion.

Is it not obvious (or at least, very likely) that where God is rejected as an authority over us, we tend to put ourselves in that authority? And if we are our own supreme authority, there is no way for us to be checked in what we justify. This is what happened with Hitler, Stalin, Mao, and Pol Pot. There was no one above them—no God and therefore no law—that they would be accountable to.

Which leads to the seemingly paradoxical conclusion that we need a worldview that contains truth that has higher authority than ourselves and that prohibits the coercion of others who do not share that worldview. Let me say the paradox again: violence against ethnic and religious minorities is best prevented by holding to a faith in the absolute claims of the biblical God, because his truth not only limits our self-exaltation but also forbids coercion as a way of getting compliance with our faith. The Christian faith comes about by the work of the Holy Spirit through the agency of God's word. Therefore, it cannot be coerced. Therefore, paradoxically, the Christian Scripture claims absolute authority, and by that authority forbids the coercion of those who deny it.

There will come a day when Jesus Christ returns to earth and establishes his kingdom in person. When that day comes, all accounts will be settled. He will separate the sheep from the goats—those who embrace his authority from those who don't. There will be a final judgment, and all unbelief and sin will be removed from the new world of justice and peace. In the meantime, we are not God. We are not the final judge. Therefore, we exalt his word, and we call all people everywhere to believe it and obey it and to see and savor him through it. But we do not use force or violence to bring about faith. Coerced Christian faith is an oxymoron. There is no such thing.

Nevertheless, I know that the total claim of the Bible on all the people of the world, and all the thoughts and feelings and actions of those people, is a staggering claim. Embracing the Bible this way would change everything. I do not take that lightly. You do not either.

A Massive Foundation

Perhaps this book has introduced you for the first time to an argument for the truth of Scripture based on the glory of God. It seems fitting that a claim of such sweeping scope would be grounded in a reality equally sweeping. In fact, this is not a mere decision before you. No one decides to see glory. And no one merely decides to experience the Christian Scriptures as the all-compelling, all-satisfying truth of one's life. In the end, seeing is a gift. And so the free embrace of God's word is a gift. God's Spirit opens the eyes of our heart, and what was once boring, or absurd, or foolish, or mythical is now self-evidently real. You can pray and ask God for that miracle. I ask daily for fresh eyes for his glory.

My argument has been that the glory of God, in and through the Scriptures, is a real, objective, self-authenticating reality. Christian faith is not a leap in the dark. It is not a guess or a wager. God is not honored if he is chosen by the flip of a coin. A leap into the unknown is no honor to one who has made himself known.

For the Simplest Person

One of the key impulses behind this argument is the concern expressed by Jonathan Edwards, that there be a way for the simplest person to have well-grounded confidence that the gospel is true—for example, preliterate Native American peoples in his day who had no familiarity with rational argumentation for the historicity of biblical events.

Edwards's claim was that "the gospel of the blessed God does not go abroad a-begging for its evidence, so much as some think: it has its highest and most proper evidence in itself. . . . The mind ascends to the truth of the gospel but by one step, and that is its divine glory."[2] I have extended that argument to all of Scripture. That is what I tried to explain and defend in this book. The point is not that Edwards's books, or mine, are designed to be read by the simplest person. The point is that the word of God emanates a spiritual light available to all.

Another way to put it is to say that this book has been an extended investigation and explanation of the words of the Westminster Larger Catechism (Question 4), "The Scriptures manifest themselves to be the word of God, by . . . the scope of the whole, which is to give all glory to God." I have taken this to mean that the whole Bible, properly understood, has this divine purpose and effect: to communicate or display the glory of God. And this pervasive aim of the Scriptures to glorify God, in what they teach and how they teach it, reveals the handiwork of God in the writing of the Bible.

The Peculiar Glory

More specifically, I have argued that the way the Scriptures convince us is by the revelation of a *peculiar* glory. In other words, the power of Scripture to warrant well-grounded trust is not by generic glory. Not, as it were, by mere dazzling. Not by simply boggling the mind with supernatural otherness. Rather, what we see as inescapably divine is a peculiar glory. And at the center of this peculiar glory is the utterly unique glory of Jesus Christ.

What has emerged, therefore, is that there is an essence or a center or a dominant peculiarity in the way God glorifies himself in Scripture.

---

[2] Jonathan Edwards, *A Treatise Concerning Religious Affections*, vol. 2, *The Works of Jonathan Edwards*, ed. John Smith (New Haven, CT: Yale University Press, 1957), 299, 307.

We have seen this in the way he glorifies himself in working for those who wait for him (chapter 13), through fulfilled prophecy (chapter 14), through the miracles of Jesus (chapter 15), and through Scripture-shaped lives of radical love (chapter 16). That dominant peculiarity is the revelation of God's majesty through meekness.

This is God's *peculiar* glory. It is at the heart of the gospel of Jesus Christ. Along with countless manifestations in Scripture, this is the central brightness of "the light of the gospel of the glory of Christ, who is the image of God" (2 Cor. 4:4). This is what bursts upon the heart and mind of the person in whom God shines with "the light of the knowledge of the glory of God in the face of Jesus Christ" (2 Cor. 4:6). This peculiar brightness shines through the whole Bible but comes to its most beautiful radiance in the person and work of Jesus Christ, dying and rising for sinners.

An Inborn Template for Glory

In one sense, everyone knows the glory of God (Rom. 1:21). It is written in nature (Rom. 1:19–20), written in our hearts (Rom. 1:15), written in the gospel (2 Cor. 4:4), and radiant through Christ (John 1:14) and the Scriptures. I have argued that this innate "knowledge" means that there is, in every human, a built-in template that is shaped for the reception of God's glory. When God opens our eyes (2 Cor. 4:6) and grants us the knowledge of the truth (2 Tim. 2:25), through the Scriptures (1 Sam. 3:21), we know that we have met ultimate reality.

This meeting—this seeing through the window of the word—has held me for almost seven decades. At the beginning, I thought I was holding a view of Scripture. Then I realized I was being held. That is my prayer for you. It is the freest of all captivities. No one considers himself enslaved when he is bound to admit that the sun has risen. Such knowledge is freedom. Blindness enslaves, not sight.

I would like to believe that by means of this book, I have been sent with the same mission as the apostle Paul when the risen Christ said to him, "I am sending you to open their eyes, so that they may turn from darkness to light" (Acts 26:17–18). When that happens, we enter a life of extraordinary purpose—to "proclaim the excellencies of him who called you out of darkness into his marvelous light" (1 Pet. 2:9).

Volume 2

If you join me in this great purpose, our work—our joy—is just beginning. Now we have a lifetime—or what's left of it—to read the Book
and see the countless ways the marvelous light is refracted in the Scriptures. Is there a way to read the Bible that lets in more light than other
ways? Does the thesis of this book carry with it implications for the way
we use the Bible—live with the Bible day in and day out? That is what
I want to write next. I would value your prayers, as I prepare volume 2
on the Peculiar Glory.

General Index

Abel, 47, 48
Abram/Abraham, 14, 91, 106, 107–8, 234
Adam, 91
Annals (Tacitus), 82
Apocrypha, 17, 41n1, 44–45, 46, 48, 48n6; books of, 44
apologetics, 272–73, 275n5; following the pathway of, 277–78
apostles, the, 115; authority of emanating from Jesus alone, 115–16, 124; choosing and preparation of the apostles by Jesus, 118–19; derivation of the term "apostles" (*sheluhim*), 120, 120n3; establishment of their foundational ministry, 121–22; guiding of by the Holy Spirit, 250; and the purpose of Jesus's authority, 117–18; and the uniqueness of Jesus's authority in the world, 117; view of themselves as "slaves" of Jesus, 120–21; the words of the apostles are Jesus's words, 119–20
apostolicity, 64; as supernatural communication, 64–66
Artaxerxes, 45

Babylonian Talmud, 44
Barnabas, 40
Bauckham, Richard, 61, 63
Bavinck, Herman, 117, 160
Bel, 218
Bengel, Johann Albrecht, 84

Bethlehem Baptist Church Elder Affirmation of Faith, 77, 77n5, 79, 127–28
Bible, the, 17, 18, 21–22, 36, 182; authority of, 32; as a book of "books," 42; books of as canonical books, 42; complete list of the books of, 41–42; divine glory revealed through, 229–30; English Standard Version of, 94; as inspired by God, 45; Jesus's Bible as the Hebrew Bible, 46–48; as a letter from the Creator, 22–23; original written languages of, 69–70; personal nature of the world described in, 23; self-attesting nature of, 211–12; and the term *biblion* (Greek: book), 42; as a window rather than a painting on a wall, 26–27. *See also* Bible, the, truth/infallibility of; biblical manuscripts
Bible, the, truth/infallibility of, 11, 32, 33, 127, 281; and divine glory as necessary to, 147–48, 151–52; doubts concerning, 172–73; the inerrancy of the Bible, 34–35, 69, 76–77, 127–28; and nonhistorians, 133–134; and unwarranted trust, 134–35; urgency of the question concerning the Bible's truth, 128–29; and the well-grounded conviction of the truth of the gospel and the Scriptures, 147. *See also* historical reasoning

Scripture Index

desiringGod

Everyone wants to be happy. Our website was born and built for happiness. We want people everywhere to understand and embrace the truth that *God is most glorified in us when we are most satisfied in him.* We've collected more than thirty years of John Piper's speaking and writing, including translations into more than forty languages. We also provide a daily stream of new written, audio, and video resources to help you find truth, purpose, and satisfaction that never end. And it's all available free of charge, thanks to the generosity of people who've been blessed by the ministry.

If you want more resources for true happiness, or if you want to learn more about our work at Desiring God, we invite you to visit us at www.desiringGod.org.

www.desiringGod.org

LOOK AT THE BOOK

Want to go deeper in your own Bible reading after reading this book? Look at the Book is John Piper's online method for teaching the Bible. It's an ongoing series of short videos in which the camera is on the text, not the teacher. You will hear John's voice and watch his pen underline, circle, make connections, and scribble notes—all to help you learn to read God's word for yourself.

www.desiringGod.org/labs